How Soda Shook Up the World

TRISTAN DONOVAN

CHICAGO
REVIEW
PRESS

Copyright © 2014 by Tristan Donovan

All rights reserved

Published by Chicago Review Press Incorporated

814 North Franklin Street

Chicago, Illinois 60610

ISBN 978-1-61374-722-3

Library of Congress Cataloging-in-Publication Data

Donovan, Tristan.

Fizz : how soda shook up the world / Tristan Donovan.

pages cm

Summary: "This social, cultural, and culinary history charts soda's remarkable, world-changing journey from awe-inspiring natural mystery to ubiquity. Off-the-wall and offbeat stories abound, including how quack medicine peddlers spawned some of the world's biggest brands, how fizzy pop cashed in on Prohibition, how soda helped presidents reach the White House, and even how Pepsi influenced Apple's marketing of the iPod. This history of carbonated drinks follows a seemingly simple everyday refreshment as it zinged and pinged over society's taste buds and, in doing so, changed the world"— Provided by publisher.

Includes bibliographical references and index.

ISBN 978-1-61374-722-3 (pbk.)

1. Soft drinks—History. 2. Carbonated beverages—History. I. Title.

TP630.D66 2013

663'.62—dc23

2013023222

Cover design: Rebecca Lown

Interior design: Jonathan Hahn

Printed in the United States of America

5 4 3 2 1

TO JAY

Contents

To the Stars

It was 1984, the height of the Cola War. Pepsi was riding high on the back of the Pepsi Challenge and an endorsement from Michael Jackson, the world's biggest star. After more than 60 years of trying to beat Coca-Cola, victory was in sight. But the Atlanta soda giant still had a trick up its sleeve to use against its fast-growing Yankee rival: it would take soda into outer space.

Coca-Cola announced to the world that NASA would take its world-famous cola into orbit when the *Challenger* space shuttle blasted off from the Kennedy Space Center in Florida in July 1985. "As more people explore outer space, it was our judgment that it would be a darn shame if people on these long voyages wouldn't have the opportunity to have a moment of refreshment with Coca-Cola," Coke president Don Keough informed *USA Today*. After all, he could have added, when you've conquered the world, the only direction is up.

Coca-Cola spent a fortune on its space mission, assigning a team of its finest engineers to build a unique soda can capable of dispensing its fizzy nectar to astronauts as they floated in zero gravity. It had taken months to develop and been tested to destruction on high-altitude flights aboard NASA's "Vomit Comet," the Boeing KC-135 that the space agency would fly on a parabolic flight path so astronauts could train in a near weightless environment.

The tough steel can featured an adhesive fastener strip so that it could be attached to the spacecraft walls to stop it from floating around. It had a special paint that would not melt in intense heat or flake in extreme cold (in which case it could float off and damage the shuttle's circuits). There was a safety lock to stop the liquid from escaping and a spout, activated by a plunger, from which Coca-Cola could be squirted down the throats of space travelers.

At the offices of Pepsi in Purchase, New York, the news that its archrival was to be first into space came as a shock. Bob McGarrah, the equipment development manager at Pepsi when Coca-Cola made its announcement, remembers the reaction: "What! Coke's going to space and we're not?" There might not have been moon bases or Martians out there to buy their fizzy drinks but this was the Cola War and the contest to be crowned soda king was on a knife edge. Pepsi couldn't let Coca-Cola be the first into space. No way. If Coke was going where no soda had gone before, Pepsi was coming too.

Roger Enrico, the president of Pepsi-Cola, ordered his staff to gate-crash Coke's orbital party. Pepsi got in touch with NASA and pointed out to the agency that "PepsiCo is strongly identified with the Republican Party and the support of President Reagan and his administration." In short, put us on that shuttle or expect trouble in Washington. What could NASA say except "OK"?

Having gotten their ticket on the same shuttle flight as Coca-Cola, Pepsi now needed a space can of its own that could pass NASA's rigorous tests. Pepsi assembled its best engineers and told them to make a space can. Fast. One of those on the team was McGarrah: "In something like 14 weeks, a really compressed period of time, we had to come up with a package that could go up in a spaceship. Everything that's going to go onto that spaceship has to be tested for things like flammability, ability to withstand a vacuum, and on and on and on. You have to create the product and go through this elaborate testing process out in New Mexico to get approval."

Working out of Pepsi's research facility in Valhalla, New York, and with support from spray technology specialists Enviro-Spray, the team raced against the clock to build the kind of space-worthy can that Coca-Cola had spent months developing. "One of the team, Scott Gillesby, was the main courier to the testing facility and he would fly back and forth to the testing grounds in New Mexico," McGarrah recalls. "He was literally in the air more than he was on the ground; flying out to the test site and back. He had to keep coming back and forth because a lot of the time the can failed."

After several weeks of ferrying prototypes back and forth, Pepsi had their can. Essentially a repurposed aerosol canister, Pepsi's steel space can contained small plastic pouches that would mix citric acid and sodium bicarbonate when the spray nozzle was pressed down. The acid and baking soda would react to produce carbon dioxide gas that would cause the pouches to expand, increasing the pressure inside the can and forcing the cola out through the nozzle. On July 8, 1985, with just four days to go before takeoff, NASA gave Pepsi permission to fly. Coke's hopes of being the first soda in space were over. As takeoff approached, the seven astronauts found themselves besieged with questions from journalists wanting the scoop on the Cola Space War. "We're not up there to run a taste test between the two," exasperated astronaut Colonel Gordon Fullerton told reporters.

The orbital Pepsi Challenge didn't take off quite as planned. At T minus 3 seconds the shuttle launch was canceled and delayed until July 29 when, finally, the world's favorite sodas made the journey into space. Back on Earth, Pepsi marked the day with newspaper ads declaring the venture "one giant sip for mankind." Once in space the astronauts tested out the cans, blowing wobbly spherical globules of zero-gravity cola around the ship before gulping them down. And when they returned to Earth the assembled press couldn't wait to find out who had won the outer space taste test. Neither, replied the astronauts. The shuttle didn't have a refrigerator, the crew explained, and warm soda just doesn't cut it.

Even worse were the zero-gravity burps from drinking carbonated drinks in space. "On Earth, that's not such a big deal, but in microgravity it's just gross," Vickie Kloeris, the food systems manager at NASA, reported on the space agency's website in 2001. "Because there is no gravity, the contents of your stomach float and tend to stay at the top of your stomach, under the rib cage and close to the valve at the top of your stomach. Because this valve isn't a complete closure (just a muscle that works with gravity), if you burp, it becomes a wet burp from the contents in your stomach." Not that Pepsi cared. "Was Coke's can better? Probably," says McGarrah. "But Coke was there and we were there too."

That either of them were there was more surprising. After all Coca-Cola and Pepsi were little more than fizzy flavored water at heart. Yet here they were traveling to space and back at the cost of millions for a publicity stunt that captivated a nation, saw the world's leading space agency told it would have to deal with the Oval Office if it didn't put Pepsi on the flight, and ended with astronauts complaining that their space cola wasn't cold enough. That soda had become this important was somehow even more miraculous than the ability to send people into space.

But humanity has always been strangely mesmerized by fizzing water. For people living in ancient times, naturally carbonated spring waters with their strange, unexplained bubbles must have seemed magical. What were they? Many civilizations concluded that these waters had healing powers or could give people strength. Others speculated that these springs were home to dangerous supernatural beings. These beliefs endured for centuries.

Hippocrates, the ancient Greek physician often regarded as the father of modern medicine, promoted the idea that mineral waters could cure disease in 400 BC. As the Romans expanded their empire across Europe, the Middle East, and Africa, they sought out natural springs in the lands they conquered, convinced that these special waters could rid them of gallstones and infections. In 216 BC, when the great Carthaginian general Hannibal crossed the Pyrenees on his way to fight in Italy, he reportedly paused his forty-six thousand troops and thirty-seven war elephants at the fizzing waters of Les Bouillens near Vergèze, France, before marching on to victory against the Romans. Today the spring where Hannibal's army rested provides the world with Perrier bottled water.

The obsession continued into the Dark Ages. In pre-Christian Scotland brides and grooms would marry while standing deep in the bubbling waters of the Marriage Well, near the banks of the River Clyde, in the belief that its effervescent waters would bless their union. At the same time, more than two thousand miles to the east, the people of Borjomi in the Caucasus nation of Georgia built stone bathtubs so that they could bathe in the area's carbonated spring water.

But even as people gathered around these waters, the mystery of why the water bubbled remained. So people began trying to figure out what created them, hoping that if they could understand that, they could re-create the phenomenon. The search for the secret of effervescence would last for centuries. In 1340 the Italian physician Giacomo de Dondi studied the hot springs of Abano Terme, hoping to uncover what gave its waters their curative power. After evaporating the water and examining the residue left behind by sight, smell, and taste, de Dondi concluded that the residue was some kind of mineral salt, a finding he believed proved that this spring's water was indeed of medicinal value.

More than two hundred years later, in 1535, the Swiss-German physician Theophrastus Paracelsus began to study the waters of Bad Pfäffer, Switzerland. Paracelsus believed that an imbalance of minerals in the body caused illness, and he tried to re-create the Swiss spring's mineral-rich waters without success. His theories did lead him to pioneer the use of chemicals and minerals in medicine. His belief that astrological talismans could cure disease proved less successful. But the 1600s finally saw some breakthroughs.

In the first half of the century the Flemish scientist Jan Baptist van Helmont identified a number of different gases through a series of experiments with mineral water, fermenting wine, and charcoal. One of these gases he named *spiritus sylvestris*, known today as carbon dioxide—the gas responsible for most of the fizz in naturally effervescent waters. In 1684 the Anglo-Irish scientist Robert Boyle published *Short Memoirs for the Natural Experimental History of Mineral Waters*. Boyle's publication drew on his own studies of well waters in and around London and set out—for the first time—a clear method for analyzing the chemical composition of mineral water.

A year later, Friedrich Hoffmann, a professor of medicine at the University of Halle in Germany, published his own study of mineral waters in which he attacked the wilder beliefs people held about bubbling water while setting out an improved method for analyzing its content and potential health benefits. Physicians and naturalists, Hoffmann wrote, "have generally remained grossly ignorant" in their studies. "We must here note and reject that common imaginary notion, as to the existence of gold, silver, lead, tin, antimony, etc. in these waters." Hoffmann also had little time for physicians who subscribed to the ancient but largely untested belief in the healing powers of mineral water. "No less preposterous has been their manner of prescribing such waters," wrote the German doctor, before dismissing such physicians as quacks.

Instead, he argued, physicians needed to pay attention to the minerals present in effervescent waters, because that was the source of their medicinal power. Based on his assessment of the composition of different waters, he identified several distinct types such as iron-containing "steel waters" and the "bitter purging waters" with their neutral salts. Steel waters, he claimed, would strengthen limbs and heal ulcers if people bathed in them, while the bitter purging waters of Sedlitz in Bohemia should be drunk as remedies for "intermitting fevers." Hoffmann also suggested that these waters could be made artificially by putting plain water, acid, and alkali in a bottle and shaking it vigorously. But when he tried to put this theory into practice, Hoffmann was unable to replicate the waters as he hoped.

In the following century, however, Europe's leading scientists would finally decode the secrets of the effervescent springs in a rush of breakthroughs. The gases of the air were identified, as were processes for producing "fixed air," as carbon dioxide was now being called, by applying acid to chalk. In 1741 William Brownrigg, the English physician who identified platinum as an element, confirmed that the gas found within the acclaimed waters of Pyrmont in Germany was fixed air. In 1750 the Frenchman Gabriel Venel demonstrated a way of duplicating the waters of Selters, Germany, before the French Academy of Sciences in Paris. Venel succeeded in creating his bubbly "aerated water," but his process also left an unpleasant residue of salts in the liquid. It was a step nearer but still far from the real thing. By 1766 Henry Cavendish, the English scientist who discovered hydrogen, had established a method for producing fixed air and testing its solubility in water.

These various strands of research into salts, gases, and the generation of carbon dioxide eventually came together when Joseph Priestley began his own experiments with mineral water. Born in the West Yorkshire village of Birstall on March 13, 1733, Priestley was a remarkable child. At the age of four he could recite all of the 107 theological questions and answers that formed the Westminster Shorter Catechism, and at school he proved himself a capable student of Greek, Hebrew, Latin, algebra, math, physics, and philosophy. When a serious life-threatening illness left him with a stutter, he began to question his Calvinist upbringing. After further theological study, he became a Presbyterian minister. But while religion was central to his life, Priestley—like many scientists of the age—was a polymath who effortlessly moved between studying history, higher mathematics, physics, and foreign languages.

Science was a particular fascination for the devout Presbyterian. He believed that science was a force for good that could improve the quality of all human life, a belief that fit perfectly with his religious convictions. One of the first scientific subjects he studied was electricity. He hoped electricity could purify fixed air produced by the burning of charcoal. It turned out it couldn't. But his experiments led him to suggest that, just like gravity, as the distance between two electrically charged objects increased, the forces of attraction and repulsion between them decreased by the square of that distance. Priestley's theory was later proved by the French physicist Charles-Augustin de Coulomb and became known as Coulomb's law, a crucial step in the development of the science of electromagnetism.

After his electrical experiments, Priestley turned his attention to mineral water and how it could be made. Like many, Priestley believed that mineral water could heal numerous ailments, and doubtless he thought that perfecting a method for producing it artificially would greatly benefit the health of all humanity. As it happened, Priestley's home in the English city of Leeds was next to a large brewery, and the smell of the fermenting grain in its vats attracted his attention. In the summer of 1767, aware that the gas produced by fermentation was fixed air, he began a series of experiments with the aim of capturing the gas emerging from the vats within plain water. Eventually he succeeded by pouring water back and forth between containers that were held above the vats of fermenting beer until the water became carbonated. The fizzy drink had been born.

In 1772, having refined the process, Priestley presented his findings to the Royal Society of London and published a paper called "Directions for

Impregnating Water with Fixed Air" that explained how to create carbonated water. Priestley's method required a narrow-necked glass vessel to be filled with distilled or filtered water before being placed upside down in a basin that contained enough water to cover its neck. A leather pipe attached to a pig's bladder would then be inserted into the neck of the upside-down container. Next, a small amount of sulfuric acid would be poured into a phial two-thirds full of chalk that had been covered with water. As the acid reacted with the chalk to produce carbon dioxide gas, the other end of the bladder, which contained a cork through which a quill had been inserted to create a narrow pipe, would be plugged into the neck of the phial.

Briskly shaking the phial would encourage the production of carbon dioxide, which would fill up the bladder. The gas could then be pumped into the upturned glass vessel through the leather pipe. Once enough carbon dioxide had been pumped in to push most of the water out into the basin, the gas-filled container would be vigorously shaken for fifteen minutes so that the water and gas would mix and produce fizzy water.

Priestley's approach was a sensation. For centuries people had been trying to duplicate the magical waters of nature and now, decades upon decades upon decades worth of study had finally produced a definitive methodology. The Royal Society and Priestley thought it was the start of a medical and travel revolution since they erroneously believed that carbonated water could cure scurvy, the horrific disease that killed at least two million sailors between 1500 and 1800. A lack of fixed air in the blood caused scurvy, Priestley argued, therefore drinking water impregnated with the gas would cure it.

The Royal Society agreed. In the same year that Priestley presented his findings, the society gave the explorer James Cook the equipment necessary to carbonate water, hoping it would prevent scurvy among his men as he set sail to find Australia. The following year, while Captain Cook continued his voyage, the Royal Society awarded Priestley its highest honor, the Copley Medal, in recognition of his fizzy water experiments. Captain Cook returned without a single incident of scurvy among the crew, but it had nothing to do with Priestley's work and everything to do with the vitamin C in the fresh fruit and vegetables he and his men collected during their journey.

Even though Priestley's carbonated water didn't end the curse of scurvy, his work altered the world in many other ways. In the 250 years that followed, the fruits of his labor reshaped cities, built nations, and made US presidents. It spawned the world's biggest brand, altered our shopping habits, and transformed our drinking habits. It ushered in consumer protection laws, funded organized crime, expanded our waistlines, and redefined sales and marketing. It would even go into space. The Age of Soda had begun, and this is the story of how those fun, fizzing, pinging bubbles changed the world around us.

1

The Beverage of Kings

The life of Jean Jacob Schweppe began like a fairy tale. He was born in 1740 in Witzenhausen, a small village of Germanic half-timbered buildings nestled among the wooded banks of the winding Werra River and famed for its cherry wines. On a hilltop to the southwest stood the fifteenth-century castle of Burg Ludwigstein, with its tall cone-topped tower overlooking a landscape of rolling countryside and forests that were the source for many of the fables that inspired the Brothers Grimm.

Most of the 1,460 people who lived in Witzenhausen back then worked in agriculture, and Schweppe's family was no exception. But Schweppe was a delicate child, and his parents fretted that their gray-eyed son would not be able to withstand the rigors of a life in farming. So when Schweppe was eleven or twelve years old, his parents asked a tinker who was passing through the village to take the boy with him, hoping that the traveling tinsmith could give their son a trade.

The tinker soon returned. The young Schweppe, he explained, had a hidden talent for precision metalwork that was far too good to waste on the lowly work of tinkering. They should get the boy an apprenticeship with a silversmith instead. Schweppe's parents did as suggested, only for the silversmith to decide that the boy's talent was too good for basic silver and gold work. So Schweppe was packed off once more, this time to become the apprentice of a jewelry maker.

On finishing his apprenticeship, Schweppe headed for Geneva, the renowned hub of watch and jewelry making. By the end of 1765 he was running a successful jewelers' shop in the city, and he had married local woman Eléonore Roget. Schweppe's talent took him far in Genevese society, and in 1777 the jewelry makers' guild named him a master jeweler.

As well as a naturally talented jeweler, Schweppe was a keen amateur scientist. He would buy and read all the science journals, and he enjoyed replicating the experiments detailed within their pages. One of the scientific papers he came across was Joseph Priestley's explanation of how to create carbonated water. The idea of re-creating the bubbling waters of nature intrigued Schweppe. Keen to find out what artificial mineral water tasted like, he built a replica of Priestley's apparatus and produced his first batch of fizzy water. Schweppe's perfectionist streak got the better of him. While impressed by Priestley's breakthrough, the master jeweler felt the resulting waters were no match for the real thing. He became obsessed with trying to improve the equipment to produce superior carbonated waters. Day after day, his five-foot-three frame hunched over scientific papers and equipment as he tried to engineer a carbonation system that would put the waters of Priestley to shame.

He had a working system in place by 1780, but he would spend the next three years perfecting it. Schweppe's big advance was the addition of a crank-operated compression pump. This pump would draw carbon dioxide gas from a gasometer and water from a tank into a barrel that would also be shaken by the turning of the crank, churning the incoming water and gas to create fizzy water. It was easier, faster, and more effective than Priestley's bladder and basin apparatus, and it allowed Schweppe to produce greater volumes of more intensely carbonated water.

Rather than waste the bubbly waters he made, Schweppe started giving them away to local doctors, hoping that they could use it to treat the city's poor. But many of those he offered his water to refused to take it for free, insisting that he charge them for such beneficial waters. Schweppe reluctantly agreed to charge a small fee to cover his expenses.

Word began to spread of the jeweler's impressive waters. By the end of the 1780s his water was even being exported outside Switzerland in ceramic stoneware bottles that Schweppe insisted on having laid flat during transit so that the moistened cork expanded to prevent the gas from escaping and the water from turning flat. As his philanthropic sideline morphed into a thriving business, the trusting Schweppe hired a friend to help him produce and sell his water. His friend used the opportunity to try to figure out the secret of Schweppe's apparatus so he could start a rival business. But on examining the equipment, the deceitful buddy found himself out of his depth. So he turned to another Genevese for help: Nicolas Paul, a brilliant mechanic who maintained La Machine Hydraulique, the pump house that supplied the fountains of Geneva with water from the Rhône.

Paul took advantage of Schweppe's double-crossing friend. After inspecting the equipment he built an inferior version for Schweppe's traitorous pal, and for himself he built a version with improved mechanics and used it to launch his own artificial mineral water business. Schweppe didn't want to compete with Paul, and instead he persuaded the talented engineer to go into business with him rather than against him. Paul brought in another partner, Henry Gosse, a Genevese pharmacist who shared Paul's interest in hot air ballooning and kept a chest containing a mummified saint—or at least what the Parisian salesman he bought it from told him was a saint—in his pharmacy, much to the disgust of his employees, who refused to go near the creepy antique.

The new business was formed in April 1790 and the combination of Schweppe's breakthrough, Paul's refinements, and Gosse's knowledge of chemistry made their imitation mineral waters even more popular. The trio started to think big. They talked of expanding into Paris, London, even Calcutta and Pondicherry in India. The partners eventually settled on starting their global expansion in London, and Schweppe landed the job of moving to the city and starting the business there. So in late 1791 the fifty-year-old Schweppe left his wife and his daughter Colette, the only one of his nine children who did not die at birth or before the age of 10, to make the journey from Geneva to London.

When Schweppe arrived in the British capital in January 1792, it was fast becoming the most populated city in the world. Its narrow cobbled streets, darkened by its tall buildings, teemed with carts, coaches, horses, people, pickpockets, rats, vagrants, and coffin-carrying undertakers. Coal fires belched out thick, choking clouds of soot, and despite the fine squares and splendid buildings that showcased the British Empire's growing wealth, the place stank. It was said that if the wind was blowing in the right direction, London could be smelled long before it could be seen. The muddy waters of the River Thames were a mass of fast-flowing garbage that doubled as the city's reservoir and sewer. With private toilets a luxury even among the rich, most people flung their excrement onto the streets, where it mixed with spoiled food and other waste before being washed by rain into open drains to putrefy while waiting for the "soil men" to come at night and shovel it onto carts so it could be dumped into the Thames. Worst of all, reported German visitor Charles Moritz in 1782, were the city's butcher shops. "Guts and all the nastiness are thrown into the middle of the street, and cause an insupportable stench," he reported to his countrymen on his return. Clean water was scarce too, and outbreaks of cholera and other diseases were a regular occurrence. In short, it was the perfect place to sell bottles of pure, healthful artificial mineral water.

The British, however, had not been idle in the twenty years that had passed since Priestley published his guide to producing artificial mineral water, and people across the country had started mineral water businesses. Priestley's friend Richard Bewley, an apothecary from Great Massingham in Norfolk, got the ball rolling. In 1767 or 1768, after Priestley told him about his experiments with carbonated water, Bewley began producing fizzy water under the name Mr Bewley's Mephitic Julep. Bewley's operation was a small one, limited by the constraints of Priestley's system, but others soon followed his lead.

Thomas Henry, an apothecary who ran a store on Manchester's King Street and one of the city's leading scientists, was one of those followers. After hearing about Mr Bewley's Mephitic Julep, Henry built a carbonation device based on Priestley's apparatus and started selling imitation mineral waters in the early 1770s. Henry regarded mineral water as a medicine, and he gave his customers strict instructions on its use. Take four ounces at a time, he would tell them, and make sure the bottle is kept tightly sealed so that the gas does not escape. But while his mineral water operation was bigger than Bewley's, Henry was only able to produce carbonated water in small quantities until he came across Nooth's Apparatus.

This superior carbonation device was the 1775 invention of John Nooth, a Scottish physician who believed Priestley's apparatus was hard to use and that the pig bladder caused the resulting waters to taste of urine. Nooth's solution was a device that consisted of three glass chambers stacked on top of each other and connected by valves. In the bottom chamber marble chips and sulfuric acid would be mixed to produce carbon dioxide. The gas would then rise into the central chamber, where it would mix with water drawn down from the uppermost chamber, which—thanks to the water inside it—also provided the pressure necessary to cause the gas to carbonate the liquid. The freshly fizzed water could then be dispensed from a faucet attached to the central chamber. The result was an eighteenth-century SodaStream, a device for making carbonated water at home that was small enough to sit on a sideboard. It also carbonated water more effectively than Priestley's apparatus.

Priestley was far from amused, however, when Nooth explained that he made this glass contraption because Priestley's method created water with a urinous flavor. The scientist-theologian responded that if the water Nooth made with Priestley's apparatus tasted of urine that would be down to a servant relieving himself in his equipment and that Nooth deserved nothing less. But even Priestley had to concede that the Scottish physician had made the superior device.

Nooth's Apparatus became wildly popular among rich Europeans. Within its first three years more than a thousand had been sold; in France, more people got their carbonated water from these devices than from bottles. Nooth's Apparatus would evolve into the gasogene, which worked on the same principle but replaced the upper chamber and the faucet of the central chamber with a soda siphon. The gasogene would still be a common sight in 1891 when Dr. John Watson spied one lurking inside 221B Baker Street during Sherlock Holmes's adventure *A Scandal in Bohemia*. Anesthesiologists also found that a slightly modified gasogene was ideal for vaporizing ether and delivering it to patients, and they used the device to create some of the very first ether inhalers.

Henry used a modified version of Nooth's Apparatus to produce artificial mineral water in large enough quantities to secure a lucrative contract with Manchester Infirmary. The success of Henry's mineral water business would eventually lead his son William to use the insights he had gained while working for his father to come up with Henry's law, one of the physical laws explaining the nature and behavior of gases. Henry's law stated that the amount of gas absorbed in water is in proportion to the pressure of the gas. This explained why carbonated water would keep its fizz when bottled under pressure but go flat when the pressure is reduced by opening the bottle. It also explained why more nitrogen is absorbed into the blood of divers at deeper depths, causing the drunken feeling of nitrogen narcosis and the risk of getting the bends, a life-threatening condition caused by the nitrogen fizzing out of the blood if the diver ascends too rapidly.

While Henry and his son fizzed up water for ill Mancunians, down in London the sight of mineral water makers roaming the streets and hawking their wares from carts was already common when Schweppe arrived in 1791. Despite the established competition, Schweppe was pleased to find that none of the British waters could match the level of fizz that his cutting-edge equipment could create. Schweppe opened a factory on Drury Lane, then a notorious slum packed with gin shops and prostitutes selling themselves for six pence. Keen to keep his carbonation technique secret this time, he added superfluous parts, hid the crank behind a useless wheel, and encased the equipment in wood so that no one could see how it worked. In spring 1792 the first waters he produced in Drury Lane went on sale, and Schweppe began sending samples to respected establishment figures, including Priestley, hoping to get glowing endorsements in return.

The endorsements never came, and Londoners ignored his waters. In July a depressed Schweppe wrote to his partners back in Geneva to tell them business was bad and he wanted to come home. They wrote back insisting that he stay. It was too soon to give up, they told him. Lonely, Schweppe asked his fifteen-year-old daughter Colette to travel to London to keep him company. It was a dangerous journey. The turmoil of the French Revolution was ongoing, and as she made her way to London that summer, an armed mob stormed the royal palace of Tuileries in Paris. While the mob massacred the five hundred Swiss Guards charged with protecting the palace, the French royal family fled through the gardens. The royals were eventually captured and imprisoned, and rumors of a counterrevolution spread panic through the country.

Despite the dangers, Colette made it to London, but Schweppe's business situation was still dire. In December Paul and Gosse decided that Schweppe was right after all, and they sent him a letter telling him to pack his bags and return to Geneva. Schweppe was furious. They had made him stay in London and caused his daughter to make a perilous journey through revolutionary France. Now, he fumed, they wanted him and Colette to risk their health and life by traveling through France in winter. Schweppe wrote an angry letter to his business partners informing them that he would not be leaving London until winter was over. But when winter turned to spring it was too late to leave. France had declared war on Britain, making travel impossible. With Schweppe trapped in London, the partnership with Gosse and Paul fell apart. Paul and Gosse opened rival mineral water businesses in Geneva, and Schweppe returned to the task of trying to build up the London operation.

Schweppe slogged away, growing the business bottle by bottle until in 1796 he finally secured the high-profile endorsements he needed to win over London's high society. The first endorsement came from Dr. George Pearson, the head physician at St. George's Hospital. The second came from the prominent physician Erasmus Darwin, who in 1794 had published *Zoonomia*, a two-volume compendium of knowledge about the animal world that set out early ideas about evolution that his grandson Charles would develop further in *The Origin of Species*. Pearson's and Darwin's support turned Schweppe into the leading producer of carbonated water in London, although the joy of this long-awaited breakthrough was tainted by the death that very same year of his wife, whom he hadn't seen since leaving for Britain. In 1798 Schweppe sold the business for the then-considerable sum of £1,200 to three businessmen from Jersey and returned to Geneva with Colette to spend his retirement tending peach trees.

The business that bore Schweppe's name would go from strength to strength, rapidly outflanking Henry's business to emerge as Britain's leading maker of mineral water. Schweppe's former colleague Paul also struggled to challenge the company's position. In 1799 Paul left Geneva for Paris, where he impressed the French Faculty of Physicians with carbonated water so fizzy that the noise of its uncorking was compared to the sound of a pistol being fired. After mild success in Paris, Paul moved to London in 1802, by which time Schweppes was beginning to export its waters throughout the British Empire. By 1806 Paul gave up on London and returned to Geneva. He died that same year at the age of forty-three.

By the time Schweppe died in November 1821, British high society had made Schweppes its mineral water supplier of choice. Schweppes waters were a common sight in the gentlemen's clubs of Pall Mall, the finest hotels, and the most exclusive restaurants. Almost every West End theater stocked Schweppes and Schweppes alone. Schweppes had even become the choice of royalty, with King William IV appointing the company as the royal household's mineral water supplier in 1831.

Schweppes wasn't the only imitation mineral water business that had caught the eye of the British king, for he had also endorsed the Royal German Spa in the seaside resort of Brighton. Opened in 1825, the spa was the brainchild of Frederick Struve, a chemist from Saxony who realized that spas no longer needed to be located at natural springs now that mineral waters could be fabricated. In 1818 he opened his first artificial spa in Dresden, which offered the city's rich a choice of waters as well as a place to relax and socialize without the inconvenient travel that going to a spa usually involved. It was an instant success, and the king of Saxony rewarded him with an Order of Merit for his innovative spa resort. Struve opened a second in Leipzig and then a third in Berlin before embarking on an expansion that would see his artificial mineral water spas popping up all across Europe, from St. Petersburg and Moscow to Warsaw and Brighton.

Like all his spas, Brighton's Royal German Spa emphasized exclusivity. The front of the building offered a Grecian portico lined with grand classical columns. Inside, an inviting staircase led its aristocratic clientele up to a finely decorated room with Ionic columns and a counter containing faucets from which they could select the mineral water of their choosing. For the rich and fashionable visitors to the English seaside resort, the Royal

German Spa became the place to be seen. In its first season, which ran from May to November 1825, it had 333 subscribers paying a guinea a week to partake of its waters. It became so popular that Schweppes struck a deal to produce and sell Struve's Brighton Seltzer Water. The artificial spa craze boomed in popularity during the 1820s and 1830s, only to lose its allure after Struve's death in 1840, by which time a new, more enduring craze had bubbled up: flavor.

No one knows who first added flavoring to carbonated water or even when, but since mixing still water with fruit juice and other ingredients was already widespread, it was an obvious thing to do to enliven the taste. By 1795 spritzers of sparkling water and wine were popular throughout Europe, and as the 1800s progressed flavored fizz became increasingly commonplace.

Sparkling lemonade was one of the most popular. Still lemonade evolved out of lemon drinks that dated back to ancient times, but the drink reached new heights of popularity in the seventeenth century when street vendors, called *limonadiers*, began wandering the streets of Paris with tanks of honey-sweetened lemonade on their backs that they would dispense to thirsty passersby. While there's no exact date for the emergence of sparkling lemonade, it was already being advertised as "aerated lemonade" to a seemingly unfamiliar audience in March 1807 by Sutcliffe & Co., a pharmacy in the city of York, which advised readers of the *York Herald and County Advertiser*: "To those who are strangers to it, an early trial is recommended." By the 1830s fizzy lemonade was widespread and being sold alongside mineral waters on the streets of London as well as being bottled by Schweppes. It would remain the United Kingdom's most popular soda until after World War II, when colas gained the upper hand.

Other sweet mixes of sparkling water and fruits followed. There were orangeades, limeades, raspberryades, cherryades, and Persian sherbets, a carbonated twist on the refreshing Persian fruit drink *sharbat*. Another still drink to get with the fizz was tonic water, also known as quinine water. Quinine came from the bark of the *Cinchona* plants, a genus native to the Andes Mountains. The bitter-tasting bark had been widely used by the Quechua people of South America, who would mix it with sweetened water to produce a drink they believed could prevent shivering in the cold. When European explorers reached the continent they picked up on the Quechua's interest in the plants, and in the early 1600s, Agostino Salumbrino, a Jesuit brother living in Lima, successfully treated patients suffering from malaria using the Quechuan shivering cure. Quinine would remain a popular anti-malaria remedy until well into the twentieth century.

In 1858, Erasmus Bond, the owner of London soft drink company W. Pitt & Co., developed the first carbonated tonic water. Since Bond envisaged it as a medicinal product to help the British in Africa and India overcome the risk of malaria, he packed his tonic water with so much quinine that even the sweetened water couldn't hide the vile bitterness of the substance. So the British abroad started using gin to blunt the acrid tonic. The gin did more than bring an alcoholic component to the beverage. At the molecular level, the structure of the essential oils of the juniper berries that give gin its flavor are similar to that of quinine. This chemical similarity causes the molecules to combine to create a more palatable drink that dampens the bitterness of the quinine. This taste-improving combination may have started as a way to help the medicine go down, but gin and tonic went on to become one of Britain's favorite cocktails. The combination proved so popular that Schweppes launched its own Indian Tonic Water in the 1870s, which rapidly eclipsed Bond's original in sales.

By the time Schweppes Indian Tonic Water went on sale, the company was the biggest soft drink company in Britain by far, selling millions of bottles of its waters and flavored drinks every year. In 1884, flush with its success, the company ventured into America and opened a plant in Brooklyn. But the company's bid for success in the United States was short-lived. In 1892 the company shut down its Brooklyn plant, having discovered that, unlike Europe with its gasogenes, tonic waters, and bottles, Americans preferred to get their fizzy kicks from an altogether different source: the soda fountain.

2

Meet Me at the Soda Fountain

It was night on July 14, 1791, when the mob reached Joseph Priestley's home in Birmingham, England. By then the furious throng was on a roll, having torched the two meetinghouses of Priestley's dissident Unitarian Church. Now they wanted the man himself.

Since his influential experiments with carbonation, Priestley had also discovered oxygen, but his religious ideas had turned the scientist-clergyman into one of the most controversial figures in eighteenth-century Britain. His incendiary 1782 book *An History of the Corruptions of Christianity* caused outrage with its all-out attack on the Anglican Church and questioning of Christ's divinity. As if that weren't enough, he wrote another book declaring that he and his followers were "laying gunpowder, grain by grain, under the old building of error and superstition, which a single spark may hereafter inflame, so as to produce an instantaneous explosion: in consequence of which, that edifice, the erection of which has been the work of ages, may be overturned in a moment, and so effectually that the same foundation can never be built upon again."

The analogy instantly reminded readers of the Gunpowder Plot of 1605, in which Catholic conspirators led by Guy Fawkes tried unsuccessfully to blow up the Houses of Parliament using barrels of gunpowder hidden in the building's cellars. Although Priestley denied that was his intention, his ill-judged words heightened suspicions about the mild-mannered preacher and earned him the nickname "Gunpowder Joe." At first his outspoken views were tolerated, but the outbreak of revolution in France hardened attitudes. Many in Britain were appalled by the French Revolution and feared that people like Priestley were out to stir up a similar revolt at home.

So when the news broke that Priestley and his fellow Birmingham radicals intended to hold a dinner at Dadley's Hotel to celebrate the second anniversary of the storming of the Bastille, fury erupted. The final straw for the city's Anglican majority was the distribution of a mischievous pamphlet purporting to be from the dinner's organizers that called on "every enemy to civil and religious despotism" to celebrate Bastille Day. Violent threats poured in and a spooked Priestley decided not to attend. The remaining guests pressed ahead but ate and left early, sneaking away from the scene before the growing crowd of protestors outside the hotel could realize they were gone. It took until the early evening before the hundreds of demonstrators realized they had been duped.

Infuriated at missing their chance to confront the radicals in person, they stoned the hotel and set off to destroy the properties of the dissidents in their midst, starting with the New Meeting House of Priestley's Unitarian Church. After setting this and many other buildings on fire, the suggestion that they head to Priestley's home rippled through the crowd. The mob began marching toward the controversial minister's residence. The terrified Priestley family could hear the rioters getting closer and closer to their home so they fled. On reaching his home on Fairhill, the mob ransacked the house, smashed up his laboratory, and set the building on fire. The flames tore through the house, reducing Priestley's extensive collection of scientific equipment, books, and studies to a smoldering pile of ash.

As their home burned, the Priestley family fled through the city's dark back streets. Eventually they reached London, but there was little sympathy for the Priestleys. When King George III finally sent in the army to quell the violence in Birmingham, he made it clear whose side he was on: "I cannot but feel better pleased that Priestley is the sufferer for the doctrines he and his party have instilled, and that the people see them in their true light." After the riots Priestley became an object of national hatred. Effigies of him were burned alongside those of fellow radical Thomas Paine. Shopkeepers refused to serve him and his family. People wrote letters accusing him of being in league with the devil and newspapers lampooned him with vitri-olic cartoons. Even the Royal Society turned their back on the man who had discovered oxygen.

By April 1794, Priestley had had enough. He and his family packed their bags and set sail for the United States, hoping—like so many before him—to find freedom in this new country with its ideals of democracy and liberty. Priestley's exit from Britain was well timed. By the time his ship docked in Battery Park eight weeks later, the British government had begun rounding up prominent radicals and charging them with seditious libel for their criti-cisms of the king, his government, and the Anglican Church. Priestley settled in Northumberland, Pennsylvania, but he spent a lot of his time in Philadel-phia mixing with the pioneers of American science. Many of the scientists he befriended in the City of Brotherly Love shared his fascination with sparkling water, especially Founding Father and physician Benjamin Rush.

Such was Rush's belief in the curative abilities of fizzing water that in 1773 he published a comparative study of three mineral water sources in Pennsylvania, which sought to identify not just their composition but also what diseases they could remedy. One of the water sources he examined was a twenty-six-foot-deep well in Philadelphia, close to the corner of Sixth and Chestnut. This water, he wrote, "has a slight fetid smell, is somewhat turbid, and after standing a few hours exposed to the air, deposits a yellow sediment." It also had "a strong ferruginous taste" that he attributed to the presence of iron. Despite this sparkling water's disagreeable aroma and fla-vor, Rush had no hesitation in recommending it as a treatment for a ragbag of ailments including hysteria, worms, kidney disease, and "foul ulcers of long standing," although he warned that it could be harmful in cases of hypochondria and consumption. The only mystery was the smell. "To what is the peculiar odor of the Philadelphia water owing," he wondered. "It has been ascribed to sulphur; but there are few direct proofs of sulphur being dissolved in a simple state in water."

Undeterred by Rush's unanswered question, Philadelphians flocked to the well and held their noses while they drank for their health. Eventually the well ran dry, so the determined citizens began searching for a way to reconnect the well to the source of this special water. Their search swiftly ended when it was discovered that the unpleasant smell that so puzzled Rush was caused by a leak in a nearby privy.

Despite such mishaps, Americans remained just as convinced as their counterparts in Europe that mineral waters had medicinal properties. Scientists investigated the properties of America's spring waters, doctors prescribed them, and citizens journeyed for miles to try them in the hope of curing their illnesses. The most highly regarded natural springs could attract huge crowds. At its peak, the iron-rich waters of Yellow Springs in Chester County, Pennsylvania, would draw as many as three hundred bathers and drinkers a day. The springs of Saratoga in upstate New York were another popular destination. According to legend, the British war hero Sir William Johnson was the first white man to visit the springs. Johnson had found fame in 1755 during the French and Indian War, when his army of colonials and Native Americans held back the French advance at Lac du Saint-Sacrement, which he promptly renamed Lake George in honor of the British king. While the British celebrated Johnson's victory, he left the battlefield permanently wounded by a lead shot that lodged itself in his upper leg. By August 1767 this persistent wound, coupled with gout, had left Johnson unable to walk. So when a group of Mohawks offered to take him to the "medicine spring," he readily accepted. After several days at the spring Johnson claimed he was well enough to walk the rough trail home without assistance.

The story is almost certainly false. Johnson was a man prone to grand fibs. His claims of military expertise were repeatedly disputed by those he commanded, and while serving as a British diplomat, he deliberately overstated the strength of the Iroquois Confederacy to boost his own standing. It is also unlikely that no other white person would have found the spring by 1767, since there were already settlements close by at that time. But no one really cared if Johnson's tale was true or not. The story of the distinguished war veteran cured by a secret Native American spring hidden in the wilderness captured people's imaginations and put Saratoga on the map. Visitors came from far and wide to sample its fizzing waters, including George Washington, who was so impressed that he later tried to buy the land around it, without success.

The fascination with the water of Saratoga and the nearby Ballston Spa was such that people began trying to bottle it. But this was an idea fraught with difficulty, as Colonel Otho Williams told Washington in a 1784 letter: "The water . . . cannot be confined so that the air will not, somehow or other, escape. Several persons told us that they had corked it tight in bottles, and that the bottles broke. We tried it with the only bottle we had, which did not break, but the air found its way through a wooden stopper and the wax with which it was sealed."

A solution to the problems that Colonel Williams described would be found by Benjamin Silliman, another fascinated visitor to the springs, and his solution would change America. The serious-minded son of a wealthy Connecticut lawyer, Silliman first visited Ballston and Saratoga in 1797 during a bout of depression. He spent a month at the springs, resting and drinking water "brisk with carbonic acid gas" before leaving, convinced that the iron-rich liquid had banished his dark moods. This visit would have had little significance were it not for an unexpected turn of events as Silliman completed his legal studies at Yale University in New Haven in March 1802.

The twenty-three-year-old planned to follow his father into the legal profession, but on finishing his exams, Yale asked if he would be interested in becoming its first chemistry professor. While Silliman's utter lack of chemical knowledge might have seemed like a severe handicap, chemistry was so new a science at the time that Yale figured it would be easier to get the capable student to learn the subject than to find someone who knew anything about it. After some hemming and hawing, Silliman accepted and set out to learn everything he could about the science he would soon have to teach.

Silliman's search for chemical knowledge began in Philadelphia, the hub of American science. There he dined with Priestley, and they discussed the practice of science, the Birmingham riots, and their opposing views of Christianity over their meal. After soaking up the insights of the city's preeminent scientists, Silliman headed to Europe in 1805 to further his knowledge and amass a collection of books and specialist equipment to bring back to Yale. During his travels in Europe he witnessed the lighting of London's first gas-powered light (which, he excitedly reported, "made noonday in the streets"), made the arduous journey to Cornwall to see its steam-powered mining operations, and found himself being questioned by police in Antwerp who suspected him of being a British spy. He also noted London's booming trade in bottled mineral waters, a sight that bubbled up again in his mind when he returned to America in 1806.

Silliman was preparing to marry Harriet Trumbull, the daughter of Connecticut governor Jonathan Trumbull. Although keen to marry, Silliman fretted that his meager teacher's salary would not be enough to support a family, and he began searching for a way to boost his income. Producing artificial mineral waters was an obvious choice. His studies of chemistry had armed him with the skills needed to create sparkling waters, his experience at Ballston had convinced him of the medicinal powers of carbonated water, and the thriving British bottled water industry had shown him that there was gold in fizz. That this business would give those who could not afford to travel to the exclusive spa towns access to these special waters also chimed neatly with his devout Christianity.

Convinced that he had hit on a way to earn his fortune, Silliman bought a Nooth's Apparatus for twenty-five dollars and struck a deal to sell his bottled water in a New Haven apothecary store. It didn't take long before the Yale professor discovered his plan worked better in theory than in practice. While demand for his water was high, bottling it was easier said than done. America's first glass house may have opened in Jamestown, Virginia, back in 1608, but two centuries later, the country's glass-making industry was still in a primordial state, and the nation relied on cheaper European imports for much of its glassware. Such was the scarcity and expense of glass at the start of the 1800s that glass windows in homes were considered a status symbol. Further, the glass bottles being produced in the United States at the time were rarely strong enough to withstand the pressure of carbonated water. Stoneware bottles, an alternative to glass, were equally unappealing due to their ineffectiveness at stopping the fizz from escaping the liquid.

Frustrated, Silliman hit on the idea of buying used British-made bottles, which were being imported to America filled with carbonated water. In October 1806 he wrote to his future father-in-law to ask for his help in securing a reliable supply of these imported bottles, explaining that since it was "quite impossible with my present means to oblige as many as call upon me for soda water, I have determined to undertake the manufacture of it on the large scale as is done in London." But almost as soon as he had found a solution to his bottle problems, world events intervened when Congress banned the import of carbonated waters from Britain.

The import ban was the latest salvo in a period of worsening relations between Britain and its former colony. At the core of the dispute was the British Royal Navy's practice of press-ganging sailors into naval service. Despite Britain's defeat in the Revolutionary War, the Royal Navy took the view that anyone born British could be forced into naval servitude and that included all those born in the United States before independence. So with little regard for its former colony's status as an independent nation, the British dragged thousands of American men from the decks of US ships and the streets of US ports to serve in the Royal Navy. Unsurprisingly, these actions infuriated the American people, but the nation's navy was no match for the British war machine, and the peace treaty between the two nations had left the issue of press-ganging unresolved. Thomas Jefferson was also wary of raising the matter, preferring to stay on friendly terms with the British while he tried to gain control of Florida.

The tension over press-ganging finally exploded in 1805 as Britain's fight with Napoleon's France intensified. Keen to contain the French emperor's ambitions, the British declared that any neutral nation that traded with its enemies could not trade with any part of its empire. But as Britain tried to use trade to punish countries that supplied the French, America was secretly helping nations to circumvent the British policy. European nations shut out by the British policy were allowed to dock at US ports and pick up duty certificates so they could pass off their cargo as originating in America even though it was never unloaded. The British were furious when they discovered America's deceit, and they retaliated by blockading New York harbor and stepping up the press-ganging of American sailors. Unable to respond militarily, America hit back by banning the import of a wide range of British goods. Eventually this dispute led to the War of 1812, but for Silliman the import ban was a show stopper, cutting off his supply of British bottles.

With his dream of replicating London's water businesses shattered, Silliman gave up on bottles and moved his equipment into the apothecary's store, where he started selling fizzy water by the glass. It was a decision forced by circumstance, but Silliman's new approach would have a profound impact on American life, for in that moment in 1806 Silliman created the first soda fountain. It was the fork in the road where America's approach to carbonated water found its own direction, one distinct from the bedside gasogenes of France and the bottled waters of Britain. This direction took carbonated water into an environment closer in spirit to the bar or the coffeehouse, and it turned soda drinking into a social, public activity open to people of all classes.

Selling water by the glass proved popular enough for Silliman to start thinking big. He moved out of the apothecary's premises and opened a dedicated store for his healthful waters in New Haven. The store struggled to turn a profit, but Silliman's belief in his business was convincing enough for three of his friends—Yale math professor Jeremiah Day, attorney Stephen Twinning, and New York apothecary Noyes Darling—to become partners in the venture. As they strived to get the New Haven store into the black, they got wind of a rumor that a similar enterprise had been founded in Philadelphia and the owner was now planning to expand into New York City. Eager to forestall this unknown competitor, the four agreed to open a store in New York as fast as possible.

In spring 1809 they opened their first soda water fountain in New York within the Tontine Coffee House, a popular spot on the corner of Wall and Walter that shared its building with the New York Stock Exchange. Darling set up three sets of carbonation equipment in the cellar, one for each type of water they would dispense—soda, Seltzer and Ballston. Soda was a plain water carbonated using bicarbonate of soda while the other two were replicas of famous natural springs. Although it would later become, like soda water, a generic term for carbonated water, their Seltzer was based on the waters of the Selters springs in Germany, which contained sodium, calcium, and magnesium salts. The Ballston water was, of course, an imitation of the waters that had captured Silliman's own imagination and contained sodium, calcium, magnesium, iodine, and iron salts as well as silica.

Each carbonator was connected to the bar above with tin pipes. At the bar level Darling hid the unattractive pipes within mahogany pillars placed a foot apart, each with a silver stopcock from which the fountain's operator would draw the pressurized water from below. The final touch was gilt urns placed on top of each pillar that displayed the name of the type of water the pillars would dispense.

While setting up the Tontine fountain, Darling discovered that the rumors of the competitor from Philadelphia were true. The challenger was Joseph Hawkins, a former secretary to the American ambassador to France, who had started his fountain business in 1807 on Chestnut Street, a short stroll from the polluted well that once got Benjamin Rush so excited. Hawkins sold his water for six cents a glass and won glowing endorsements from local physicians including Rush and the pioneering surgeon John Syng Dorsey. Flush with the success of his Chestnut Street business, Hawkins was now preparing to make his move on New York City. But Hawkins wasn't the only threat to Silliman and his friends, as an Irishman named George Usher had also opened a soda fountain on Broadway.

As the summer of 1809 approached, the scene was set for a clash of the soda fountain pioneers, and it didn't take long before the cash-strapped Silliman and his partners found themselves on the back foot. The Tontine Coffee House might have been a prime location but sales were disappointing. Within a few weeks its owner had resorted to sticking labels on wine bottles that encouraged customers to mix it with soda water to drum up business. Silliman's rivals also had distinct advantages. Hawkins's custom-made carbonation apparatus was far more precise and reliable than Silliman's cranky and outmoded equipment and, much to Silliman's annoyance, both he and Usher had access to a reliable supply of bottles capable of withstanding the pressure of their sparkling waters.

Usher in particular proved to be a formidable and forward-thinking rival. There appear to be no first-hand records of Usher's motivations and approach, but Silliman and his colleagues' correspondence highlights how the Irishman's approach captured the imagination of New Yorkers. While Silliman emphasized the health benefits and science behind his replica mineral waters, Usher made his fountain a stylish venue for the city's fashion-conscious residents. He provided free newspapers and novels for his clientele to read while they sipped his waters so they could "combine amusement with utility in this novel and salutary establishment." The Irishman also allowed men and women to mingle at his fountain and opened on Sundays. As the competition between the two businesses intensified, Silliman relented on his opposition to serving women, but he stubbornly drew the line at doing business on the Sabbath.

Usher's innovative streak didn't end there, either. He made a point of making his waters extra bubbly and ice-cold. The latter was an especially daring move for the time. A great many people believed that drinking cold drinks was dangerous, possibly fatal. Doctors warned patients to avoid cold drinks, and those who dared to sip icy water often poured some on their wrists before drinking in the hope that it would prevent them from dying of the shock of imbibing the chilled beverage. But with the oppressive summer heat bearing down and the healthy image of carbonated water, Usher's chilled drinks overcame people's fears of death by cold soda. The growing appeal of cold soda water presented another challenge for the cash-poor Silliman. Ice was an expensive commodity in the days before refrigeration. Supplies were limited by how much ice could be gathered in the winter and stored at a low enough temperature to remain solid. To get around the expense of buying ice, Silliman tried chilling his water by having the fountain operator pour the liquid over ice, only to find that New York's ice came from stagnant ponds and that no New Yorker would want to drink a beverage that had come into contact with such ice.

As summer turned to fall, Silliman's venture was struggling. Even the opening of a second fountain in the City Hotel had failed to turn things around. Despite his business struggles, Silliman finally married on September 17, 1809, and the newlyweds headed for Newport, Rhode Island, to enjoy their honeymoon. But while he honeymooned, trouble was brewing back in New York. A visiting sailor had died unexpectedly after drinking at a soda fountain, and his death was quickly attributed to chilled water. Panicked by the news, New Yorkers stopped going to the soda fountains, wiping out the trade overnight. Something had to be done and fast.

With Silliman away, Darling was left in charge. He froze, unsure of how to remedy this sudden turn of events. In contrast Usher, ever the canny businessman, wasted no time. He made a public point of throwing out the wooden casks he had been using to store his water, and he replaced them with brand new copper ones. The copper casks came with a host of benefits. The metal made it easier for him to cool his water, and the airtight design helped retain the bubbles. The copper also looked more attractive to the public, and since doctors had declared that copper was an excellent tonic, it reassured people that Usher's water was safe to drink. Customers defected from Silliman's establishments and joined the queues at Usher's fountain.

Silliman returned from his honeymoon in October 1809 to find his business was finished. Darling bore the brunt of Silliman's failed soda dream, having racked up debts of $40,000, a sum equivalent to more than $740,000 in today's dollars. Faced with this debt mountain, Darling vanished, leaving behind a letter implying he had committed suicide. He later resurfaced in Pittsburgh before vanishing again as he sought to evade his creditors. Meanwhile Silliman sold his equipment and the City Hotel operation to his rival Joseph Hawkins. Silliman, with his science and health–focused appeals to the public, had misjudged the desires of his customers. They might have wanted the curative fizz but they were just as, if not more, keen on having somewhere to go that was fun and inviting.

Silliman and his friends might have walked away bruised, but the soda fountain concept that they pioneered thrived. The business model established by Usher, Hawkins, and Silliman during that competitive New York summer spread like wildfire as entrepreneurs latched onto the idea of profiting from soda water. In the decade that followed, fountains sprouted in cities and towns across the Eastern Seaboard before moving, step by step, ever westward toward the frontier. As the soda fountains spread they weaved themselves into everyday life, unseating tradition as they converted people to the refreshing appeal of ice-cold drinks. The curative carbonated waters that were once only available to the richest citizens were now everyday commodities, available in plentiful supply on Main Street. As Adlard Welby, an English visitor to Philadelphia in 1819, reported in a book about his travels to America: "During the hot season, mineral waters (chiefly soda), sometimes mixed with syrups, are drank in great abundance. The first thing every American who can afford five cents . . . takes on rising in the morning, is a glass of soda water: many houses are open for the sale of it, and some of them are fitted up with Parisian elegance."

Welby's words not only provided a snapshot of how rapidly the soda fountain entrenched itself in American life within its first decade but also pointed to how this new retail experience was evolving with ever more eye-catching interior decoration. The move toward more elaborate fountains was underway even as the 1809 contest of the pioneers drew to a close. After taking over Silliman's City Hotel fountain, Hawkins gave it an overhaul. He ditched the plain gooseneck spigots and installed a marble fountain where consumers could choose between three fizzy waters that would gush from the mouths of sculptured eagles. This fantastical fountain design was just the beginning. As the 1800s progressed a decorative arms race that would last a century broke out between competing fountains as they vied for customers by reaching for ever greater heights of bling and downright bad taste. From exotic polished marble and silver spigots to sculptures of near-nude nymphs, coats of arms, Greek gods, and wild animals, the displays of the soda fountain became ever more elaborate as the manufacturers that formed to service the fountains jostled to produce the most talked-about designs.

One leading light of fountain manufacturing was the Englishman John Matthews, who immigrated to America in 1832. Matthews learned how to build fountain equipment back in Britain while working as a teenage apprentice for Joseph Braham, the inventor of the hydraulic press. On arriving in New York he opened a soda fountain on Gold Street and assembled a fountain of his own design that produced carbon dioxide by applying sulfuric acid to marble—a process that had replaced the use of bicarbonate of soda. (Even so, people kept calling the resulting beverage "soda.") Unlike many fountain owners, however, Matthews had big ambitions. After getting his own fountain up and running, he started buying his competitors. He swallowed Usher's old business, snapped up businesses with valuable patents for soda fountain equipment, and began designing, manufacturing, and building fountains to sell to others. Matthews became one of the kingpins of the soda business, and like his competitors, his company began producing ever more exotic fountain apparatus. Among them was the $2,976

Frost King. The Frost King knew nothing of subtlety. Aimed at upmarket stores in large cities, it boasted glass nozzles, bronze fittings, gas illumination, sixty jewel stones embedded in its frame, and carvings of medieval fantasies in its polished marble exterior.

Matthews's rivals also pulled out all the stops. The equally successful James Tufts of Medford, Massachusetts, was just as prone to grandiose designs. He moved beyond the white Italian marble used in the early fountains and introduced marble of attractive red, velvet black, chocolate laced with white frosting, and—most expensive of all—the majestic swirls of Mexican onyx. But his most excessive creation came in 1876 when he unveiled the ultimate in soda fountain excess at the Centennial Exposition in Philadelphia: the Arctic Soda Water Apparatus. This monster fountain stood thirty-three feet high, weighed thirty tons, and measured twelve feet in diameter. It could dispense twenty-eight types of water and store seventy-six different flavoring syrups and was capped off with hanging ferns, a chandelier, and a device for spraying perfume into the air. This lavish beast ended up at Coney Island after the exposition. In 1886 it was moved to the premises of the Famous Clothing Company, a department store in St. Louis. Shoppers came from miles around to get a glimpse of Tufts's most outrageous creation. Its fame, however, was short-lived. In November 1891 a fire tore through the department store, destroying both the Famous Clothing Company and its spectacular soda fountain.

Other developments in fountain design were more practical. Gustavus Dows of Lowell, Massachusetts, launched his fountain-making enterprise in the late 1850s after becoming fed up with the tiring and hand-numbing task of shaving ice for the drinks served at his older brother's soda fountain. He built a fountain that housed a crank-operated ice shaver as well as tanks for storing flavoring syrups. He named his creation the Ice Cream Soda Apparatus and sold it to fountains throughout the United States for $225 each. Despite its name, Dows's fountain had nothing to do with ice cream soda as we know it today. The reference was a nod to the pre–Civil War practice of mixing sweet cream into soda water.

The modern-day ice cream soda, or float, came a few years later. There are numerous stories about the origin of ice cream soda, but the most convincing claim is that of Robert McCay Green, a small-time fountain manufacturer who introduced it during an 1874 exhibition at the Franklin Institute in Philadelphia. Worried that the lavish creations of bigger rivals such as Dows and Matthews would overshadow his more modest fountain designs, he started looking for a way to stand out from the crowd. Green thought about how people would often drink a soda while eating ice cream, and he decided to combine the two by serving sodas with a dollop of ice cream dunked into the fizz. When the exhibition opened he handed out flyers with a call to action: "Something new! Green's Ice Cream Soda, try it and tell your friends."

The first day was a disaster. Green sold just eight dollars of ice cream soda. Undaunted, Green returned the next day with a new ploy. He went around the exhibition offering teenagers a free ice cream soda if they came to his fountain at a set time. When the time came a throng of young men and women gathered around his fountain. The youthful crowd caught the interest of others, and then the teens to whom he gave the free ice cream sodas began telling others of this unusual but tasty fusion of food and drink. By the end of the exhibition Green was raking in $200 a day. After the exhibition, news of this new recipe spread far and wide. People began asking their local soda fountains to make it for them. Fountain owners, by and large, weren't too pleased about this. It took longer to make than a standard soda drink, and even worse, it took longer for people to consume it. This meant that customers hogged precious seating space for even longer—especially important at a time when ordering a drink and taking it away to gulp down on the streets was socially unacceptable. As irritating as the ice cream soda was for store owners, it was too popular with the public to ignore, so the reluctant fountain owners served it. Green's creation would also provide the inspiration for the sundae, which—the story goes—was invented in Evanston, Illinois, during 1890 after the pious town council banned the serving of ice cream soda on Sundays. Unwilling to be bossed around by these city fathers, one druggist got around the rules by serving ice cream covered in soda syrup that he only served on Sundays. Word of his Sunday treat spread to Chicago before being adopted by fountains throughout the nation.

While the fountains thrived, bottled soda struggled to make similar inroads. Although the War of 1812 derailed Silliman's ambitions, it ultimately helped America's glass industry by prompting the imposition of import tariffs on foreign goods in 1824. This tax amounted to just over a penny a bottle, but that was enough to eliminate Europe's price advantage and make the business of glass making a more profitable venture. And as America's glass industry gathered momentum, bottled soda became a more common sight.

One of the first people to see the potential in bottled soda was Eugene Roussel. Born in France in 1810, Roussel worked as a perfumer in Paris before moving to the United States in July 1838. He settled in Philadelphia and opened a store at 75 Chestnut Street. Roussel's emporium sold toiletries imported from France and Britain, ranging from perfumes and fragrant soaps to skin creams and hair dyes. He also sold bottles of lemon-flavored mineral water, an idea inspired by the bottled waters on sale in Paris. Roussel's flavored water, which came in French-style glass bottles, proved an instant hit with his wealthy clientele. During 1839 he sold 120 to 180 bottles a day and its enduring popularity led him to bring his soda to New York in 1845. Before the end of the 1840s, Roussel had sold his Philadelphia store to focus full-time on his flavored fizz, which by then was even being advertised in the frontier state of Wisconsin.

Yet while Roussel's upscale soda business thrived and inspired dozens of competitors, the bottling of carbonated drinks was still dogged by the challenge of how to retain the fizz. Throughout the 1800s people experimented with hundreds of different approaches to sealing bottles. There were the egg-shaped bottles that relied on the liquid engorging the cork, but even then the gas would seep out—and if sealed incorrectly, the cork was liable to shoot out due to the pressure inside the container. Another method involved placing glass-ball stoppers in the neck of the bottle. The bottle would then be sealed by pulling the ball up using a hook embedded within it so that the stopper wedged itself in the neck to create a seal. To open the bottle, drinkers would push down on the hook to force the ball back into the bottle. While this approach kept the fizz, the ball was hard to wash, increasing the risk of the drink becoming contaminated. Another approach was the swing stopper, which is still used on bottles of Grolsch lager. This method used wire to hold the stopper tightly in place and allowed drinkers to pop open the bottle using a wire lever attached to the neck. It was easier to clean than the ball stopper but more expensive to make.

It was not until the end of the nineteenth century that the sealing problems plaguing bottled soda were finally resolved with the invention of the Crown Cork bottle cap by William Painter in 1892. The edges of these single-use metal caps would be crimped around the neck of bottles by machine to provide an airtight seal. The caps were cheap and the machine-based sealing method meant soda could be bottled faster than by the hand-based methods that preceded it, a point underscored by Painter's 1898 invention the Crown Soda Machine. This machine condensed the soda bottling process into a single device that was capable of mixing the syrup and water, filling the bottles, and attaching the caps. It streamlined the bottling process and paved the way for the mass production of bottled soda that followed in the twentieth century.

While soda bottlers struggled with sealing technology, the fountains dominated, offering cheaper, colder beverages and more flavors to choose from, thanks to the ever-expanding range of flavoring syrups being created. As in Europe, the exact origin of the use of flavoring syrup in America is unclear, but it was certainly happening in 1807, when Townsend Speakman began stirring up his Nephite Julep, a mix of fruit juice and soda water, for the customers of his Philadelphia apothecary store. By the middle of the 1800s, visitors to the soda fountains faced a bewildering range of flavoring options to liven up their soda water. There were familiar fruit flavors, exotic plants, alcoholic concoctions, and—since fountains were often located in pharmacies—even the medical ingredients that druggists would use to cook up the lotions, pills, and potions that they sold to the public with unsubstantiated claims about their benefits.

Soda drinkers could spice up their fizzy water with enduring favorites such as wintergreen, vanilla, or cherry, or they could opt for something more unusual such as hock, syrup of violets, or celery. To keep people interested, soda fountain operators, who were now nicknamed soda jerks due to the jerking motion they made when pumping out water for their customers, started mixing up new taste combinations for customers to try.

Some mixed sweet cream into the cool bubbling water to create the original cream sodas. Others made chocolate syrups and used them to create chocolate-flavored soda waters that proved a big hit with women. Men tended to opt for the egg sodas, in which soda water and uncooked egg white were stirred together to produce a beverage with a foamy head. The egg sodas eventually spawned the original version of the egg cream, where cream, egg yolk, and soda met. Other soda jerks reached for the chemical cabinets of their stores and chucked in phosphoric acid to create phosphates, a type of soda that offered a pleasing acidic tang.

It was a fad business. For years egg cream would be all the rage, then everyone would go nuts for phosphates before dumping them for some new exciting soda combination. This constant stream of new spins on soda in nineteenth-century America was driven by competition, with fountains hoping to win business by whipping up flavors that couldn't be found elsewhere. Yet while the soda jerks and pharmacists concocted new, head-turning combinations, there were plenty of enduring favorites such as orange, lemon, vanilla, and the 1800s wonder plant sarsaparilla.

Native to Central America, the sarsaparilla plant had long been regarded by the native people as having medicinal properties, and when the first samples were taken back to Europe in the 1500s it gained a reputation as a cure for syphilis. After the initial excitement about its discovery died down, the plant fell into disuse for many years until the patent medicine boom of the 1800s reignited interest in its medical potential. Physicians reassessed sarsaparilla and declared that as well as curing syphilis, it was also effective against scrofula and skin ailments. Some went so far as to add cancer, rheumatism, hepatitis, and gout to the list of diseases this wonder plant could treat. In 1820 the renewed hype was convincing enough to earn sarsaparilla syrup a place in the first United States Pharmacopeia, which also included soda water among its definitive list of medicines. For soda fountains this was a double win. Not only did they get to promote the health benefits of their carbonated water, but the addition of sarsaparilla syrup also let them effortlessly tap into the appeal of the patent medicine. Soon sarsaparilla was one of the most popular flavors at the fountains, providing an early indication of how the soda business would soon embrace both the cookbook of quack medicine and its advertising rulebook too.

3

The Medicine Men

The soda fountain wasn't the only health craze taking America by storm in the early 1800s. As the fountains arrived on Main Street, thousands of people were embracing the ideas of Samuel Thomson, the Pied Piper of quackery. An illiterate pig farmer turned herbal healer, Thomson was an unlikely health icon, but by the 1810s his firebrand approach to medicine had won him legions of devoted followers.

Born in February 1769, Thomson grew up poor on an isolated New Hampshire farm. The nearest doctor lived more than ten miles away, so his family relied on the folk medicine of a neighboring widow for their medical care. "The whole of her practice was with roots and herbs, applied to the patient, or given in hot drinks, to produce sweating; which always answered the purpose," Thomson recalled many years later.

The widow's cures fascinated the young, sickly boy, and he would often help her hunt for herbs and roots in the fields and woods. He dreamed about becoming a "root doctor" who would travel the nation dishing out herbal brews to raise the ill from their sickbeds. But it seemed like an unattainable dream. He was, after all, needed on the family farm, and by the time he turned sixteen he had dismissed his herbalist fantasies as childhood folly.

Not that he forgot about the herbs. When he got sick he turned to the old widow's medicine rather than seeking help from physicians, and every time he recovered he became even more convinced that his roots and herbs could remedy anything. His conviction grew deeper in 1789 when both he and his mother contracted measles. As Thomson's mother lay dying in her bed, doctors battled to save her but their treatments proved ineffective. After nine weeks of fever she died. As usual Thomson refused to see the doctors, dramatically declaring he would rather die than accept their "unnatural" cures. So when he lived and his mother died, he once again concluded his root brews saved him, and came to believe that the doctors killed his mother with their dubious cures.

So a year later when his wife fell gravely ill after giving birth to their first child, he called in the root doctors and when she recovered he decided it was time to follow his dream. He began administering his remedies to his family and neighbors. Then, as word spread, he began treating people for miles around. With his services in high demand he abandoned his pigs and began wandering New England selling his medical expertise. Thomson's homespun medicine centered on expelling disease by inducing vomiting, sweating, or bowel movements in patients. To make patients sweat he would prescribe steam baths and to make them vomit he would feed them *Lobelia inflata*, a vomit-inducing plant also known as Indian tobacco, which Thomson believed could cure just about everything. Armed with his baths and Indian tobacco, Thomson went from town to town promoting his remedies while delivering furious rants against the medical profession, which he regarded as no better than "Java's deadly trees."

Doctors initially laughed at the heavy-browed backwoodsman with his pukeweed and wild-eyed rhetoric, but as Thomson's reputation grew it became clear that his diatribes against the medical profession were resonating with the public. In one case he so whipped up an Illinois crowd with his angry denunciations that they went on the rampage, killing a medical student and seriously injuring his teacher. Worried doctors began pressing for laws to curb his activities, but Thomson simply claimed such action was proof of the grand medical conspiracy he spoke about, winning over even more people in the process.

Thomson's star continued to rise for the next thirty years. He patented his medical system and began selling the right to use it to individual families for $500 a time on the condition that they kept the system a secret. By 1839 Thomson claimed to have sold one hundred thousand of these "family rights," enough to have made him a billionaire in today's money. But Thomson's followers did not keep the secret. Many of those he sold his family rights to taught others about his cures, and some opened schools that taught Thomsonian medicine. Thomson remained furious with those who divulged his secrets until October 1843, when he died while trying in vain to fend off an unidentified fever with his roots and his herbs.

Thomson's salesmanship may have been new but his folk remedies drew on a long tradition of using roots and herbs to produce medicinal teas or beers. Such brews were common in medieval Europe, where the poor would brew drinks made from roots, bark, herbs, and berries that would gently fizz with the gas of fermentation. Known collectively as "small beers," these low-alcohol beverages not only contained plants that people believed had health benefits but, thanks to the alcohol within them, were actually safer than the dirty, parasite-ridden stream and river water they would otherwise have had to drink. One of the most popular and enduring small beers was dandelion and burdock, which was being made in the British Isles by 1265 and, according to legend, was the product of divine intervention. The legend attributes the creation of dandelion and burdock to the Italian priest Saint Thomas Aquinas, who had been praying to God for inspiration. After finishing his prayers, the thirteenth-century Catholic saint headed into the country and, trusting in God to provide, made a drink from the first plants he encountered. The resulting weed brew aided the priest's concentration, enabling him to develop the arguments he set out in his influential guide to Christian beliefs, *Summa Theologica*.

The practice of brewing small beers came to North America as the Europeans began their exploration of the New World. Spruce beer made from the branches of the conifer tree became a favorite among the early colonists. One early advocate of spruce beer was Sir William Vaughan, a Welsh poet and aristocrat who made it his life's mission to establish a settlement on Newfoundland. Vaughan hoped to create a New Wales to rival New England and the new Scotland of Nova Scotia that the Scottish were talking of establishing. He bought land on the chilly island, and in 1616 he paid a group of Welsh families to travel there and establish the settlement of Cambriol.

The families did little more than erect some meager shacks that barely got them through their first winter, but Vaughan was undeterred. He sent a second group and, from his comfortable home in Britain, started supplying them with medical advice that included the recommendation that they drink spruce beer rather than strong liquor. The spruce beer wasn't enough. The colonists endured years of harsh winters, pirate raids, and attacks from French settlers of Canada who repeatedly set their crops on fire before the bid to create New Wales fizzled out in the 1630s.

While New Wales vanished from the map, spruce beer endured. By the time of the Revolutionary War, spruce beer was so popular that the British were giving their soldiers seven drinks of it a day. Not to be outdone, George Washington added a quart of spruce beer to his troops' daily ration of peas, oatmeal, and salt pork. Even as late as 1887 spruce beer was common in what could have been New Wales, with the *Canaseraga Times* reporting that "the fishermen of Newfoundland, Labrador and the Gulf of St. Lawrence drink large quantities of spruce beer." By then, however, spruce beer had been overshadowed in the United States by another small beer descendant: root beer.

Root beer emerged almost at random and with little consistency in its composition, save that it was a drink of roots, herbs, berries, and barks brewed to a family recipe. Some recipes harked back to the earlier small beers with the inclusion of dandelions, spruce, or birch bark, the core ingredient of birch beer. Others used bark from the Joshua tree, which—thanks to its saponin content—gave the resulting brew a foamy head reminiscent of regular beers. More often homemade root beers featured licorice root, sarsaparilla, vanilla, wintergreen, and sassafras.

Wintergreen was a popular flavoring often used in chewing gum and toothpaste while sassafras, like sarsaparilla, had become highly prized in sixteenth- and seventeenth-century Europe as a treatment for syphilis and gonorrhea. So great was the desire for sassafras in Britain at the start of the 1600s that when the English explorer Captain Martin Pring carried out his 1603 survey of Maine, New Hampshire, and Cape Cod he did so with the sole aim of bringing home a ship loaded with the plant. Pring's voyage was an immense success. He returned to the English port of Bristol with a full cargo of sassafras and profited greatly from his efforts. So did Sir Walter Raleigh, whom Queen Elizabeth I had awarded a monopoly that gave him trading rights over all cargo from the New World. The sassafras voyage encouraged Pring to make further expeditions, expeditions that would lay the foundations for the trade routes that later led to the colonization of America.

For years these root beer recipes were passed down through the generations and, despite being fizzy thanks to the fermentation process, had little to do with the sparkling waters being sold in bottles and at soda fountains. But in the second half of the 1800s, entrepreneurs began to look at the idea of taking root beer out of the home and into the stores and fountains. The earliest known attempt to turn root beer into a commercial product came in 1866 when Henry Smith and Hiram Snow of Dover, New Hampshire, hatched a plan to sell bottled root beer. The duo envisaged their drink, Smith's White Root Beer, as a summer beverage, and they sold it in stoneware bottles. In common with the homemade root beers, their drink was carbonated by fermentation and counted sarsaparilla, life-of-man root, prince's pine, spruce oil and sassafras among its ingredients. Whether Smith's White Root Beer achieved much success is unknown as all that remains of their efforts is a patent application and a few intact bottles. But just a few years later a farmer's son from New Jersey would complete root beer's transformation into a commercial product.

Charles Elmer Hires started his pharmacy career with a dollar-a-day job at a drugstore in Salem, New Jersey. After learning the ropes in Salem, he moved to Philadelphia, where he trained to become a pharmacist before opening his own drugstore, complete with a flashy octagonal soda fountain fashioned from dusty pink Tennessee marble. By the time he married in 1875 at the age of twenty-four, his drugstore was doing decent if unspectacular business. But all that was about to change.

For his honeymoon Hires and his wife went to stay at a boardinghouse on a New Jersey farm near Morristown. During their stay their hostess offered the teetotal Quaker couple her homemade "herb tea," a root beer brewed using berries, bark, roots, and herbs collected from local fields and woods. While her drink gained its fizz from the fermentation of yeast rather than artificial carbonation, the brewing process was cut short so that the beverage had no more than a trace amount of alcohol but was lightly carbonated. Impressed by her refreshing temperance beverage, Hires asked her for the recipe. The generous hostess happily obliged, detailing the process and even going to the trouble of taking Hires out to the woods and fields to point out the exact sixteen plants she used to create her beverage. As the woman pointed out the ingredients, the businessman in Hires stirred. Collecting all this stuff seemed terribly time consuming, he thought. Would it not be better to make an extract and sell it so that all that needed to be done was to add yeast, sugar, and water? Also, he thought, if an extract was produced on a large scale then the finest ingredients from across the world could be used, rather than whatever happened to grow nearby.

Hires returned to Philadelphia inspired, and he set to work creating a powdered root beer extract that he envisaged as the perfect marriage of quality and convenience. With the aid of two local physicians he identified roots, berries, barks, and herbs that would make his drink healthy as well as tasty. The final recipe included sarsaparilla, wintergreen, spikenard, birch bark, Italian juniper berries, and dog grass. In keeping with his belief in abstinence from alcohol, the young businessman named his beverage Hires Herbal Tea and readied himself to introduce it at Philadelphia's 1876 Centennial Exposition. But when he told his plans to his friend Reverend Dr. Russell Conwell, the Baptist minister who had found fame with his motivational "Acres of Diamonds" speech, the clergyman objected. "For Heaven's sake don't call it herb tea," Conwell exclaimed. "Our hard-drinking Pennsylvania coal miners will never touch it under that name. Call it root beer." Hires did as he was told and renamed the drink Hires Root Beer just in time for the exposition, where he handed out free glasses of his temperance beverage to crowds wowed by James Tufts's enormous, perfume-spitting Arctic Soda Water Apparatus.

Despite the free samples and name change, sales of Hires Root Beer would remain sluggish until a chance meeting changed Hires's fortunes. One morning while Hires traveled to his store on the Market Street cable car, a man named George Childs sat next to him. The two began talking and Childs, the publisher of the *Philadelphia Public Ledger* newspaper, told

Hires, "I have had a taste of your root beer, and think it fine. Why don't you advertise it?" Hires explained that all his money was tied up in his business and he had none to spare. "Let the advertisements make money for you," responded Childs, who then offered to delay billing Hires for any ads he bought until he was making enough money from his root beer to settle the bill. Shortly after, Hires placed his first advertisement.

"Sales increased slowly at first, and then more rapidly, until I felt justified in asking the *Ledger* for a bill," recalled Hires years later. When the bill came it was a shock. "It amounted to more than $700! I nearly had heart failure, for while I knew advertising cost money, I had no idea that it cost *that* much. That was really the turning point of my career as an advertiser, for I found courage enough to let the advertising go on running while I was paying off the $700. For the next 10 years I put every penny of profit from the root beer business back into advertising."

As sales grew so did Hires's commitment to advertising his root beer extract, a packet of which would cost twenty-five cents and could produce five gallons of the drink. His promotional campaigns became bolder and bolder, setting the tone for not just the soft drink industry but advertisers everywhere. He pushed Childs to let him run ads over two newspaper columns rather than the standard one-column width, and he became one of the first advertisers to buy an entire page of a US newspaper. Soon he was timing the publication of his daily newspaper ads to coincide with hot weather so that people were more likely to see the promotions for his refreshing drink while feeling thirsty. By 1884 Hires Root Beer ads were appearing in papers throughout the United States and Canada.

Hires's promotional assault didn't end there. He opened a printing division within his company that produced a blizzard of promotional cards, lithographs, booklets, and pictures, many of which emphasized the link between Hires and Christian temperance with painted scenes from the Old Testament or quotations from scripture. He hired seventy-three salesmen to travel the length and breadth of America, going from town to town sticking his booklets into letterboxes. The lithographs and cards were sent to stores to help jolt customers into buying some Hires Root Beer extract. To improve brand recognition among children, Hires came up with the Hires Root Boy, a chubby infant mascot who always wanted one more root beer.

The scale of Hires's promotional campaign was unheard of for a soft drink. It was a campaign worthy of the biggest-spending patent medicine makers, who had set the pace for advertising ambition for most of the 1800s with their brazen claims, spectacular medicine shows, and giant billboards. Hires's promotional push caused a rapid rise in sales. Within five years he had gone from selling enough extract to make 11,520 glasses of his root beer every year to selling enough to make nearly 1.5 million drinks. As the mustached business tycoon noted in an interview: "Business success is built upon two foundation rocks. One is to make your product as nearly perfect as possible. The second is to be energetic and tireless in selling it." Hires's recipe for success would not be lost on two new carbonated drink brands that burst into life a few years later in the mid-1880s, both fueled by their creators' interest in patent medicine and dreams of wealth: Moxie and Coca-Cola.

Moxie started out in 1876 as Moxie Nerve Food, a nostrum invented by a spiritualist named Dr. Augustin Thompson. Born in Union, Maine, in 1835, Thompson trained as a blacksmith before deciding to become a doctor while serving in the Union infantry during the Civil War. On being discharged in July 1865 he enrolled at the Hahnemann Homeopathic College in Philadelphia, a medical school that taught the theories of Samuel Hahnemann, a German with a distrust of mainstream medicine to rival that of Samuel Thomson. Hahnemann believed that "like cures like," so if a substance induced symptoms similar to a specific disease then it would cure that illness. After finding his medicines often proved toxic, he decided his cures would work safely if diluted and devised a dilution method so extreme that what he gave patients was nothing more than water. It was outlandish quackery, but in an age when professional medicine often failed to deliver results, his remedies caught on. By 1875 there were six thousand homeopathic doctors at work in the United States alone.

Thompson lapped up Hahnemann's theories, and on completing his studies in 1867 he headed to Lowell, Massachusetts, doctorate in hand. On reaching the industrial textiles town he opened a homeopathic practice.

Within ten years it was the largest homeopathic practice in New England, but by then Thompson was captivated by the stories about the druggists who had gotten into the patent medicine business and were now making incredible profits.

Thompson decided to make some nostrums of his own and in 1876 launched Moxie Nerve Food. He told his customers that this powerful, dark brown potion was named after his good friend Lieutenant Moxie, whom he met while studying at the United States Military Academy at West Point. Lieutenant Moxie went on to discover a nameless miracle plant in the Strait of Magellan. This turnip-shaped plant, he continued, is the basis of Moxie Nerve Food and has incredible curative powers. It could, Thompson claimed, "recover brain and nervous exhaustion; loss of manhood, imbecility and helplessness." Not only that but "paralysis, softening of the brain, locomotor ataxia, and insanity when caused by nervous exhaustion" too. Not to mention restoring the appetite, banishing tiredness, and curing alcoholism.

In common with most patent medicines sold at the time, the sales pitch for Moxie Nerve Food was nothing but lies. Thompson never attended West Point. Lieutenant Moxie didn't exist nor did the magic turnip from South America. The main flavorings were sugar, wintergreen, and gentian root extract, resulting in a drink that tasted like a bitter root beer with a licorice-like aftertaste. The Moxie name was likely borrowed from the landscape of Maine, where there is a Moxie Falls, Moxie Mountain, and Moxie Cove.

Despite being sold on the back of a tale as fictional as the amateur plays Thompson took to writing in his twilight years, Moxie Nerve Food achieved modest success. But it still wasn't the patent medicine hit Thompson had hoped to create. So in 1884 he carbonated his potion and relaunched it as a soda that he sold in twenty-six-ounce bottles and as a fountain syrup. To help promote his drink, Thompson hired Frank Archer, a former soda fountain clerk from Lincoln, Maine. Archer quickly proved himself as a man with a knack for attention-grabbing gimmicks. His first stunt was the Moxie Bottle Wagon, a giant recreation of the drink's bottle in which a salesman would sit and sell soda through a hatch. Launched in the summer of 1886, Archer ordered the enormous bottle to be hauled around New England by horse-drawn cart, knowing that wherever it went it was bound to get people talking about Moxie. Soon Archer had a fleet of Moxie Bottle Wagons roaming the northeastern states.

In 1907 Archer went one better with a thirty-five-foot replica Moxie bottle that toured expositions around New England before becoming a fixture at the Pine Island Amusement Park in Manchester, New Hampshire. In 1919 the company, feeling the bottle had run its course, sold off the giant bottle to a local man called Louis Messier. Messier turned the oversized promotional item into a tower-like extension for his two-bedroom cottage, creating an instant landmark and prompting jokes in newspapers about old ladies living in shoes. It remained part of the house until 1999 when it was finally dismantled. Coupled with more traditional advertising, Archer's zany promotions turned Thompson's reinvented nostrum into the leading soda of the Yankee North with sales of just under 2.3 million bottles in 1899. By then, however, an upstart from the south called Coca-Cola was nipping at its heels.

John Pemberton, the creator of Coca-Cola, was born in July 1831 in Knoxville, Georgia, and like the creator of Moxie, he found himself drawn to the world of alternative medicine. In 1850 he became a student at the South Botanico Medical College, one of the schools that taught Samuel Thomson's medical system and had so angered the firebrand herbalist in his final years. On completing his studies, Pemberton—in true Thomsonian tradition—became a "steam doctor" and set to work trying to sweat the ailments out of patients. In 1853, while still working as a steam doctor, he married Cliff, the fifteen-year-old daughter of a plantation owner. She gave birth to their only child, Charles, a year later. Pemberton eventually tired of sweating patients and in 1855 he and his family moved to Columbus, Georgia, where he opened a drugstore selling medicines, cigars, perfumes, dyes, and surgical instruments. The business thrived. But in spring 1861 as Pemberton wrote to his mother-in-law telling of his success, dark clouds were forming on the horizon.

A few days after writing to Cliff's mother, the seven Confederate states announced their secession from the United States in response to Abraham Lincoln's election victory and the new president's opposition to slavery. A month later civil war broke out. Life continued as normal for the Pembertons for a while, but in May 1862 as the fighting intensified and the Union made gains in Tennessee and Virginia, Pemberton closed his store and enlisted in the Confederate cavalry. Pemberton became a lieutenant colonel in the Third Georgia Cavalry but soon quit because he didn't like taking orders. So instead of going to war he formed a militia cavalry that would fight to protect Columbus should the Yankees make it that far.

That moment finally came on Easter Sunday, April 16, 1865, in what would prove to be the final battle of the Civil War. The Confederate strategy was to prevent the Union troops from crossing the Chattahoochee River and entering the city. So they burned down one of the city's two bridges and gathered at the remaining crossing to face the Northern forces. Just after nightfall the Battle of Columbus began with Pemberton's cavalry among the Southern forces gathered for the last stand of the Confederacy. During the two-hour battle for the bridge, Pemberton was wounded: shot and slashed by a saber that sliced him open from abdomen to chest. Against the odds Pemberton survived the battle. The Confederacy did not. Ten days later the war was over.

The South had been crushed. Many of its cities were in ruins and its people were defeated and malnourished. A sense of moroseness infected the defeated states and patent medicine sales boomed as citizens searched for nostrums capable of ridding them of the disease and deep depression that blighted daily life. This was especially true in Atlanta, which was particularly hard hit in the war. The city had formed in 1837 as Terminus, a collection of shanty homes, whorehouses, and saloons stuck at the southern end of the Western and Atlantic Railroad, which stretched north to Chattanooga and was intended to be extended east to Augusta. By 1860 this dead-end hamlet had changed its name to Atlanta and become a railroad hub where nearly ten thousand people lived. But when General William Sherman of the Union army reached the city in November 1864 on his way to capture the port of Savannah, he ordered Atlanta to be leveled. As the general recalled in his memoirs when his forces finally left for Savannah, "Behind us lay Atlanta, smoldering and in ruins, the black smoke rising high in the air, and hanging like a pall over the ruined city." Atlanta, however, would rise from the ashes like a phoenix.

Instead of brooding on its destruction, Atlanta rebuilt itself with a new vigor, rallying around the vision of a New South as championed by Henry Grady, the editor of the *Atlanta Daily Herald* and, later, the *Atlanta Constitution*. Through his newspapers Grady pitched his vision of Atlanta as the place where the New South would be forged. "There was a South of slavery and secession; that South is dead," he remarked in an 1866 speech. "There is a South of union and freedom; that South, thank God, is living, breathing, growing every hour. . . . From the ashes [General Sherman] left we have raised a brave and beautiful city; somehow or other we have caught the sunshine in the brick and mortar of our homes and have builded therein not one ignoble prejudice or memory."

To illustrate the need for a new, industrial South he told the story of a poor Georgia farmer who, when he died, was buried in a coffin made in Cincinnati. The nails that sealed his coffin and the clothes he was buried in also originated from the factories of the North. So too his marble headstone, which came from Vermont, and the Pittsburgh-made shovel that dug his grave. All Georgia did, he noted, was provide a body and some cotton. Atlanta took Grady's impassioned vision to heart and in the final decades of the 1800s turned itself into a boomtown. In 1870 there were just 2,200 residents. Ten years later it was a thriving city of 37,000 people. By 1900 there were 90,000 citizens living there. In just thirty years Atlanta went from smoking ashes to a modern city with paved streets, electric lights, streetcars and tall office blocks that cast long shadows over the churches that once dominated its skyline.

At the center of this fast-growing metropolis were the patent medicine men. Postbellum Atlanta was the national capital of patent medicine, packing in more quacks per head than any other US city. And it was the city's insatiable appetite for nostrums that drew Pemberton to its bright lights, dazzling energy, and potential for profit in 1869. Pemberton opened a drugstore in Kimball House, an upscale hotel with more than three hundred rooms and a steam-powered elevator. He hoped to find plenty of business there for his Globe Flower Cough Syrup and Extract of Stillingia blood purifier. But his business crashed and burned. By 1872 he was bust, and he would have to spend the next seven years paying off the debts from the failed venture. Undeterred, Pemberton started making nostrums to sell to Atlanta's drugstores, including a rheumatism cure called Prescription 47-11. It was while cooking up these new patent medicines that he read an article by Sir Robert Christison, the president of the British Medical Association, reporting on how he managed to climb the Ben Vorlich mountain in the Scottish Highlands by chewing coca leaf.

Peruvians might have been using coca leaf as a stimulant for centuries, but the chemists and physicians of Europe and North America only started taking an interest in this unusual plant after 1855, when the German chemist Friedrich Gaedcke isolated its active ingredient—cocaine. The plant's reputation grew further in 1859 when the Italian doctor Paolo Mantegazza wrote about his experiences of chewing coca leaf while out in Peru. So impressed was Mantegazza that he boldly declared, "I would rather have a life span of 10 years with coca than one of 10,000,000 centuries without coca." On reading Mantegazza's enthusiastic endorsement, Angelo Mariani, a Corsican chemist and businessman living in Paris, started looking for a way to turn this new wonder plant into a product he could sell. He tried it in teas, in lozenges, and in pâtés before, in 1863, he combined it with red wine to create a coca-wine cordial called Vin Mariani.

Mariani sold his cocaine-laced wine as a luxury tonic and sent cases to the rich and famous along with a request for an endorsement and a photo. When celebrities responded with praise, he would use their words and image in his advertisements and to gain publicity in newspapers across the world. Among those who became advocates for Vin Mariani were Pope Leo XIII, who took to carrying it around with him in a hip flask, and the prolific inventor Thomas Edison, who spoke of how the drink kept him awake. Another fan was the sculptor Frédéric Auguste Bartholdi, who declared that if he had been drinking Vin Mariani when designing the Statue of Liberty he would have made it hundreds of meters high rather than forty-six. And he very well might have because Vin Mariani was rather potent. The recommended dose was three full claret glasses of Vin Mariani a day, equivalent to a line of cocaine spread over a day washed down with three glasses of 22 proof wine.

Mariani's coca wine became a global success, well known not just in Europe but also in America. It inspired so many copycats that the French businessman began running advertisements warning his customers about "the many worthless, so-called coca preparations" and the dastardly people who made them. One of those dastardly people was Pemberton. Having read about the wonders of cocaine, which was still legal at the time, the Atlanta druggist gave it a try and reported "a feeling as though the body was possessed of a new power formerly unknown to the individual." Impressed, he joined the coca-wine bandwagon by launching French Wine Coca in 1884. To promote this buzzy brew, Pemberton ran advertisements listing the multitude of ills his coca wine could allegedly treat, including "nerve trouble, dyspepsia, mental and physical exhaustion, all chronic and wasting diseases, gastric irritability, constipation, sick headaches, neuralgia."

As Pemberton began selling his French Wine Coca for a dollar a bottle, cocaine's reputation was at its peak. A year earlier Austrian ophthalmologist Karl Koller discovered the drug was an effective and revolutionary local anesthetic allowing eye, throat, and nose surgery to be performed on conscious patients. His famous Viennese friend Sigmund Freud was writing about its value as an antidepressant and about his own use of cocaine. Back in America, former president Ulysses S. Grant told the country how he was using cocaine to ease the pain of the throat cancer that would kill him in July 1885, and the Hay Fever Association had declared it their official remedy. There was no shortage of cocaine to buy either. Stores and mail-order businesses offered not just cocaine itself but coca-leaf cigarettes, ointments, and sprays too. All were available for anyone to buy over the counter.

In light of the interest in cocaine, French Wine Coca's launch couldn't have been better timed. By the summer of 1885 Pemberton had sold hundreds of bottles of his coca wine and finally, at the age of fifty-four, his run of bad luck in Atlanta seemed to be over. He relocated his business and his family to a two-story redbrick house on Marietta Street, where he turned the basement into a manufacturing lab and the ground floor into an office and storage room. The top floor became his home. In January 1886 he founded the Pemberton Chemical Company and began work on a new product, one he could sell to the five soda fountains that were now open in Atlanta. What exactly drew Pemberton to making a soda fountain syrup is unclear. Certainly the brisk trade at the fountains would have appealed to his business sense, but another factor may have been the growing clout of the temperance movement.

The temperance movement had started in 1826 with the formation of the American Society for the Promotion of Temperance in Boston. By the middle of the century it had become a national political force with thousands pledging to abstain from alcohol and hundreds of local campaign groups spread across the country. As the 1850s ended, the states of Maine, Michigan, and Nebraska introduced laws against the production and sale of hard liquor. But as the Civil War approached, political support for the movement evaporated as politicians focused on the issue of slavery. By the time the first shots were fired, temperance had disappeared from the political agenda and the state-level alcohol restrictions were being dismantled.

The temperance movement spent years in limbo before returning with a vengeance in 1873 when Eliza Thompson of Hillsboro, Ohio, gathered a group of women and began holding daily "pray ins" outside drugstores that sold alcohol-laced medicine. After six months of Thompson and her Christian soldiers turning up every day to pray and sing hymns, all but one of the drugstores stopped selling alcoholic medicine to get them to go away. Word of this victory spread, and similar bands of women formed across America. They gathered outside saloons, Bibles in hand, praying for the souls of those within. Some of the saloons went out of business as their customers were driven away; others renounced alcohol and signed the pledge of abstinence. By Christmas 1874 this countercultural movement had organized itself into the Women's Christian Temperance Union (WCTU).

Unlike its pre–Civil War predecessors, the WCTU was utterly determined to wean America off alcohol. It presented alcohol as a national evil, arguing that alcohol not only caused alcoholism but also made women prostitutes and men wife beaters. Hundreds of thousands of women joined the WCTU, turning it into the first mass movement of women in American politics.

The temperance message found plenty of support in Fulton County, Georgia, and its county seat of Atlanta. In 1885 the electorate of Fulton County narrowly voted in favor of going dry. The move wasn't a threat to Pemberton's French Wine Coca, since it only shut the saloons, leaving drugstores free to keep selling their boozy bitters and alcoholic "med-icines." But with local prohibition due to start in July 1886 it is possible that Pemberton feared alcoholic medicines could be next or that he figured soda fountains would pick up most of the regular customers from the bars. Whatever his exact reasoning as prohibition loomed in Atlanta in spring 1886, Pemberton started developing a soda fountain syrup based on the coca leaf that had already fueled his success.

To give his syrup an added punch he added another wonder drug that was getting the medical world all excited: the kola nut. This chestnut-sized seed came from the bean-like pods of a slow-growing West African tree, the most cultivated variety of which, *Cola acuminata*, originated in the lands east of the Volta River that now form Nigeria and the Congo River basin. The kola nut, which ranges in color from dark reds and browns to creamy whites and pinks, had been an important commodity in sub-Saharan Africa for thousands for years and played an extensive role in many African cul-tures. In some areas a kola nut would be planted with the umbilical cord of newborn children in recognition of a successful birth, and the tree that grew would become the property of that child. It was a feature of social life, used as a gift to welcome friends and guests to the home, and it had medical uses too. Even as late as the mid-1990s in rural areas, it was being used to treat guinea worm and to ease the pain of childbirth. The African trade in kola nuts was so big that by the 1100s the nut had reached Arabia, where doctors wrote of its warming effects and ability to ease stomachache. The stimulant properties of the caffeine and theobromine within the nut also made it a favorite among African armies. Askia Mohammad, the great ruler of the Songhai Empire in the late 1400s and early 1500s who converted his lands to Islam, supplied kola nuts to his armies. In return they helped him turn his kingdom into the largest nation ever seen in West Africa.

So when European explorers began entering Africa in the 1500s, they quickly picked up on people's devotion to this stimulating nut. One sixteenth-century Portuguese explorer reported that "the black population would scarcely undertake any enterprise without the aid of kola." Later that century kola tree seedlings made their way to Jamaica at the request of Caribbean slave masters who wrote to a trader in Guinea with an urgent plea for the plant "to avert, as far as practicable, those attacks of constitutional despondency to which . . . Negroes were peculiarly liable."

By the late 1800s, the British and French empires had spread the tree to Martinique, Sri Lanka, Zanzibar and beyond, and interest in its medical and military applications was reaching a fever pitch. By 1870, kola was being mixed with sugar and vanilla to produce tonics for the invalid, and in 1880s British soft drink companies, including Schweppes, were selling fizzy kola tonics and kola champagnes. The kola champagne made by London's Pure Water Company even won an endorsement from the *Times* newspaper, then seen as the voice of the British establishment, which informed its readers that the drink was "especially good for keeping the brain clear and active." The rise of the kola drinks so worried British hot chocolate maker Cadbury that it began running ads to discourage people from drinking the stuff.

The world's militaries were also captivated by the potential of kola in the 1880s. A US Navy medical inspector administered kola paste in hot milk to a thirty-six-year-old woman plagued with an irregular heart beat, fatigue, dyspnea, and headaches, and he reported, "The general condition has materially improved, the heart's action is more regular, and the attacks of dyspnoea and faintness have nearly disappeared. The most characteristic effect seems to have been an immediate relief of a sense of fatigue, a sense of *bien-être* and cheerfulness to which the patient had been long a stranger." The British military tested kola on soldiers stationed in India and found that it reduced their appetite and thirst while boosting their energy levels. The German War Office was impressed enough with its kola experiments to order thirty tons of the stuff for its troops.

The kola nut buzz wouldn't last. The nut failed to live up to the hype, proving no more intoxicating than two large cups of filter coffee, but in 1886 it was still a wonder drug, so Pemberton mixed it into his cocaine-laced soda syrup. The bitter taste of kola dominated the drink, so he added plenty of sugar to mask it. Eventually he cut the kola back to a trace, replacing it with cheaper synthetic caffeine to either save money or further reduce the bitterness. Next in went citric acid, which gave the drink a pleasing tang similar to that of phosphate sodas. Then more sugar to offset the vinegar-like taste of the acid. Falling back on his Thomsonian know-how, Pemberton then added a combination of flavoring oils that included vanilla, nutmeg, elixir of orange, lemon, lime, oil of coriander, cinnamon, oil of cassia, and neroli. Finally, to give the drink its dark brown color, he added caramel, a popular coloring among patent medicine makers at least partly because it made it hard for customers to see if an insect or other undesirable object had slipped into the bottle by accident.

In April 1886 Pemberton began testing his new drink on customers of Willis Venable's soda fountain, which was housed within Jacobs' Pharmacy on Peachtree Street just three blocks from the Pemberton Chemical Company building. Venable would report back on customers' reactions and Pemberton would adjust the mix before sending a new batch of syrup for testing. As Pemberton slaved over his essential oils and brass kettle, moving ever closer to the ideal formula for his soda, a man named Frank Robinson knocked on his door.

Born in 1845, Robinson grew up in East Corinth, Maine, and had come to Atlanta with his friend David Doe to launch an advertising agency based around their "chromatic printing press" with its ability to print in color. Advertising agencies were a relatively new concept at the time. The earliest agencies developed on the back of the patent medicine business, which dominated advertising in America to such an extent that it was largely responsible for the rapid growth of US newspapers in the 1800s. Initially the agencies formed to carry out the onerous task of placing ads in the ever-growing sea of newsprint, but as the century progressed they began offering to help businesses write and create their ads too. Robinson and Doe had been pointed in Pemberton's direction by a newspaper reporter whom they asked to help them identify businesses that might be interested in their services. But instead of leaving with the Pemberton Chemical Company as a client, Robinson and Doe became convinced that Pemberton's new coca and kola soda could make a fortune. They put their advertising agency on hold and went into partnership with Pemberton, handing over $6,000 each to buy their way in. Robinson then got his brother and father to shovel an additional $7,000 into the venture. Pemberton's landlord, Edward Holland, also joined the partnership, giving the company its premises in exchange for a share of the business.

By early May 1886 Pemberton had a formula he was happy with, and Robinson and Doe began planning how to sell this novel soda. At Robinson's suggestion the drink was christened Coca-Cola in an alliterative nod to its coca and kola content—despite protests from Venable, who thought it was a difficult name to remember. On Saturday May 29, 1886, the first Coca-Cola ad appeared in the *Atlanta Journal* in a blaze of exclamation marks and rat-a-tat-tat buzzwords: "Coca-Cola. Delicious! Refreshing! Exhilarating! Invigorating! The New and Popular Soda Fountain Drink, containing the properties of the new wonderful Coca plant and the famous Cola nuts. For sale by Willis Venable and Nunnally & Rawson." But if Pemberton and his investors expected to reap Hires-like success they were to be disappointed.

Shortly after the drink launched, the stomach and intestinal problems that had plagued Pemberton since his injury at the Battle of Columbus struck again. Pemberton retreated to his bed and, if the later claims of his former associates are to be believed, to the comfort of the painkilling morphine he had become addicted to since the Civil War. With Pemberton bedridden, the Coca-Cola project began falling apart. Atlanta's soda fountains managed to move less than fifty dollars worth of Coca-Cola that summer despite the ads and the heat. Doe lost faith. He packed up the printing press that he and Robinson came to Atlanta with and left to seek his fortune elsewhere.

Robinson, despite his quiet demeanor, was made of sterner stuff. He soldiered on, carefully inking out Coca-Cola's now famous logo by writing its name in Spencerian script, which established itself as the standard handwriting style for American business in the late 1800s thanks to its mix of speed, legibility, and elegance. Robinson felt Coca-Cola's big problem was getting people to try it in the first place. So in spring 1887 he started giving prominent Atlantans tickets they could exchange for two free glasses of Coca-Cola; his goal was to get them talking about it. He also began producing a mountain of advertising materials, including five hundred streetcar signs and more than fifteen hundred posters. By early summer 1887 Robinson's advertising blitz was paying off. Orders poured in not just from the soda fountains of Atlanta but from all across Georgia and even from fountains in Alabama and Tennessee. But just as Coca-Cola began making progress, Pemberton's fading health struck again.

In early July he returned to his sickbed, this time convinced he wouldn't be leaving it again. Desperate for money, Pemberton sold a two-thirds stake in the rights to Coca-Cola to Venable and a patent medicine manufacturer named George Lowndes in exchange for an interest-free loan of $1,200. When Robinson and Holland found out, they felt betrayed and asked local lawyer John Candler to intervene. Candler visited the bedridden doctor, who admitted he had sold the rights but insisted that it was always he who owned them, not the Pemberton Chemical Company. Besides, the cash-strapped Pemberton added, I've got no money, so there's nothing for you to get out of me. Candler informed Robinson there was nothing that could be done to regain the rights.

Meanwhile Lowndes and Venable's Coca-Cola business was struggling. Lowndes had taken on the job of sales only to find that Venable had failed to cook any of the syrup needed to fulfill the orders he had taken. Within a few weeks of working together the pair agreed to sell. In December 1887 they found their buyer in Woolfolk Walker, the salesman for the Pemberton Chemical Company. Walker bought the rights for $1,200, which he borrowed from his youngest sister, persuading her to hand over the money that she and her husband were saving to buy a home.

By the time Walker bought the controlling stake in Coca-Cola, Frank Robinson was working for Candler's brother Asa Griggs Candler. Asa was a highly successful local druggist who had left his hometown of Cartersville, Georgia to seek his fortune in Atlanta. He arrived in the city in July 1873 with just $1.75 in his pocket and found work at a Peachtree Street pharmacy run by George Howard. Candler worked his way up to chief clerk before quitting in 1877 to start his own business and marry Howard's daughter Lizzie. By 1887, when he met the down-on-his-luck Robinson, Candler had not only a thriving drugstore but a line of successful patent medicines such as Botanic Blood Balm, De-Lec-Ta-Lave toothpaste, and Everlasting Cologne. Candler took Robinson on as a part-time bookkeeper but had little interest in his new employee's constant chatter about how he should invest in Coca-Cola. But then Candler paid a visit to Venable's soda fountain while suffering from a headache, Venable suggested he try a Coca-Cola, and to the drug maker's amazement the headache disappeared. On April 10, 1888, he wrote to his brother Warren: "You know how I suffer with headaches, well some days ago, a friend suggested that I try Coco-Cola [sic]. I did and was relieved. Some days later I again tried it and was again relieved. . . . I determined to put my money into it and a little influence."

Within days Candler had bought Pemberton's remaining third of the business in return for writing off the $550 debt the drink's inventor owed him, and he gave $750 to Walker for another third to gain control of the drink. Four months later Pemberton was dead. On August 16, 1888, at the age of 57, the man who invented Coca-Cola died from gastroenteritis, leaving his widow facing a future of poverty. His son Charles would follow his father to the grave six years later after overdosing on opium.

On gaining control of Coca-Cola, Candler put Robinson back in charge of promoting the drink. Their first act was to change the formula. Candler reduced both the cocaine and kola to mere traces, only stopping short of their complete removal out of concern that the Coca-Cola trademark would be at risk if the two ingredients it was named after were no longer present. Robinson and Candler also worried about the recipe being stolen, so they gave the ingredients code names. Merchandise No. 1 was the sugar. The caramel became Merchandise No. 2 and the synthetic caffeine Merchandise No. 3. The phosphoric acid was recast as Merchandise No. 4 while the combination of kola and coca extract was code-named Merchandise No. 5 and the preservative glycerin became Merchandise No. 6. Finally there was Merchandise No. 7x, the top-secret blend of flavoring oils.

In early 1889 Candler completed his acquisition of Coca-Cola by paying Walker $1,000 for his remaining third. On getting the money, Walker hot-footed it out of Atlanta and headed for Arkansas, leaving the $1,200 debt to his sister unpaid.

With Robinson back masterminding the promotions, a new sweeter formula, and the ownership questions sorted, Coca-Cola was back in action, and in the summer of 1890 sales hit 8,855 gallons—four times the amount sold the year before. In early 1891 business was going so well that Candler shut his drugstore so he could concentrate on making his medicines and Coca-Cola. He set up a factory on the second and third floors of a building in a run-down part of Decatur Street, much to the annoyance of the second-hand clothing store below, which regularly had its stock ruined by hot, sticky Coca-Cola syrup that had boiled over and seeped through the floorboards. Coca-Cola sales were growing, but Botanic Blood Balm remained Candler's big seller, so weekdays were devoted to cooking up this "blood purifier" while Coca-Cola syrup was confined to weekends. This soon changed.

In early 1892 Candler formed the Coca-Cola Company in the hope of selling enough shares to raise $50,000 to spend promoting the drink. The share sale earned just $7,500. With promotional funds tight, Robinson suggested a novel solution. The company could give away coupons that could be exchanged for a free glass of Coca-Cola at any soda fountain that stocked the drink. The company would then reimburse the fountains. It would, Robinson argued, introduce people to the drink and encourage consumer demand for Coca-Cola at the soda fountains. Candler agreed to the plan and soon the company was dishing out thousands upon thousands of coupons all over the South, each bearing the words "Good for a 5¢ glass of Coca-Cola at the soda fountain of any druggist."

In a few months they had given out enough for a million free Coca-Colas in what was the first-ever promotional coupon campaign. Robinson's marketing innovation would be copied countless times by companies across the world and become a mainstay of business promotion. It also sent Coca-Cola sales soaring, even though Candler almost suffered a heart attack every time the bills from the soda fountains landed on his desk.

As the twentieth century dawned, the Coca-Cola Company was selling 281,000 gallons of its syrup every year and had established itself as the leading soda of the South. Moxie remained ahead, but the gap was narrowing fast. But as Hires, Moxie, and Coca-Cola began to eclipse the generic flavors of the fountains and pushed soda success to ever greater heights, these brands found themselves butting up against another fast-growing force in American society: the temperance movement.

Hires was the first to feel the movement's wrath. In 1895 the WCTU realized that root beer was brewed with yeast and therefore contained alcohol. Fearing that many of its members were at risk of being conned into drinking an alcoholic beverage branded as a temperance drink, it called for a national boycott of root beer and started printing literature to warn tee-total citizens about this sinister brew. Other temperance groups rallied to the call and teetotalers began turning their back on root beer, even though newspapers joked that more people would want to drink it now that they knew it had alcohol in it. The temperance movement's root beer backlash hit Hires hard, and sales began to plunge. Hires spent the next three years battling the temperance movement that he personally supported to prove that their boycott was misjudged. He eventually emerged victorious after publishing a chemical analysis that showed that the level of alcohol in a Hires Root Beer was less than that in a loaf of bread. Embarrassed, the WCTU quietly dropped its boycott in 1898.

Coca-Cola faced a tougher challenge. By 1900 cocaine was no longer seen as a wonder drug and was increasingly being talked of as a danger-ous and addictive narcotic. Candler may have slashed the cocaine back to the merest of traces, but the image of Coca-Cola as the cocaine soda had stuck in people's minds. Soda fountain customers continued to order it by nicknames that gave knowing nods to its Peruvian connection—names like dope, coke, "a dose" or "a shot in the arm." Matters only worsened in July 1898, when Congress imposed a tax on medicines to raise money for the Spanish-American War. Since Candler had registered the Coca-Cola Com-pany as a medicine manufacturer, it found itself caught by the new tax. Keen not to pay more tax, Candler sued the federal government on the grounds that Coca-Cola was a beverage not a medicine. When the case reached court in 1901 Candler got his tax back but the hearings also dredged up the issue of cocaine yet again. In their defense the federal government lawyers noted that Coca-Cola contained the medical drug cocaine, a point Candler confirmed. To defuse the situation Coca-Cola called in Dr. George Payne, secretary of the Georgia State Board of Pharmacy, who informed the court that "a man would explode" before he could drink enough Coca-Cola to get a cocaine high.

A year after this uncomfortable court examination of Coca-Cola's cocaine traces, a further blow came when the news broke in July 1902 that a railroad cashier in Virginia had tried to commit suicide by cutting his throat with a penknife and was now in jail charged with lunacy. A friend of the man told the *Times* of Richmond, Virginia, that the man's "breakdown was not so much due to the use of liquor as to the Coca-Cola habit, which had a hold upon him."

Cocaine was back in the news in June 1903 when the *New-York Tribune* interviewed Colonel J. W. Watson of Georgia, who issued a stark warning about how the "cocaine sniffing" habit was growing at an alarming rate in Atlanta, particularly among the city's black population. "I am satisfied that many of the horrible crimes committed in the southern states by the colored people can be traced directly to the cocaine habit," he told the paper. Action was needed to curb this habit before a generation lost their minds, he continued, before noting that the drug was present in "a soda fountain drink manufactured in Atlanta and known as Coca-Cola" and that "men become addicted to drinking it, and find it hard to release themselves from the habit."

Candler had had enough. He traveled to New York to find a way of ridding his drink of the troublesome drug. In New York he found Dr. Louis Schaefer, the German founder of the Schaefer Alkaloid Works, who said it was possible to remove all the cocaine from the coca leaf, allowing Candler to keep the coca in his drink while also banishing the cocaine taint. Candler put Schaefer in charge of producing Merchandise No. 5, and Schaefer developed a method for eliminating every last molecule of the cocaine from the coca leaves. By the end of 1903 Candler could confidently declare that Coca-Cola was cocaine free. But if Candler thought he could finally put his drink's drug problems behind him, he hadn't reckoned with Dr. Harvey Wiley, the chief chemist of the Department of Agriculture, who now had Coca-Cola firmly in his sights.

4

A Snail in a Bottle

On October 1, 1902, a dozen young men sat down to eat a meal laced with benzoic acid and America held its breath. They were the Poison Squad, hired by the federal government to dice with death for the sake of the nation's health. For five dollars a month they would munch on additive-loaded feasts to find out if they were harmful, and their fate gripped the country.

Newspaper reporters clamored to get the exclusive on their latest toxic dinner. People in soda fountains gossiped about what might happen to these human guinea pigs. The era's most famous blackface minstrel showman, Lew Dockstader, composed a ditty in their honor: "If ever you should visit the Smithsonian Institute, look out that Professor Wiley doesn't make you a recruit. He's got a lot of fellows there that tell him how they feel, they take a batch of poison every time they eat a meal. For breakfast they get cyanide of liver, coffin shaped, for dinner, undertaker's pie, all trimmed with crepe. For supper, arsenic fritters, fried in appetizing shade, and late at night they get a prussic acid lemonade."

The Professor Wiley that the vaudeville star referred to was Dr. Harvey Wiley, the chief chemist at the Department of Agriculture and the mastermind behind the Poison Squad. He was a bureaucrat but one far removed from the shy, faceless pen-pusher that description brings to mind. In 1902 the very name of this tall, broad-shouldered chemist struck fear into the hearts of patent medicine manufacturers with their misleading medicines and nostrums and caused the social reform campaigners of America's growing Progressive movement to swoon.

Wiley grew up on the southern Indiana farm where he was born on October 18, 1844. His pious parents raised him on a diet of bread made from unbolted cornmeal and a brand of fundamentalist Christianity that regarded whistling and fishing on a Sunday as terrible sins. The religious sermons didn't stick. Wiley left home an agnostic, but he did inherit his parents' taste for pure, unadulterated food and their zealous sense of righteousness. After leaving the family farm he got a medical degree from Indiana Medical College, but instead of becoming a doctor he turned to chemistry, gaining a second degree from Harvard and becoming Indiana's state chemist. In 1883 Washington called and he was appointed chief chemist at the Department of Agriculture.

The science of chemistry had progressed in leaps and bounds since the start of the 1800s. The days of Yale asking law students to become professors of an embryonic science were over. Chemistry was now a science that had given humanity the ability to alter the very nature of the world around us. Nowhere was chemistry's great leap forward as evident as in food and drink. A flood of new artificial flavorings, sweeteners, colorings, and preservatives had made it possible to change what people put in their stomach beyond all recognition. Wiley was deeply suspicious of this mania for adulterated and manufactured food, but what annoyed him most was the thought that people no longer knew what they had on their plates. After all, how could anyone trust that their meat was what they thought it was, when chemicals could change how it tasted, how it looked, and how long it took to spoil? So on arriving in Washington, the iron-willed bureaucrat made it his goal to usher in a new era of purity in American food and beverages.

But while Wiley had a fanatical streak and an intimidating glare, he was also a skilled political operator capable of winning people over with his charm, wit, and eye for headline-grabbing stunts. The drama of the Poison Squad was his biggest stunt yet. Its creation swelled public interest in the issues he held dear as well as arming him with more data to help nudge politicians into seeing things his way. That all of the Poison Squad walked away from their meals unharmed was merely a bonus.

In 1905, a few years after the Poison Squad's creation, a freelance reporter named Samuel Hopkins Adams contacted Wiley asking for help with his current investigative assignment. Adams had been hired by *Collier's* magazine to probe the patent medicine business, and he wanted Wiley's help in identifying what substances and so-called medicines were of greatest concern. With Wiley's support, Adams dug deep into the world of the nostrum makers, discovering the poisons lurking in popular medicines and the lies they used to sell their products. On October 7, 1905, *Collier's* published the first article in Adams's ten-part "The Great American Fraud" series. It became one of the most significant pieces of journalism ever written. It ripped away the curtains hiding the pathetic truth of this Wizard of Oz industry. The articles picked apart the bogus claims of the health-giving pills, shamed the newspapers that had turned a blind eye to their shameful practices in order to feast on their ad dollars, and exposed opium-addiction and alcoholism "cures" that were themselves packed full of liquor and opiates. In December 1905 President Theodore Roosevelt responded to the resulting clamor for government action in his annual address: "I recommend that a law be enacted to regulate interstate commerce in misbranded and adulterated foods, drinks, and drugs."

The man who would write that law was Wiley, and when the Pure Food and Drug Act passed in June 1906 he became its enforcer. The act didn't destroy the patent medicine business, but it blew the legs out from under it and ended a century of nostrum mania in America. But the snake oil salesmen were not the only ones who needed to worry about Wiley's law, for the campaigning chemist already had soda, and Coca-Cola especially, on his hit list.

Wiley disapproved of soda. He believed that people should "be contented with water, which is the only real thirst quencher and the one beverage for which you can safely form a habit." He had heard the rumors about the cocaine-laced soda of the South but was too busy fighting nostrum makers to focus on it. Then in spring 1907 the US Army banned the sale of Coca-Cola from its bases after receiving complaints that it contained alcohol and cocaine. Coca-Cola was, understandably, horrified by this decision and sprang into action. Coca-Cola lawyer John Candler contacted the

War Department to inform them that these claims were false and the ban unjust. The War Department responded by asking Wiley to investigate the claims. Wiley already viewed Coca-Cola with suspicion, but his concerns about this southern menace only deepened when his deputy Dr. Lyman Kebler returned from a tour of the South with wild tales about the popular soda. Kebler painted a vivid picture of Coca-Cola fiends hanging out in Atlanta soda fountains, of soldiers driven wild by mixing whiskey and Coke, and of four-year-old children drinking it from beer jugs. Kebler's tales fueled Wiley's determination to use his new powers to stop this dangerous beverage.

The summer came and went without word from Washington, so Candler caught a train to the capital and find out what was going on. On arriving he was informed that Wiley had completed his tests and found Coca-Cola to be free of cocaine and that the tiny amount of alcohol in the syrup was acceptable as a preservative. But instead of reporting his team's findings to the War Department, Wiley had homed in on the caffeine content of the drink and was using the Poison Squad to test the toxicity of the stimulant in the hope of proving that its presence made Coca-Cola harmful. Wiley believed caffeine was a dangerous, habit-forming drug. In speeches he talked about "tea and coffee drunkards" and once claimed: "In England, I have seen women who, if they were denied their tea at four o'clock, would become almost wild." Wiley figured that if he and his Poison Squad could build a case against caffeine, then instead of giving Coca-Cola the all-clear he could attack the southern menace on a new front. All he needed was enough time to show that the government should be concerned about the beverage's added caffeine.

Having learned of Wiley's intentions, Candler secured a meeting with Secretary of Agriculture James Wilson and urged him to force Wiley to issue his report on the cocaine and alcohol content of Coca-Cola. Six days later on October 16, 1907, Wiley's report was released. It confirmed that the claims that Coca-Cola was an alcohol and cocaine laced beverage were nonsense, but the government chemist used the opportunity to publicly moan about how he and the Poison Squad were not given enough time to investigate the caffeine content of the drink. Despite his objections Amer-

ican troops were once again able to buy Coca-Cola for their canteens that
November.

Wiley seethed at having his hand forced by the soft drink company, but
rather than give up, he became even more determined to continue his fight
against Coca-Cola and its caffeine content. He hatched a plan to charge
Coca-Cola under the Pure Food and Drug Act for adulterating its drink
with caffeine and failing to say so on its labels. All he needed to do this was
permission to seize a shipment of Coca-Cola syrup that had crossed a state
border. That, however, was going to be tricky.

In 1906 Wiley had fallen out with Roosevelt after lecturing the president about the dangers of saccharin, an artificial sweetener discovered in
1879. For the president this was a rant too far. "Anybody who says saccharin
is injurious to health is an idiot," Roosevelt thundered, pointing out that
his own doctor gave him the sweetener every day. Wiley found himself
excommunicated. The president refused all of the chemist's subsequent
requests for meetings and appointed a committee of scientific experts to
keep tabs on Wiley's activities. Wilson began refusing to approve any case
Wiley wanted to pursue unless two or more officials from the Bureau of
Chemistry also supported the action.

In March 1909 Wiley requested permission to confiscate a shipment of
Coca-Cola syrup headed for New Orleans. Roosevelt's experts blocked it.
Wiley tried repeatedly to get permission to seize various shipments of the
soda syrup but time after time he was blocked. Eventually Wilson, probably thinking the obstinate official needed the message spelled out to him,
wrote a letter telling Wiley to leave Coca-Cola alone. Unknowingly the
agriculture secretary had just given Wiley the stick of dynamite he needed
to explode the political roadblocks holding him back.

Wiley leaked Wilson's letter to the *Atlanta Georgian*, an antiestablish-
ment newspaper that had it in for Coca-Cola chief Asa Candler. It had
already threatened to expose the dire conditions at the Decatur Orphans'
Home, where Candler was a trustee. The newspaper contacted Wilson
and told him that if he did not give Wiley the green light for his Coca-
Cola investigation they would publish his letter. The agriculture secretary
relented on the condition that the case was not heard in Washington, DC,

but somewhere in the Coke-friendly South. He and Wiley settled on Chattanooga, Tennessee. "It is remarkable what the fear of publicity will do," Wiley remarked afterwards.

On the evening of October 20, 1909, a team of federal agents gathered on the Tennessee-Georgia border and laid in wait for a truck that was making its way from Atlanta to Chattanooga loaded with Coca-Cola syrup. When the truck crossed the state line into Tennessee, the agents pounced and seized its cargo of forty barrels and twenty kegs of the soda syrup. Earlier that day Kebler paid an unexpected visit to the Coca-Cola syrup plant in Atlanta and, despite the plant manager's pleas, began poking around. Howard Candler, Asa's oldest son and vice president of operations at Coca-Cola, returned from lunch to find federal inspectors combing the factory. The inspectors said they had come to collect a sample of Merchandise No. 5, the coca leaf and kola nut extract used in the drink. Unsure what to do, Howard gave them the sample and told them to leave, before going to find his father. Asa ran to the scene, catching the inspectors as they were heading out the door. Furious at the intrusion, he demanded they give the sample back, but the federal inspectors refused and left for Washington to start analyzing the secret Coca-Cola ingredient.

The seizure of the syrup at the border and the Merchandise No. 5 sample from the plant was followed by a lawsuit filed in the federal court in Chattanooga. It charged the Coca-Cola Company of breaching the Pure Food and Drug Act by failing to declare that caffeine was added to the drink and by calling itself Coca-Cola when coca and kola were barely present in its product. The second accusation was especially worrying for the company. If it lost the case on that count, its trademark would be lost, and with it the entire business. Coca-Cola was now in a fight for its very survival.

For one Texan rival of Coca-Cola, this situation was fabulous news. Dr Pepper was born in a Waco pharmacy and soda fountain called the Old Corner Drug Store in December 1885, five months before John Pemberton created Coca-Cola. Back then Waco was the epitome of a Wild West town with its dusty streets, saloons, and gunfights. Cowboys and outlaws would come from miles around, attracted by its legal brothels, which would remain in operation until 1912. Charles Alderton, the Old Corner Drug Store's Brooklyn-born pharmacist, invented the drink that became Dr Pepper after noticing that customers were growing bored with the soda fountain's usual favorites of sarsaparilla, lemon, and vanilla. Keen to revive interest, he started experimenting with new flavor combinations, eventually settling on a unique combination of twenty-three flavors mixed with the popular tang of phosphoric acid. The result tasted unlike anything else available at America's soda fountains. Impressed by his pharmacist's creation, the Old Corner Drug Store's owner Wade Morrison agreed that they should offer his unusual fruity soda to customers. The city's soda fountain loafers loved it and, since the drink had no name, they began to ask the soda jerk to "shoot a Waco."

Morrison decided the drink needed a name and opted for Dr Pepper. The inspiration, he told his customers, was Dr. Charles Pepper, with whom he had worked in Rural Retreat, Virginia, before moving to Texas in 1882. While working for the Virginia physician, Morrison fell in love with the doctor's daughter, but Dr. Pepper believed their romance was premature, so Morrison left. The drink, he explained, was named in honor of his lost love. What Morrison's wife, Carrie, whom he married while working as a pharmacist in Round Rock, Texas, thought of this romantic yarn isn't recorded, but she need not have worried, because the story was just that: a story. There was a Dr. Charles Pepper who lived in Virginia, but at the time when Morrison headed west, he was working in the town of Bristol, not Rural Retreat. What's more, his daughter, Ruth, was just eight years old at the time. But it was a good romantic tale to spin at the soda fountain when people asked about the drink's name.

As word spread of Alderton's creation, other soda fountains around central Texas started asking to buy the syrup. Morrison and Alderton began cooking up the syrup in the cramped basement of the Old Corner Drug Store but found themselves unable to keep up with demand, so Morrison turned to Robert Lazenby, the clever but hot-headed founder of the Circle "A" Ginger Ale Bottling Company.

Born in Johnson County in 1866, Lazenby grew up in Waco and launched his soda business there in 1884. His Circle "A" Ginger Ale quickly found success, and by the time Morrison asked for his help with Dr Pepper he had a second bottling plant in St. Louis, Missouri. Together with Alderton they formed the Artesian Manufacturing and Bottling Company, named after the artesian water wells that were once common in Waco. They promoted Dr Pepper as a drink of purity, strength, and discretion, adopting the slogans "Vim, Vigor, Vitality" and "King of Beverages." Their advertising presented proud lions, the stoic King George V of Britain, Native American chiefs on the hunt, and curvaceous nude women reclining as the sea waves swelled around them to preserve their modesty. Alderton and Morrison would quit the business before the century was out but under Lazenby's stewardship, Dr Pepper entrenched itself in Texas and began reaching out into other states. By 1901 Dr Pepper had even put in an appearance at a stall in Rag Town, the Oklahoma encampment where thousands of people had gathered to bid for 1,126 lots of land near Anadorko that were being auctioned off by the federal government. On the day of the auction an estimated twenty thousand people had gathered. When the sale was over, they and the Dr Pepper stand selling them bottled soda vanished.

As part of his efforts to take Dr Pepper beyond the Lone Star State, Lazenby exhibited the drink at the 1904 Louisiana Purchase Exposition World's Fair in St. Louis. Even by the grand standards of world's fairs, this was a biggie. It cost $50 million to put on, and the site for the seven-month event packed 1,500 buildings into 1,240 acres. By the time the fair ended in December 1904, around twenty million people had visited the site. The exposition popularized the concept of convenience food, with visitors treated to an enormous selection of sweet drinks, instant hot snacks, and sugary treats. As well as Dr Pepper, Coca-Cola, and Hires Root Beer, many visitors got their first taste of iced tea, peanut butter, Jell-O, ice cream cones, and cotton candy. The event also popularized hot dogs and hamburgers as we now think of them. Most of these products existed before the event, but the coming together of these sweet beverages and handy snacks in St. Louis showed them in a new light. Instead of being a collection of disparate products, they could now be seen clearly as part of a new all-American cuisine unified by common traits of being quick, tasty, instantly satisfying, and rarely, if ever, demanding the use of a knife or fork. It was the moment that fast food was born, and soda was clearly an integral part of this culinary revolution.

Dr Pepper also sought to widen its appeal by emphasizing its lack of caffeine, cocaine, and other "injurious drugs." One ad showed the heroic Roman centurion Horatius fending off the armies of Clusium accompanied with the words: "Dr Pepper stands alone on the bridge defending your children against an army of caffeine-doped beverages as the great Horatius defended Rome." So when Wiley got his claws into Coca-Cola, Lazenby wrote him an opportunistic letter offering his full support for the caffeine crackdown and presenting him with a copy of the Dr Pepper formula to show that his drink was free of such drugs. Lazenby's opposition to caffeine wouldn't last. In 1917 he changed his mind about caffeine and added the stimulant to the drink's mix.

Another competitor that would have welcomed Wiley's clash with Coca-Cola was a copycat from North Carolina called Pepsi-Cola. Pepsi's creator was Caleb Bradham, the son of a rich businessman. Bradham was born in Chinquapin, North Carolina, on May 27, 1867. He went to the University of Maryland to study medicine, but when his father's business collapsed in 1891 he found himself unable to afford the fees and quit. He moved to New Bern, a North Carolina lumber town located at the meeting point of the Trent and Neuse rivers. There he became a teacher, and when the local drugstore owner died in 1893, he bought the business and became the town's pharmacist.

Bradham's Drug Store had the usual mix of soda fountain treats, general goods, and medicine, but the conscientious pharmacist also liked his gadgets. He had a prescription case for storing medicines with a skull and crossbones painted on it that would sound an alarm if someone opened it. Instead of offering customers a piano and some sheet music to play as some soda fountains did, he had a primitive jukebox machine that would play selections of violin or piano music in exchange for a nickel. The chatty pharmacist also enjoyed playing soda jerk, mixing up new drinks for his friends and fountain regulars to try.

In the summer of 1898 he decided to create a cola, but one designed to help customers suffering from indigestion and free from the narcotic taint of kola nut, cocaine, alcohol, and caffeine. His friends gave his cola the thumbs up and christened it Brad's Drink. Bradham wasn't too keen on this and decided he had better come up with a different name, eventually settling on Pepsi-Cola in August 1898. The cola part of the name was an obvious nod to the cola flavor of the drink, while the word Pepsi referred to his goal of making an indigestion-easing beverage. Whether the word Pepsi came from the digestive enzyme pepsin or dyspepsia, the medical name for indigestion, or both isn't known.

Promoting it as a safe, drug-free, and cleanly made cola, Bradham slowly built Pepsi up over the next five years. He began selling it to other fountains, opened a bottling plant in New Bern, and advertised widely. By the time he married his wife, a nurse named Charity Credle, in January 1901, he was beginning to believe his drink could make it big. In 1902 he sold nearly eight thousand gallons of his syrup to fountains across the mid-Atlantic states of North Carolina, Virginia, Maryland, Pennsylvania, and New York. By the end of the year he had founded the Pepsi-Cola Company. He began finding bottling plants around the United States to bottle his drink, sent a squad of wall painters to comb the nation for places to paint Pepsi ads, and even landed a celebrity endorsement from world-record-holding race car driver Barney Oldfield who said, "It's a bully drink—refreshing, invigorating, a fine 'bracer' before a race, and a splendid restorer afterwards." By 1907, as Wiley's men moved in on Coca-Cola, Bradham was selling more than one hundred thousand gallons of syrup every year and was confident enough in the drink's future to register its trademark in Canada and Mexico.

Despite Pepsi's growth, Coca-Cola paid it little attention. For the Atlanta firm it was just another imitator, one of hundreds of me-too colas that had burst into life to cash in on the success of Pemberton's creation. Besides, with Wiley's legal action threatening its future, the company had more to worry about than some North Carolina upstart with comparatively paltry sales. In March 1911 the case finally came to court, and from the start the Chattanooga hearings were a media circus. Newspaper reporters descended on the Tennessee city to grab the scoop on this epic clash between the preacher of purity and the famous but controversial soda.

The buildup to the first day in court set the tone. Fearing Coca-Cola might try to influence the jury, federal agents were sent to Chattanooga to keep tabs on the jurors and make sure they had no links to the soft drink firm or secrets that could derail the case. Coca-Cola responded by sending private detectives to Chattanooga to watch the federal government's spies. Then there was Wiley himself. Just before the trial the sixty-six-year-old married Anna Kelton, a prominent suffragette half his age. The couple used the trip to Chattanooga as their honeymoon. Journalists followed every move of this celebrity couple, reporting back to their readers on where the two had dined and what these icons of the Progressive Era had picked from the menu.

On March 13, 1911, the hearings began. Wiley's lawyers told the court that Coca-Cola had adulterated its drink with caffeine, "a poisonous ingredient." They accused the company of using colorings and flavorings to cover up the muck hidden in its syrup and, contrary to its name and the coca leaf and kola nut pictures on its labels, the drink contained almost no coca or kola. The federal lawyers informed the court that the syrup it had seized was found to contain flies, bees, mice, and spiders. A Department of Agriculture inspector told how he visited Coca-Cola's syrup plant in July 1909 and saw a black man cooking the syrup while wearing "a dirty undershirt," "an old, dirty pair of trousers," and tatty shoes with bare feet poking out. This man, he added, was sweating and chewing tobacco while making the syrup, and both his spittle-covered tobacco and perspiration went into the mix. The factory, he continued, was also filthy, covered in cobwebs and with syrup-cooking kettles encrusted with crystallized sugar. Other prosecution witnesses informed the court that the beverage kept boys awake at night, tempting them with masturbation, that lab rabbits died when given the company's syrup, and that a Philadelphia streetcar conductor was now in an asylum after being driven mad by his twelve-a-day Coca-Cola habit.

Coca-Cola's legal team responded by deftly picking apart Wiley's collection of flimsy evidence. James Gaston, the black Coca-Cola syrup worker, informed the court he had never chewed tobacco in the twelve years he had worked at the company. The insane streetcar conductor's doctor confirmed that his patient did hear voices and see visions but that had nothing to do with him drinking Coca-Cola. It turned out that the rabbits had not been given syrup but large doses of Merchandise No. 5, the potent mix of kola and cocaine-free coca leaf that was only used in minuscule amounts in the actual syrup. With the government case collapsing around him, Wiley suddenly remembered an urgent appointment in New York City and grabbed the first train out of Chattanooga. At the end of the hearing the federal case had unraveled to such an extent that the judge directed the verdict, ruling that people expect caffeine in Coca-Cola and understand it as a branded product rather than a drink of kola and coca.

Coca-Cola emerged from the courtroom victorious, and to celebrate, the company published a booklet declaring that there is "not one indivisible atom of cocaine in a whole ocean of Coca-Cola." But the drink's enemies were down, not out. In March 1912 Wiley stepped down as chief chemist of the Department of Agriculture and landed a gig as a columnist for *Good Housekeeping* magazine, a platform from which he continued to rage against Coca-Cola. That same year a little-known film director called D. W. Griffith, who would later find fame with his controversial 1915 movie *The Birth of a Nation*, responded to the case with a short silent film entitled *For His Son*. The film told the story of a physician who develops a drug-laced soda called Dopokoke, which hooks its customers and makes him rich, only for his son to become an addict and eventually die from his soda-fueled drug habit.

The federal government was not about to give up its legal fight either. The Chattanooga verdict had undermined the whole Pure Food and Drug Act by allowing a product to name itself after ingredients it barely contained. Unwilling to let this key piece of legislation become toothless, the government vowed to fight the case all the way to the Supreme Court. But while the lawyers rallied for a second round, the Coca-Cola Company could get on with establishing itself as America's number-one drink, a campaign that had come on in leaps and bounds during the first decade of the twentieth century.

The first big development was Coke's largely unintentional move into the bottled drinks market. The first man to bottle the drink was Joe Biedenharn, the jolly and bushy-eyebrowed owner of a candy store in Vicksburg, Mississippi. Biedenharn began selling Coca-Cola at his soda fountain in 1890 and loved it so much he couldn't help himself from trying to introduce all his customers to it. In summer 1894, with demand for Coca-Cola soaring, Biedenharn figured that his rural customers would appreciate being able to buy it in bottles and began using his syrup supplies to put the drink in plain bottles that he then sold in his store. "I did not say anything to Mr Candler about it, but I did ship [him] the first two-dozen case of Coca-Cola I bottled," he told the *Coca-Cola Bottler* magazine in August 1944. "Mr Candler immediately wrote back that it was fine. He made no further comment at all that I remember."

This informal arrangement reflected the Coca-Cola chief's general disinterest in bottled drinks, which he believed were often produced in filthy conditions. By the start of 1899 the only other step Candler had taken toward bottled Coke was to give the company's New England wholesaler an option to bottle the soda, an option it never used. So when two Chattanooga lawyers turned up at his office in mid-July 1899 to ask for the rights to bottle his drink throughout the United States, he could barely be bothered to meet them; his mother was on her deathbed and the company had a five thousand gallon backlog of syrup orders to fill.

The men who came to see Candler that July were Benjamin Thomas and Joseph Whitehead. The idea of making their fortunes bottling Coca-Cola came from Thomas, a grocer's son born in Maysville, Kentucky, in 1861. Although trained as a lawyer, the sandy-haired baseball fan dreamed of becoming a successful businessman and, being an optimistic soul, believed it was just a matter of finding the right idea. He finally found that idea in 1898 when he signed up for the US Army to do his bit in the Spanish-American War. The army sent him to Manzanillo, Cuba, to work as a quartermaster's assistant. While there he noticed how popular a bottled pineapple soda called Piña Frío was with Cubans. He wondered why his own favorite drink, Coca-Cola, wasn't sold in bottles. When he got back home later that year, he was convinced that bottled Coca-Cola was the money spinner he had been searching for. He persuaded his friend Whitehead, a tax attorney born in Virginia, to join him in the venture and the pair headed to Atlanta to strike the deal of their lives.

At the meeting with Candler they explained how they would open a bottling plant in Chattanooga and then expand to the rest of the United States. Candler didn't think much of their plan. Bottling was an expensive business, needing huge upfront investment in machinery, real estate, horses for distribution, bottles, and boxes, before even a single drink could be sold. Despite his pessimism about their venture, Candler offered them a deal. He would give them the bottling rights to everywhere except Mississippi, New England, and Texas on the provision that they adhere to quality standards set by the Coca-Cola Company. The pair rushed back to their hotel and drafted a contract that would give them the perpetual right to bottle Coca-Cola in almost every part of the United States. It also fixed the price of the syrup they would buy from the Coca-Cola Company at one dollar a gallon. Candler signed. As the excited pair left, Candler told them not to come crying to him when it all went wrong.

A few months later they understood why Candler had been so discouraging. They had spent all their money and an extra $2,500 from an investor named John Lupton to open their first bottling plant, and it wasn't going well. The bottling machinery of the time was cranky and slow. Because of the pressure of carbonation, exploding bottles were a regular occurrence, a hazard that meant the employees had to wear wire-mesh masks like those of a fencer to protect themselves from flying glass. One day the rope suspending a keg of syrup snapped, drenching the plant's manager in gallons of thick, sticky gloop. The pair realized that at this rate it could take months, maybe years, to earn back enough money to open a second bottling plant. Their hope of a national Coca-Cola bottling empire seemed impossibly distant.

The three investors decided to rethink the business. Instead of trying to open bottling plants they decided to dice up the country into tiny pieces and sell the exclusive right to bottle Coca-Cola in these areas. They would make money from selling the rights and then take a cut from the money these bottlers spent buying Coca-Cola syrup. In short, the people who bought the rights would fund the expansion of their bottling empire. While the three businessmen agreed on the principle, they differed on the details of the contracts they would offer bottlers, so in early 1900 they took a map and split America in two. Thomas got the mid-Atlantic states, Whitehead and Lupton the South and the Midwest. In 1901 they sold just five franchises between them, but the following year they made twenty-nine deals. In 1905 they sold nearly two hundred. Lupton parted ways with Whitehead and took control of the western states. By 1919 there would be nearly one thousand Coca-Cola bottlers, each with a slice of America to call their own. The arrangement made Coca-Cola bottling one of the first franchised businesses in America, and almost everyone involved got exceedingly rich.

Lupton, Thomas, and Whitehead made millions from their cut of syrup sales. The Coca-Cola Company in Atlanta saw its syrup sales rocket. The bottlers got rich too, thanks to their local monopolies on selling bottles of what was fast becoming America's favorite carbonated drink. Lupton used his millions to build a ten-bedroom mansion complete with a gym, two swimming pools, a ballroom, and a bowling alley. Oklahoma bottler Virgil Browne bought a Louisiana sugar plantation and a 110-foot boat that he christened by smashing a bottle of Coca-Cola against its bow. Biedenharn and his sons used some of their Coca-Cola fortune to help a small aerial crop-dusting business expand into airmail and passenger flights. Today that company, Delta Air Lines, is one of the biggest airlines in the world.

The immense wealth of the Coca-Cola bottling "family" also found its way into countless acts of philanthropy, as bottlers used their wealth for the good of their communities and to build goodwill toward their product. They funded hospitals, bought sports equipment for schools, created endowments for universities, and lavished money on libraries and churches. In some cases they quite literally built cities. Thomas helped to develop the Tennessee town of Lookout Mountain. Lupton funneled his soda millions into the construction of Lupton City, Tennessee, to house the hundreds employed at his textile factory, providing them and their families not only with homes but also with a cinema, a church, a public swimming pool, a post office, and a school.

With so much money sloshing around the Coca-Cola bottling network, it didn't take long before people began trying to get some of it for themselves too. The primitive and clunky bottling technology of the 1890s meant it wasn't unusual for the odd piece of glass to get chipped off a bottle somewhere along the line and slip unnoticed into the drink. Mechanized cleaning and sterilization of bottles was also in its infancy in the 1890s, as were effective bottle seals. The invention of the bottle cap improved things immensely by offering a cleaner and more effective seal, but its arrival did little to quash public fears about unexpected "extras" in their bottled soda.

Stories abounded about gruesome finds. Glass chips, soil, sawdust, straw, cigarette ends, insects, spiders, feathers, human hair— the list seemed endless. Many of the claims were imaginary, but it happened often enough in reality to keep the tales of creepy crawlies lurking in bottled beverages circulating, and there was no shortage of lawyers ready to represent drinkers who said they had encountered dubious additions to their soda. Carbonated drink bottlers found themselves faced with claims about bottled frogs, mental agony inflicted by cola-drowned worms, soda spiked with poison, and exploding glassware. Much of the time they paid the claimant off to avoid the risk of adverse publicity. But as the number of claims mounted, Coke bottlers joined forces and in 1914 founded the Coca-Cola Bottlers' Association, which kept tabs on repeat claimants and would handle the threats of legal action. One of its first acts was to look into getting insurance for its members, only to find the type of insurance it wanted didn't exist. The association ended up working with an insurance company to create the first liability insurance policy in the United States.

Claims about unpleasant finds in bottled fizzy drinks also rewrote the world's law books. On August 26, 1928, May Donoghue, a shop assistant from a poor area of Glasgow in Scotland, took a tram to Paisley to visit a friend. The pair met at the Wellmeadow Café, and Donoghue's friend bought her a nonalcoholic ginger beer and ice cream float. The café owner opened the ten-ounce brown bottle of ginger beer, poured some over her ice cream and served the float. Donoghue tucked into the treat. After a while Donoghue's companion topped off her friend's float by pouring the rest of the ginger beer over her ice cream and that's when, Donoghue later claimed, a decomposed snail plopped into her float. Having already consumed most of the drink, the thirty-year-old woman was horrified. A few days later she went to the Royal Glasgow Infirmary to be treated for gastroenteritis that she believed was caused by the rotting gastropod.

She decided to sue but found that she couldn't take action against the café since her friend had bought the float. So she tried to sue David Stevenson, the Paisley company that made the ginger beer, but the Scottish courts rejected her claim on the grounds that she had no contract with the company. Determined not to give up, she took her battle for compensation to the House of Lords, Britain's highest court. In December 1932, in one of the most significant legal decisions ever made, the lords sided with the Glaswegian single mother, ruling that a contract was unnecessary—the manufacturer of the drink had a duty to take reasonable care to protect its customers from harm. Since the decisions of the House of Lords were treated as common law not just in Britain but throughout the British Empire, the verdict instantly changed case law in Australia, Canada, India, Jamaica, New Zealand, and beyond. Yet even though the case transformed the law across the world, to this day no one knows if the snail that started it all even existed.

Twelve years later, another soda bottle incident confirmed a similar principle in US law. Gladys Escola, a waitress at a restaurant in Fresno, California, in the early 1940s, had just taken in the latest delivery of Coca-Cola from the local bottling company. She was placing the bottles one by one in the restaurant's refrigerator when the bottle she was holding exploded in her hand. The glass cut deep, slicing a five-inch-long wound that severed blood vessels, nerves, and muscles. She sued the bottler, the Coca-Cola Bottling Company of Fresno, and their legal fight ended up at the Supreme Court of California in July 1944. The court backed Escola, and Chief Justice Roger Traynor ruled that manufacturers were liable for harm caused by defective products even if they were not negligent, a principle that has since become enshrined in law throughout America. The precedents set by the cases brought by Escola and Donoghue strengthened consumer protection throughout the world, and it all started with a possibly fictitious snail drowning in ginger beer and an explosive bottle of Coca-Cola.

While the Coca-Cola bottlers were learning to joust with customers over flies and frogs in the 1910s, back in Atlanta the Coca-Cola Company embarked on altogether different legal campaign. In the wake of Coca-Cola's success, hordes of copycat colas had flooded the market and sly soda fountain owners were serving customers cheaper imitators while telling them they were getting the real thing. Asa Candler's answer was direct. He told his salesmen to punch soda fountain owners they caught substituting rival drinks as Coca-Cola. "Those first salesmen would say to the substitutors: 'Now, if you don't quit this, the next time I come here, you and I are going to have some trouble,'" John Powers, an early Coca-Cola salesman, told the company's *Refresher USA* magazine in 1976. "One dealer told me he was once scared that the salesman I succeeded was going to punch him in the eye."

Thumping wayward soda jerks might have quenched Candler's thirst for justice but it did little to stop the rising tide of imitators. The list of Coca-Cola copycats at this time was enormous, numbering in the hundreds. Aside from Pepsi-Cola, people could drink Candy-Kola, Gay Cola, Roxa-Kola, Taka-Kola, Its-a-Cola, Afri-Kola, and Kiss-Kola. Some played on the way southerners pronounced Coca-Cola to come up with Co-Cola and Coke-Ola or sought to appeal to cyclists by christening their beverage Bicy-Cola. Others, like Kaw-Kola, harked back to their inspiration's early days by lacing their syrup with plenty of cocaine. There was even Klu Ko Kolo, an Atlanta-based copycat hoping to cash in not just on Coca-Cola but on the revival of the Ku Klux Klan that followed D. W. Griffith's 1915 movie *The Birth of a Nation*.

Most of these mimics didn't get very far. Roxa-Kola never made it beyond eastern Kentucky, where it was created in 1906. But by the early 1910s clones such as Pepsi-Cola and Chero-Cola began to morph into something threatening. Chero-Cola originated in John Pemberton's old home city of Columbus, Georgia, and was invented by a dour pharmacist named Claud Hatcher. Hatcher had moved into the soda bottling business in 1905 to produce drinks to sell in his family's wholesale grocery store. He started out with a ginger ale called Royal Crown Ginger Ale before coming up with his Coca-Cola approximation Chero-Cola. After achieving local success he began selling bottling franchises, and by 1914 sales had topped $600,000 a year and were growing fast.

As copycats grew in number it was clear that Coca-Cola needed something more effective than salesmen with a good right hook, and Candler's nephew Sam Dobbs believed he had the answer. The son of Asa's older sister, Dobbs grew up in rural poverty. His childhood home was a one-room shack in Carroll County, Georgia, and he reached adulthood with just six months of schooling to his name. He moved to Atlanta in 1886 to work for his uncle Asa and to be tutored by another uncle: Bishop Warren Candler, a leading figure in the Southern Methodist Church that formed in 1844 in response to the Methodist Episcopal Church's decision to oppose slavery. Dobbs loved Coca-Cola from the moment he first tasted it at an Atlanta soda fountain; he would drink more than a dozen a day. So when his uncle gained control of the business, he couldn't wait to get started.

Dobbs fizzed with bright ideas about how to sell more Coca-Cola, and as he rose up the company ranks in the 1890s and 1900s he left a trail of innovations behind him. He gave the company's salesmen generous expenses to make being a Coca-Cola peddler a prestigious job. He also ordered the sales force to teach soda jerks across the country how best to serve Coca-Cola. Working with Frank Robinson, Coca-Cola's gentlemanly marketing guru, Dobbs masterminded the first wave of Coca-Cola ads to be painted on walls, starting with one on the side of the Young Brothers Pharmacy in Cartersville, Georgia. As his list of achievements grew, so did Dobbs's ambition. He became convinced that he should be the next boss of Coca-Cola rather than Asa's eldest son, Howard. Fueled by a mix of burning ambition and jealousy, Dobbs set out to prove to his uncle that he, not Howard, was the real successor in waiting.

He began to undermine and sideline the mild-mannered Robinson until Asa put Dobbs in charge of advertising in 1906. Coca-Cola's advertising had changed drastically since the dry, wordy promotions of the 1800s, largely thanks to the Massengale Advertising Agency, the Atlanta advertising agency hired by Robinson in 1902. Massengale's modern, forward-thinking promotions showed Coca-Cola as part of daily life. The problem was that these scenes showed the wealthy at play: well-dressed women relaxing with a Coke after a day's shopping, theatergoers sipping the cola in the intermission, and top-hatted aristocrats in fancy new automobiles. Dobbs wanted more egalitarian ads that could connect with a broader audience. On becoming the company's advertising chief, he sidelined Massengale and brought in D'Arcy, a young advertising agency that had made a splash at the 1904 World's Fair in St. Louis, creating a spectacular artificial waterfall that used water piped in from the Mississippi River to promote Cascade Whiskey.

Dobbs and D'Arcy took Coca-Cola advertising to a new level. Out went fusty and prim Victorian women, and in came young, attractive, girl-next-door types who showed a little bit more leg and had a twinkle in their eyes. In 1908 they constructed a thirty-five-foot billboard alongside the Pennsylvania Railroad, which connected Philadelphia with New York City. The sign showed a giant pharmacist in white overalls using a ceramic Coca-Cola urn to dispense water pumped in via a four-hundred-foot pipeline connected to the city mains. The following year they hired an airship to float around the skies above Washington, DC, while carrying a huge Coca-Cola sign. Dobbs's advertising skill also landed him the job of president of the Associated Advertising Clubs of America in 1909. He used this position to launch a "truth in advertising" campaign that urged advertisers to clean up their act and adopt honest promotions. Dobbs's initiative led to the creation of one of the earliest codes of conduct for advertisers, and his efforts to weed out crooked campaigns earned him a place in the American Advertising Federation's Hall of Fame.

As he sought to build his power base in the company, Dobbs started taking an interest in its legal affairs. He allied himself with Coca-Cola lawyer Harold Hirsch and, keen to stop company salesmen from brawling with potential customers, Dobbs encouraged Hirsch to use the courts to destroy the copycat colas. Hirsch responded by launching a campaign of legal action that would see more than five hundred imitators dragged before the courts over the next thirty years for trademark infringement. In 1916 alone the company successfully sued 153 imitators. Soon brands like Candy-Kola, Coke-Ola, and Kos-Kola were being stamped out of existence. Coca-Cola's northern nemesis Moxie took note and started suing its own imitators Toxie, Noxie Kola, and Proxie out of existence.

In July 1913 Coca-Cola's desire to crush its clones in court prompted Hirsch to ask the company's bottling network to develop a distinctive Coca-Cola bottle for use throughout the United States. The idea of a uniform bottle had a lot of appeal. Refrigerators were still some years away, so stores kept bottled drinks chilled in tubs filled with ice and water. To get a drink, customers had to reach into the cold water and fish out a bottle. Since most soda bottles were indistinguishable by touch, customers usually wouldn't know what they had until they had dragged it out of the icy water. Sometimes they wouldn't even know after pulling out the bottle, because the paper labels often came off in the water. A bottle distinct enough to be instantly recognizable by touch and sight would fix this problem and boost sales. It could also be patented, adding an extra layer of legal protection against the copycats, and would double as a promotional tool by helping Coca-Cola stand out from the competition. In short, Hirsch envisaged a bottle that wasn't just a container but a package capable of reinforcing a brand, lifting sales, and providing more ammunition for the legal team.

Word of Hirsch's appeal for design suggestions eventually reached the Root Glass Company, a glassworks in Terre Haute, Indiana. The company's founder Chapman Root gathered his top men together and asked them to create a design to submit to Coca-Cola. What happened next is now the stuff of claim and counterclaim, but what seems to be the most reliable version of events is this: Alex Samuelson, the Swedish plant superintendent, asked what Coca-Cola was made of. The men scratched their heads. No one knew. So auditor Clyde Edwards and bottle mold supervisor Earl Dean headed to the city's Emeline Fairbanks Memorial Library. The librarian dug out a copy of *Encyclopaedia Britannica* and they looked up coca and cola but found little to inspire them. But while flipping through the encyclopedia they chanced upon an illustration of the cocoa pod with its ribbed, pumpkin-like segments. Although the chocolate-producing plant had no connection to Coca-Cola, Dean thought it would make a good basis for a bottle design and sketched out a copy of the cocoa pod. That night he developed a design: a bottle with ribs like those of a cocoa pod running from its neck to its base. The following day Dean produced a mold and the first prototype of his bottle design in green glass. Other versions of the story have Dean creating the mold and Samuelson designing the bottle based on the cocoa pod because Edwards got coca and cocoa mixed up at the library.

Whatever the details, the end result was the same: a distinctively ribbed, green glass prototype bottle with a thin neck that widens into a bulbous middle with the Coca-Cola logo embossed onto it, before tapering away until the very bottom, where it widens slightly to form the base of the container. The design was patented in November 1915 and sent to the committee of seven Coca-Cola bottlers charged with picking the winning design. In early 1916 after several days of discussion the Root Glass Company's "contour bottle" won the vote six to one. After being selected, the bottle underwent further changes. The fat middle became less bulbous and the tapering between it and the base made less drastic, changes that gave the bottle a more appealing hourglass figure and made it better suited to the rigors of bottling plant production lines. By 1918 every Coca-Cola bottler was using the new bottle, and the royalties had made Chapman Root the richest man in Indiana.

The contour bottle was a packaging masterpiece, instantly recognizable by touch and in silhouette. The distinctive cocoa pod–inspired ribs ensured that even when a broken fragment of the glass was found, it was clear that it came from a Coca-Cola bottle. Raymond Loewy, the industrial designer who created some of the most iconic designs of the twentieth century, including Lucky Strike cigarette packets and Studebaker's classic Avanti car, called it "the most perfectly designed package in use today." It became one of the best-known packages in the world, gaining an iconic status to rival that of Robinson's handwritten Coca-Cola logo. In 1960 the Coca-Cola bottle was so well recognized that it became one of the few items of packaging to be awarded a trademark.

While Dobbs and Hirsch had set to work destroying the competition with unique bottles and a blizzard of lawsuits, Asa Candler had been thinking about his future. He doubted that fizzy pop had much of a future and had started investing his fortune in real estate, erecting Candler Building skyscrapers across North America, including a seventeen-story tower in Atlanta that was the city's tallest structure when it opened in 1906. He also used his wealth to help build the Atlanta suburb of Druid Hills and to bankroll Emory College's transformation into Emory University.

He started thinking about selling Coca-Cola and moving on, but with the federal government case over caffeine that threatened the company's all-important trademark dragging on, no one was willing to buy. Candler still lacked a buyer in 1916 when he decided to run for mayor of Atlanta. So he quit the company, divided up his shares among his five children and his wife, and appointed his son Howard president of the business. He went on to win the election by a comfortable margin.

With his uncle gone, Dobbs saw an opportunity to finally become the boss of Coca-Cola. He found a potential buyer of the company in Ernest Woodruff, the battle-hardened Atlanta businessman who ran a bank called the Trust Company of Georgia. Woodruff had a reputation as a ruthless operator who did whatever it took to advance his business interests. Once he bought a bunch of houses in a red light district in Atlanta, where he planned to build a factory for one of his companies. After evicting the prostitutes and pimps, he made sure they and their customers stayed away by spending night after night patrolling the street with a shotgun.

Like many people in Atlanta, the Candlers knew who Woodruff was and they didn't like him, so while Woodruff was interested in buying Coca-Cola, he knew they wouldn't make a deal with him. Aware that this was the case, Dobbs offered to play deal maker by encouraging the Candler family to sell their shares to Woodruff and his partners. Dobbs's bridge building worked. In 1919 Woodruff's coalition of bankers bought the Coca-Cola Company for $25 million. Howard Candler was moved into the chairman's seat, and Dobbs was rewarded for his role in the takeover with the post of company president that he had coveted for so long. But his soda boss dreams rapidly turned sour when, just a few months after taking charge, Coca-Cola was plunged into crisis.

The problem was sugar. World War I had shattered Europe's sugar industry, which had been dominated by the sugar beet growers of the newly dismantled Austro-Hungarian Empire, causing a global shortage of the sweetener. Wartime price controls had kept sugar prices stable at nine cents a pound, but on December 1, 1919, the federal government lifted the restrictions. With sugar in short supply, prices skyrocketed. Within a few weeks the cost of sugar had climbed to twenty cents a pound and continued to rise. The price spike sent shock waves through the fizzy drink industry. Sugar was the main ingredient in the syrups they used to make their sodas, and in just a few days the price of this crucial commodity had more than doubled.

For Coca-Cola this was a serious problem. Coke was now one of the biggest consumers of sugar in the world, gobbling up nearly one hundred million pounds of the sweet stuff every year. Soon Coca-Cola profits were being sucked into a sugar price black hole that threatened to ruin the company. By early May 1920, with sugar prices hitting twenty-eight cents a pound, Candler decided Coca-Cola needed to protect itself against further increases and ordered the company to buy half a year's supply of sugar for an eye-watering sum. To pay for all this sugar, Coca-Cola borrowed millions from Wall Street banks. As collateral for the loan, the company handed over the sole copy of its secret formula, which was promptly locked inside a New York City bank vault. Coca-Cola wasn't the only soda company thinking this way. As the crisis deepened, Pepsi-Cola, Chero-Cola, and Moxie all started buying up sugar in large quantities.

Then in early August 1920 sugar prices collapsed, the speculative bubble bursting as eastern Europe's sugar beet producers got back on their feet. Within days the price of sugar had slumped to ten cents a pound. The soft drink giants that had bet on further price rises had miscalculated and were now saddled with mountains of overpriced sugar. For Moxie it was the beginning of the end of its days as a national force. In 1920 the company was still ahead of Coca-Cola in sales and riding high on its successful "What this country needs is plenty of Moxie" wartime ads, which turned the soda's name into a byword for a can-do attitude. Moxie had also scored a hit with its off-the-wall Horsemobiles. These attention-grabbing promotional vehicles consisted of model horses welded onto automobile chassis that Moxie salesmen could drive while riding the horses. These strange motor vehicles became a regular sight in New England and attracted huge crowds wherever they went. But the sugar crisis caused Moxie to slash its advertising budget, a move that destroyed its sales momentum. By 1925 sales of the Massachusetts soda had peaked.

Compared to Pepsi-Cola, Moxie got off lightly. Bradham's sugar-buying spree brought his company to its knees. Desperate, he tried selling his business to Coca-Cola without success. In 1922 he found himself with little choice but to file for bankruptcy. Pepsi-Cola was dead. Chero-Cola was also badly wounded by its sugar-buying error and received a further blow when Coca-Cola's lawyers won a trademark suit that forced it to drop the word cola from its name. Within a few years Chero, as it would now be called, was fading fast.

But over at Coca-Cola, the sugar crisis became a means for Woodruff to tighten his control over the business. Relations between Woodruff and Dobbs had deteriorated rapidly since the takeover. Dobbs resented Woodruff's constant interference, and Woodruff had became increasingly fed up with Dobbs's objections to his plans. The sugar crisis brought these tensions to the fore. They clashed over how to handle the company's network of bottlers, who were rebelling over increases in the price of Coca-Cola syrup due to the spike in the value of sugar. Woodruff wanted the company to impose a price and the bottlers to lump it. Dobbs wanted a compromise that would split the burden of high-price sugar between the company and its bottlers. Dobbs got his way, but when the cost of sugar plunged, Coca-Cola still had large stockpiles of the sweetener that it had bought at the peak of the price bubble and so couldn't reduce the price it charged bottlers for its syrup. The bottlers responded by suing the company.

The pair also fought over advertising. Dobbs wanted a bigger promotional budget so that he could keep advertising Coca-Cola during the winter when sales of the drink would fall off. Woodruff wanted larger dividends and opposed Dobbs's high-spending ad plan. Dobbs regarded Woodruff as a man ignorant of the power of advertising; Woodruff regarded Dobbs as a man out to waste his money. The disagreements came to a head in September 1920 when Woodruff and his boardroom allies showed Dobbs who was the real boss of Coca-Cola by blocking his request for more advertising funds. The following month Dobbs resigned.

With Dobbs gone, Woodruff reinstated Howard Candler as president. After all, Coca-Cola was in trouble, and Candler already had experience running the business. Candler wasn't keen on the job but took it, in part, out of a sense of duty toward the business that his father had built. Candler successfully steered Coca-Cola out of the sugar crisis. Unlike Moxie, Coca-Cola kept advertising its product, which helped sales continue to rise. More sales not only meant more money for repaying the loans the company had taken out but also caused its expensive sugar mountain to erode faster. By summer 1921 most of Coca-Cola's sugar stockpiles were gone and the company had reached an out-of-court settlement with its bottlers.

Despite his success in pulling Coca-Cola out of the crisis, Woodruff and the company's board were unhappy with Candler. They felt he lacked the fire needed to take Coca-Cola forward, and they hadn't forgotten that it was Candler who bought all that sugar in the first place. The board wanted a more go-getting boss, and there was an obvious choice: Woodruff's son Robert, the vice president of the Cleveland-based White Motor Company. Robert accepted the offer to become Coca-Cola's president but on one condition: that he would be free to run the business as he saw fit and that his father would butt out. Ernest agreed and in April 1923 the thirty-three-year-old replaced Candler as the president of Coca-Cola.

By then the mess caused by the sugar crisis had been cleaned up and Coca-Cola had weathered the storm. In fact all of the company's problems seemed to have been solved. All of its competitors were in retreat. The overpriced sugar mountain was gone and the debts incurred from buying it had been repaid. Even the Wiley case that had dogged the company for years had been settled, after Coca-Cola agreed to reduce the amount of caffeine in its drink and the government agreed not to challenge its trademark. Finally, the cola king was ready to cash in on the soda boom that the introduction of Prohibition had just kickstarted.

5

The Bar Is Dead, Soda Is King!

On January 17, 1920, America ran dry. Years of vigorous campaigning by the temperance movement had ended in victory; the demon liquor had been slain and was now banned throughout the United States.

For the triumphant prohibitionists, the Eighteenth Amendment that introduced the ban and the Volstead Act that enforced it marked the dawning of a new era. No longer would drunken American men beat their wives or blow their pay in smoky saloons. Instead the new American male would be a model citizen. He would hold down a job, save his money for his family, and go to church. Firebrand temperance campaigner Reverend Billy Sunday envisaged the birth of dry America as an express elevator to utopia. "The slums soon will be only a memory," he proclaimed as the nation headed for last orders. "We will turn our prisons into factories and our jails into storehouses and corncribs."

Prohibition's puritan supporters believed their "noble experiment" would banish every social ill, but not every American greeted the ban with joy. As wet America's final hours approached, the *New York Evening Post* wrote of "liquor stampedes" as New Yorkers scrambled to stockpile alcohol to see them through the dry days ahead. For the nation's breweries, Prohibition threatened nothing less than ruin. With their core business abolished, they started hunting for new sources of profit to mine. Some reinvented themselves as car part manufacturers, hoping to cash in on the fast-growing automobile market. A few took to smoking hams. Others retooled to become ice cream producers, among them Budweiser brewer Anheuser-Busch.

Many sought salvation in near beer, the super-low-alcohol beer permitted under Prohibition since its alcohol content was under 0.5%. The trouble was that near beer verged on tasteless since the boiling process that removed the alcohol also destroyed the chemicals that gave beer its flavor. The resulting liquid was a bland, buzz-free beer substitute that food critic Waverley Root described as a beverage that "might have been dreamed up by a puritan Machiavelli with the intent of disgusting drinkers." Despite these shortcomings, near beers such as Miller's Vivo and Anheuser-Busch's Bevo sold briskly at first, although their appeal was short-lived. Near beer sales peaked at three hundred million gallons in 1921 but come 1929 annual sales had dwindled to one hundred million gallons.

Another business lifesaver the breweries clung to was carbonated soft drinks. Many breweries became bottling plants for existing soda brands; a few went a step further and invented fizzy drinks of their own. The Independent Breweries Company syndicate of St. Louis came up with IBC Root Beer, only to collapse in 1923. Green River was another, more successful brewery soda. Developed in 1919 by the Schoenhofen Edelweiss Brewing Company of Chicago, Green River was a lurid green, lime-flavored soda that became a sensation in the Midwest. To draw attention to its drink, the brewery commissioned Eddie Cantor of Broadway's famous Ziegfeld Follies revues to compose a promo tune that is one of the earliest examples of popular music being used to promote soda pop. Cantor's song, "Green River," pitched the emerald liquid as the only soft drink suitable for despondent drinkers facing life under Prohibition. "Since the country's turned prohibitin', I've been in a bad condition," the lyric went. "Every soft drink that I try, just makes me want to cry. Take it back from whence it came, all your drinks are much the same. I tried one here today, and believe me when I say: For a drink that's fine without a kick, oh, Green River!"

This ditty wasn't the last song Green River would inspire. In 1969 the rock band Creedence Clearwater Revival scored one of its biggest hits with "Green River," a song partly inspired by singer John Fogerty's childhood love of the drink. "In my neighborhood, if you went to the soda fountain at the pharmacy, you could order different fizz drinks," he recalled in Hank Bordowitz's biography of the group *Bad Moon Rising*. "One of the drinks was a Green River, a bottle of syrup that fit into the dispenser upside down. The drink was a green, lime drink on ice with fizz water, a soggy green snow cone. That's what I would order and it made me the happiest."

But while Prohibition forced breweries into the soda business against their will, the companies that built the industry could barely conceal their delight. Soda makers had never knowingly missed an opportunity to align themselves with the temperance movement, and just like the Reverend Sunday they saw a bright future ahead—one where the greenbacks that once filled bar tills flowed into their coffers instead. The soda trade papers danced gleefully on the grave of the liquor business. The *Ice Cream Journal* described the soda fountain as "the new American bar" while *Drug Topics* boldly proclaimed, "The bar is dead, the fountain lives, and soda is king!"

This attitude wasn't hubris. Prohibition forced the saloons and bars out of business. Restaurants that relied on liquor sales for their profits increased their food prices to compensate, only to watch their diners drift away to the soda fountains that were now offering cheap snacks to complement their staples of sodas, shakes, and sundaes. To welcome the refugees from the bars, fountain operators concocted soda recipes designed to appeal to those more used to the punch of rum than the sweet bubbles of cola. They added dashes of pepper, pinches of salt, even cayenne chili pepper extract to give their drinks an added kick. And as the barflies moved to the soda fountains, so did the newly unemployed barkeeps. The teenage and medically trained soda jerks of old were out. In their place were professional bartenders who had honed their skills and chat in the saloons. The new breed of soda jerk was exemplified by the kind of acrobatic fountain wizardry that Buster Keaton's character tried, disastrously, to imitate in the 1927 movie *College*.

Within months of Prohibition's introduction, drugstore soda fountains had replaced bars and taverns as the social epicenters of Main Street America. But it wasn't just soda drawing in the customers. Under the Volstead Act, drugstores became the only place where alcohol could be purchased legally, provided it was for medicinal purposes. Strangely, the need for medicinal alcohol grew rapidly after Prohibition. In 1921 alone, pharmacists withdrew more than eight million gallons of medicinal whiskey from federal warehouses, twenty times the amount they dispensed before Prohibition. Soda fountains also did a roaring trade serving their regulars with drinks that were anything but soft. The J-Bar at the Hotel Jermone in Aspen, Colorado, reinvented itself as a soda fountain but spent most of its time whipping up Aspen Crud, a cocktail of vanilla ice cream soda laced with bourbon that became an illicit favorite with the Sunday after-church crowd.

The authorities weren't dumb, however. Soon drugstores were playing cat and mouse with the law enforcement agencies that began raiding pharmacies and seizing barrels of suspect medicine. In one 1929 raid federal agents busted a soda fountain liquor ring in Meridian, Mississippi, after receiving reports that young men and women were "getting hilarious" on their Coca-Colas. The fountains had been offering customers a mix of Coca-Cola and Jake, the most notorious black market liquor of all. Bootleg booze had a reputation for harshness and dubious ingredients, but Jake took the danger of illicit liquor to a whole new level. Formed from fermented Jamaican ginger, this perilous beverage contained an adulterant that was supposed to fool the feds but proved highly toxic. Within weeks of going on sale, the vicious drink had left an estimated 15,000 to 100,000 people impotent or partially paralyzed for life. The hobbling walk of those crippled by the drink became known as "Jake leg."

But for the hip young things of the Jazz Age, the illegality and danger of moonshine were all part of the thrill and romance of Prohibition drinking. Alcohol was never far away from the rebellious bobbed-haired flappers and their male counterparts, the sheiks, as they swung their way through the Roaring Twenties. To counter the harsh burn of bootleg liquor they turned to soda-based cocktails or mixed drinks, which had been uncommon in the days before Prohibition, when soda was more often used as a chaser than as a mixer for alcohol. In speakeasies they would order "set ups" of cracked ice and ginger ale or club soda into which they could discreetly slip a measure of bathtub spirit from their handy and oh-so-chichi hip flasks. Cola may have overtaken ginger ale as America's favorite fizz by the dawn of the Jazz Age, but the appeal of the latter as a mixer drove its sales to new highs in the 1920s.

It is often claimed that ginger ale was first developed in Ireland by the American apothecary Dr. Thomas Cantrell around 1850, but drinks bearing the same name were being advertised as early as 1818. Regardless of its exact origin, ginger ale was a variation on ginger beer, the sweet, dark, yeast-fermented drink that had become popular in Britain during the early 1800s. Initially there was little difference between ginger ale and ginger beer, but over time ginger ales evolved into ginger-flavored drinks carbonated with soda water rather than yeast that were clear rather than cloudy.

Ginger ale lived in the shadow of ginger beer for several years until the introduction of Cantrell's Belfast ginger ale turned the drink into an American favorite. Cantrell's drink inspired a wave of what are now called golden ginger ales. One of the drinks inspired by Cantrell was Vernor's, the 1866 creation of Detroit pharmacist James Vernor that gained a reputation for being so fizzy it caused people to sneeze. Vernor's ginger ale became a regional favorite in Detroit and Michigan and stands today as America's oldest surviving soda brand.

The next leap forward for ginger ale came in 1900 courtesy of Canadian pharmacist John McLaughlin, the reserved Presbyterian son of a carriage maker from Enniskillen, Ontario. McLaughlin entered the soft drinks business in 1890 using the dowry from his marriage to Maud, a haughty redhead from a wealthy New York family, to open a Toronto store where he sold bottles of sarsaparilla, lemon, and cream soda under the brand name Sanitary. In 1900 he added a ginger ale to the range, but his wife and customers found his drink too syrupy for their tastes, so he began work on a lighter colored and less sweet version. Four years later he launched McLaughlin's Pale Dry Style Ginger Ale, a new form of ginger ale that offered a lighter, less pungent taste. A year later he renamed it Canada Dry and, at his wife's suggestion, started promoting it as "the champagne of ginger ales."

Canada Dry spread rapidly through the Canadian provinces, and while most people drank it straight, McLaughlin's dry ginger ale also gained a reputation as a mixer thanks to its mellow taste. In 1923 the drink's appeal as a mixer prompted two businessmen, Perry Saylor and James Mathes, to buy the business for a cool million dollars. The Canadian-born Saylor and his American partner took Canada Dry into the United States with a direct appeal to Prohibition drinkers. They billed it as a New York nightclub favorite, sold it in miniature champagne-style bottles and rode the speak-easy boom to enormous success. In just four years Canada Dry went from selling 1.7 million bottles a year to more than 50 million in 1926. Almost everyone who bought Canada Dry used it as a mixer, with surveys suggesting that as many as three-quarters of ginger ale drinkers used it to mask the taste of bootleg liquor.

Ginger ale became so big during Prohibition that even the notorious gangster Al Capone got in on the act, setting up ginger ale and club soda bottling plants so that he could monopolize the mixer market in Chicago. He and his older brother Ralph "Bottles" Capone, who was put in charge of the mobster's soda operation, made millions from the business. The marriage of soda and alcohol established during Prohibition would prove to be one of the temperance movement's most enduring legacies, prompting a change in American drinking habits that still lingers on today.

But while Canada Dry built an empire in the speakeasies, Coca-Cola was enjoying even greater success. By the time Robert Woodruff took charge in 1923 the company was in great shape, with the challenges of the late 1910s resolved. The 1920s lay before the company ready for the taking, and Woodruff used this rosy inheritance to turn Coca-Cola into the epitome of modern business. During the first twenty-five years of his leadership, Coca-Cola would not just dominate the fizzy drink industry but transform how *all* businesses operated and weave its product into the very soul of America. Woodruff's Coca-Cola captured the spirit of the 1920s. It was an age of bold dreams, expansive plans, and modernist thinking in which synthetic plastics, refrigeration, cars, color advertising, radio, airplanes, and telephones fundamentally reshaped the world. One of the fruits of this push for the modern was a vision of the corporate boss as a decision-maker reliant on the expert knowledge of PR specialists, lawyers, researchers, salespeople, and advertising creatives to run their businesses. Woodruff was nothing if not a professional manager. Under his stewardship Coca-Cola became a firm at the cutting edge of modernist corporate management.

One of the first signs of the cigar-puffing six-footer's determination to modernize, standardize, and improve was his early push to clean up

Coca-Cola's bottling plants. Bottled Coca-Cola sales were still behind those made at the soda fountains, but the lucrative potential of the home and take-away market was obvious. The only hurdle was the lingering image of unsanitary bottles that still put many people off. For Woodruff, cleaning up the bottlers was a priority, and, the company legend goes, he witnessed the problem firsthand shortly after becoming president when he visited a Coca-Cola bottling plant. Inside he found piles of broken glass, dust-covered machinery, and pools of spilled Coca-Cola syrup swarming with flies. Furious, he told the bottler that if the plant wasn't clean by the next day they would no longer be a Coca-Cola bottling plant. "But Mr. Wood-ruff," pleaded the bottler, "it don't do no good to clean up. The next day it'll look like this again." Woodruff removed his cigar from his mouth and growled: "You wipe your ass, don't you?"

Woodruff began issuing edicts to the company's twelve hundred bottlers that dictated everything from employee dress codes and delivery truck color schemes to hygiene standards and the exact amount of syrup to be used in each bottle. To enforce these rules he formed a quality control department to monitor their output and used local advertising support as a carrot and a stick. Bottlers who did what they were told got advertising support, those who did not found Coca-Cola advertising dollars vanished from their territory. By 1928 more Coca-Cola was being sold in bottles than at the soda fountain, where Woodruff continued his push for a standardized beverage by getting soda jerks to serve the drink in the now iconic bell-shaped Coca-Cola glasses that came with a mark showing exactly how much syrup to pour in.

Woodruff's quest for standardization was fueled by his ardent belief that the image mattered as much as the product's actual quality. Coca-Cola the liquid might be unremarkable but the brand that came with it was anything but. For Woodruff, Coca-Cola was not just a drink but a lifestyle choice, and its public image was as crucial as any ingredient in its secret formula. In fact the secret formula would play a vital role in Coca-Cola's efforts to turn its soda into a corporate totem. In 1925 the company relocated the lone copy of the formula from the New York bank vault, where it had been held since the sugar crisis, back to Atlanta in a blaze of publicity. Then it made public the procedures surrounding the mysterious document—policies that seemed more appropriate for a state secret than a soda recipe. Employees needed approval from the board to even look at the document, and only two Coca-Cola employees were permitted to know the recipe at any one time. The secret formula was more than a trade secret; it was now a holy relic—a divine object of mystery sealed deep within an impenetrable vault.

This was myth-making on a Wizard of Oz scale: any chemist worth his or her salt could decode much of the formula, as the hundreds of cola copycats had proved, and there wasn't really anything that special lurking in the liquid. But that was, in many ways, the point. It wasn't the drink that mattered so much as what customers believed it to be. And the task of telling them what to think about the drink fell to Archie Lee, the company's advertising mastermind.

Born and raised in Monroe, North Carolina, Lee grew up dreaming of writing literary novels and leaving an impression on the world. "I feel that to work just for money's sake would be a desecration," the idealistic youth once wrote to his mother. "I want to do something really worthwhile. I would die happy if it should be just one recognized and lasting thing." Lee's search for greatness took him into journalism, but after several years as a reporter he made the leap into advertising by joining Coca-Cola's ad agency D'Arcy, where he took charge of the Coke account in 1923. Today Lee's approach seems obvious, but in the 1920s it was groundbreaking. Most advertisers were still stuck in a rut of verbose text-heavy promotions that often resorted to dry, functional detail or to scare tactics to win business. Lee had little time for such approaches. "The offering of a product is blunt selling," he wrote in a 1945 letter summarizing his beliefs about advertising. "Presenting the idea from the consumer angle is using imagination."

He presented Coca-Cola not as a mere beverage that would quench your thirst but as something symbolic of innocent everyday pleasure. He commissioned artists such as Norman Rockwell and McClelland Barclay to paint scenes of happy times, sociability, and rural tranquility that he then complemented with a message condensed into a bite-size slogan, short enough for motorists to absorb from a roadside billboard in a single glance. Messages like "Thirst knows no season" and "6,000,000 drinks a day." Simple, eye-catching, and backed with a budget capable of putting these ads in front of millions of eyeballs, Lee's creations set the tone for the future of advertising. Lee's most memorable slogan, "The pause that refreshes," came in 1929. It and the myriad variations on that theme he created captured the public imagination so effectively that the company was still using the slogan twenty years later. Its impact was still being remembered seventy years on, when the industry journal *Advertising Age* named it one of the ten best campaign slogans of the twentieth century.

Lee's gentle nostalgia and positive sell captured something about the American spirit, and as the 1920s went on, people began more and more to think of Coca-Cola as representative of America. People began talking about things being "as American as Coca-Cola," and in the southern states Coca-Cola cake, a moist chocolate cake made with the soda, became a common sight at picnics and church events. The suspicion that surrounded the drink before the First World War was gone. Now Coca-Cola was part and parcel of American life. Nothing illustrated this change in public attitudes as much as the reaction to the news that the Women Christian Temperance Union of Arkansas City would devote 1929 to stamping out the "hydra-headed menace of Coca-Cola." Instead of finding the public rallying to their crusade, the temperance activists watched their short-lived campaign get lampooned in the newspapers and dismissed as a joke.

Many of Lee's campaigns drew on the insights that came from Coca-Cola's statistical department, another of Woodruff's innovations. Formed in 1923, the department brought a scientific edge to the company's operations. It gathered vast amounts of data about traffic patterns in towns and cities throughout the United States, so that the company could pinpoint exactly which billboards would have the most impact. It identified the most valuable retailers in the country so Coca-Cola's sales force could visit them twice as often as less lucrative stores. It analyzed the shopping habits of forty-two thousand drugstore customers and then used the results to teach soda fountain operators how to sell more Coca-Cola and how to encourage Coke drinkers to buy additional items. The statisticians also enabled the company to start accurately predicting future sales and profits—no mean feat for a company of Coca-Cola's size in a computerless age. And in late

1928 Coca-Cola's statistical department sent a warning to Woodruff that an economic crash was coming.

The soda pop giant's numbers men were right. The Roaring Twenties had been a decade of speculation, excess, and a widespread belief that share prices would keep going up and up and up. But this party came to a screeching halt in October 1929 when the stock market crashed. In the space of a week millions were wiped off the value of stocks, erasing personal and business fortunes. To recover from the losses US banks began refusing to lend money to Germany to help it rebuild, prompting the German economy to collapse, which frightened American shareholders even more. Soon there were runs on the struggling banks, and businesses across America started going bust, leaving millions out of work. The Great Depression had begun.

As the economic crisis deepened, people stopped buying soda as they tried to make ends meet. Soon the soda fountains and retailers that the fizzy drink industry relied on were going under in the thousands. "There has been a tremendous loss in outlets," Coke's vice president of sales Harrison Jones told Woodruff in a 1932 memo. "We have found that practically all bottlers are experiencing an inability on the part of many of their small outlets to buy more than one case and pay cash. In many cases, when the truck calls in the morning, the dealers are required to ask them to come back later in the day, until such time as they can get enough money to pay the cash for a case of Coca-Cola."

Coca-Cola responded with more advertising. While Moxie and others slashed back their advertising budget, Woodruff kept spending big—a move that made Coca-Cola even more visible than ever. "In the last four years there has been less advertising of every kind and character than at any time in fifteen years," wrote Jones. "Since we maintained our advertising showings in all media we have stuck out as a sore thumb, and have been more dominant unquestionably than at any time before in our history." The company's ad budget went further too. Billboard owners didn't have enough advertisers to fill their boards, so instead of leaving their poster sites vacant, they gave Coca-Cola space for free, enabling the company to blanket America in Lee's visions of a happier America.

Lee fulfilled his end of the bargain by finally producing a campaign good enough to convince people that Coca-Cola was an all-year-round drink rather than a summer treat with a series of Christmas ads painted by Haddon Sundblom. Born in Muskegon, Michigan, in 1899, the Swedish American artist had already made his name in advertising with his work for Maxwell House and Palmolive by the time Lee asked him to illustrate Coca-Cola's 1931 Christmas ad. Lee wanted an illustration of Santa Claus having a refreshing pause with a Coca-Cola, and Sundblom was happy to oblige for the appropriate fee. Partially inspired by Clement C. Moore's poem "A Visit from St. Nicholas," Sundblom painted a smiling, ruddy-faced Santa toasting the audience with a glass of Coca-Cola. He modeled the character on his retired friend Lou Prentiss. "He embodied all the features and spirit of Santa Claus," Sundblom explained. "The wrinkles in his face were happy wrinkles." The advertisement proved so successful that Coca-Cola made its Santa advertisement an annual event, with Sundblom illustrating every one of them until 1964.

It is often claimed that Sundblom's ad created the look of the modern-day Santa Claus with his red suit, black leather belt, white beard, and bobble hat. But the reality was that Sundblom simply latched onto the emerging consensus about how Santa looked. Traditionally Santa and his European forerunners had come in all shapes and sizes. Sometimes he was tall and skinny; at other times he was the squat, pipe-puffing elf from Moore's poem. Santa's garb also varied from the bishop's clothing of the Dutch Sinterklaas, who would kidnap naughty children, to Britain's Father Christmas, who wore green robes, to the present-day red-and-white outfit. Despite Santa's mixed-up origins in folklore, paganism, and Christianity, by the time Coca-Cola hired Sundblom, the idea of St. Nick as a fat man with a big white beard dressed in red was already becoming the archetype of the Yuletide gift giver.

In fact, not only was Sundblom's depiction simply tapping into a wider trend, but this popular vision of Santa had even been used to promote soda pop before. The Santa in White Rock's 1915 Christmas ads looked much like Coca-Cola's Santa, although he preferred to make his festive deliveries of the Wisconsin soda firm's drinks by automobile or biplane rather than by sleigh and magic reindeer. A few years later in 1923, White Rock was running Christmas ads in color magazines showing a Santa almost indistinguishable from Sundblom's enjoying a whiskey and a White Rock ginger ale while catching up on his mail. Luckily for Santa, Prohibition didn't apply in Lapland. But while Coca-Cola's Santa was not by any stretch of the imagination the origin of the modern-day St Nick, it probably sealed the deal once and for all with its ubiquitous year-in, year-out Christmas advertising muscle.

Not that all its extra advertising, Coke-guzzling Santas, and statistical wizardry worked miracles. Coca-Cola sales flatlined in the Depression, the growth of the 1920s replaced with stagnation. Compared to most of its rivals, though, this was a good result. Charles Hires watched sales of his root beer fall off a cliff, dropping 60 percent between 1930 and 1935. Nor were sales of Hires's temperance drink helped by the end of Prohibition in April 1933. The noble experiment had proved little more than the naïveté of the temperance campaign. In the hope that the return of the liquor industry could help the moribund economy, the federal government consigned the Volstead Act and Eighteenth Amendment to the trash can of history.

The return of alcohol worried the soda industry. In the first six months of Prohibition, soda sales leapt by 200 percent and kept rising all the way up to the Great Depression. The question now haunting the industry was whether the repeal of Prohibition would reverse all of that. Would people still want a Coke when beer was readily available? Would they still need ginger ale in their drink when distilled liquor didn't taste like gasoline? The breweries hoped not. Schoenhofen Edelweiss greeted the end of Prohibition by sidelining Green River, the soda that saw it through the dry years, and refocusing on beer. Soon the breweries that survived by making smoked ham and ice cream were poised for a glorious return.

At Coke, vice president of sales Harrison Jones was particularly twitchy. He wrote to Woodruff warning that the brewers would be a serious threat to Coca-Cola. They were buying ads like crazy, he noted in one memo. In another he urged Woodruff to launch a Coca-Cola beer to grab a share of the expected post-prohibition liquor boom. Woodruff dismissed the proposal. Coca-Cola made Coca-Cola, nothing else. At first it looked as if Jones was right. After several years of flat sales, 1934 saw Coca-Cola's revenues dip by about 25 percent to $31.2 million. But the hit was short-lived, and in 1938 the company's annual sales reached a new high of $75.8 million. Coca-Cola had survived once again.

Coca-Cola wasn't the only soda company to buck the trend for decline in the Depression. Another success story was the lemon-lime drink 7Up. Its creator Charles Leiper Grigg was born in 1868 in a log cabin in Price's Branch, a tiny hamlet in Montgomery County, Missouri, with a population of just twenty-five people. As a child Griggs became obsessed by mail-order catalogs and the array of wonderful goods on offer within their appealing pages. He was still obsessing about catalogs at the age of twenty-two when he wrote to a St. Louis mail-order company to tell them that their catalog wasn't up to scratch and explained how it could be improved. "If you think you can do better, come to St Louis and do it," the firm replied. So he did.

Grigg spent the next three decades working in various St. Louis companies. In 1918, he ended up as an advertising executive for Whistle Orange Soda, the creation of local businessman Vess Jones. But Grigg didn't get along with his new boss, so in 1919 he walked and started work on an orange soda of his own. He obtained funding for the new company from his friend Edmund Ridgway, who had made his fortune investing in mining. In 1920, Grigg launched Howdy—a lightly carbonated but very sweet orange-flavored soda. Although Griggs and Ridgway had built a network of nearly four hundred bottlers by the mid-1920s, Howdy struggled, overshadowed by the rapid rise of Orange Crush, a rival orange soda from Chicago. Orange Crush was booming on the back of doctors recommending orange juice as a source of vitamin C, because the soda contained orange juice rather than the essential oils of the fruit's peel that were used in Howdy. Grigg found his beverage under attack from rivals for its lack of juice, and new laws forced him to label Howdy an orange-*flavored* drink rather than an orange drink. He hated the obsession with juice and pulp, and he refused to change Howdy's formula "simply in order to line up with a pseudo-consumerist notion that the addition of orange juice makes a better product."

But the market had spoken, and by 1927 Grigg had started searching for a new drink to make his millions. He settled on the idea of creating a lemon soda. As one of the simplest flavors around, lemon sodas abounded, with around six hundred brands on sale in the United States alone during the late 1920s. But Grigg saw opportunity in this fiercely competitive sub-market due to the lack of a market leader. Grigg spent months perfecting his new drink, eventually settling on a lemon and lime flavored beverage that fizzed more than the average soda.

The drink also harked back to soda's origins in patent medicine thanks to the inclusion of a trace of lithium citrate. Although better known today as an antidepressant, lithium's use in pharmacology only began after World War II. Lithium's main medical use in 1929 was as an alternative to table salt in the wake of research linking salt with hypertension and heart disease. This ill-advised substitution would continue until evidence of severe side effects and deaths prompted an outright ban on the sale of lithium salts in 1949; the ban also forced the removal of the substance from Grigg's drink.

But in 1929 this was all to come, and Grigg was keen to highlight the alkali metal's presence in his new drink, so much so that he named his beverage Bib-Label Lithiated Lemon-Lime Soda. Someone must have had a quiet word, though, because shortly after its October 1929 launch Grigg changed the name to 7Up. Why Grigg picked 7Up remains a mystery, but there's no shortage of speculation. Some stories say Grigg got his inspiration while gambling with cards or dice. Another claims he saw a cattle brand with the shape of a seven and a *u*, while another tale suggested the seven represented the number of ingredients and the up referred to the fizz. Whatever the reason, looking back everything seemed stacked against 7Up.

It had launched just two weeks before the stock market crash, and it still had to find a way to stand out from its hundreds of competitors. But 7Up had some advantages. For a start it had Howdy's bottling network to tap into, giving it instant reach across America, and because the drink was lower in sugar than most sodas, it was cheaper to make, which made it an appealing option for other cash-strapped bottlers. It also successfully promoted itself as a hangover cure, running a "7Up for 7 hangovers" campaign that pitched the drink as capable of easing the effects of overdrinking, oversmoking, underdrinking, mental lassitude, overwork, overeating, and over-worry. After sales of 7Up syrup reached 5,920 gallons in 1930, the drink began a steady rise. In 1933 syrup sales topped 174,000 gallons before shooting up to 2,074,000 gallons a year by 1936, after Grigg's post-Prohibition decision to start promoting his soda as a mixer that "tames whiskey" and "glorifies gin."

As 7Up raced to the top of the lemon soda league in 1936, Coca-Cola was marking its fiftieth anniversary with a party for its employees. By then Jones's fears about beer had subsided, and the flamboyant and towering Coca-Cola sales chief was convinced that Coke was here to stay. "There may be war," he told the assembled Coca-Cola men and women in a tub-thumping speech. "We can stand that. There may be revolutions. We will survive. Taxes may bear down to the breaking point. We can take it. The Four Horsemen of the Apocalypse may charge over the Earth and back again—and Coca-Cola will remain." But even as he uttered those words Coca-Cola's dominance was under renewed attack from an old foe reborn. Pepsi-Cola was back.

In 1922 the original incarnation of the Pepsi-Cola Company had gone down in flames, a victim of the sugar price bubble. While the drink's creator Caleb Bradham retreated to the North Carolina drugstore where it all started to eke out a life of obscurity, Wall Street investor Roy Megargel bought the tattered remains of the Pepsi dream. Megargel tried to bring the drink back from the dead but soda fountains snubbed it, bottlers ignored it, and Coca-Cola's advertising juggernaut crushed it. By 1931 Megargel's Pepsi was on its deathbed. Then, just as all looked lost, Charles Guth called.

Guth came from a family of confectioners. His Russian father, Emil, owned a Baltimore confectionery business, and his two elder brothers, who were born in Russia before the family moved to America, were already making candy for the store by the time Guth was born in 1876. Guth followed in his father's footsteps, starting in 1899 with a candy store of his own in Baltimore before building and selling three successful chocolate businesses. By the middle of the 1920s he had hit on his biggest success yet: a chocolate drink named Mavis.

Despite his trade, Guth was no sweetie. In 1913 he shot and killed his chauffeur after the driver attacked him with an axe for firing him. He bribed Coca-Cola bottlers to produce Mavis on the side, much to Coca-Cola's annoyance. Guth also liked to be imposing despite his five-foot-six frame, so he had the desk in his office placed on a raised platform so that employees and those who did business with him would have to look up to him. Then there were his ruthless dealings with the Loft family, who owned the New York candy store chain Loft Inc. In August 1929 Guth persuaded them to swap Loft shares for a stake in Mavis. Within seven months of the deal Guth had used his shares in Loft to install himself as the company's president and seize control of the family business.

After his devious takeover of Loft, the gray-eyed tycoon bought two more New York candy store chains—Happiness and Mirror. By 1931 he controlled an empire of 225 candy stores, many of which had soda fountains selling Coca-Cola. Guth figured that since his stores went through thirty thousand gallons of Coca-Cola syrup every year, Loft deserved a discount and the right to buy directly from Atlanta headquarters rather than the local distributor. Coca-Cola disagreed. Guth threatened to stop selling the drink. The response from Atlanta remained the same.

Furious at Coca-Cola's unbending attitude, Guth decided he would carry out his threat by picking up the pieces of Megargel's shattered dream. He struck a deal with the Pepsi owner. Guth would pay $12,000 for the rights to Pepsi and give Megargel a royalty on sales and a one-third share in the resurrected business. Megargel readily agreed and signed over the business. To pay for the rights, Guth took $10,500 out of Loft's bank account and established the third Pepsi-Cola Company in July 1931 with him and Megargel as the only shareholders. Guth then set about reformulating Pepsi.

Guth didn't like Pepsi. He regarded its taste as unsatisfactory, so he ordered Loft chemist John Ritchie and his assistant Thomas Elmezzi to fix it. But Guth's sweet tooth made it a challenging job, and his constant demands for a sweeter beverage eventually resulted in something closer to sugar water than cola. "We'd bring him a sample, and he'd say 'No, no, no, you've got to make it sweeter,'" recalled Elmezzi in his biography *The Man Who Kept the Secret*. "We'd wait a couple of hours and bring him the same sample. 'Oh that's good.'" After a few weeks of tests the chemists eventually hit on one that their boss thought was "about right" and Guth ordered

Loft's soda fountains to start selling the new Pepsi-Cola, which now also included caffeine.

Guth knew what would happen next. Another of Woodruff's business innovations was the trade research department, a division that was charged with investigating retailers who might serve a cola other than Coca-Cola when people asked for a Coke. Its investigators, a motley crew of ex-athletes and security guards, acted like a private police force. Retailers resented and feared them. These Coca-Cola cops would visit soda fountains hoping to catch out soda jerks. If a suspect beverage was served they would collect a sample to send to Coca-Cola's labs for analysis, demand samples of the syrup, and threaten legal action. To make sure any lawsuits were successful, the investigators worked in pairs so that they could confirm each other's recollection of events in court. Sometimes they would come back to the same fountain day after day waiting for a slip-up.

But Guth did not run an easily frightened mom-and-pop outfit. Knowing that Coca-Cola's undercover spies would soon be swarming over his stores, Guth issued written orders to his soda jerks telling them that "under no circumstances is Pepsi-Cola to be offered for Coca-Cola or compared with it." As an extra precaution he offered a $10,000 reward to any customer who was offered a Pepsi when they asked for a Coca-Cola at one of his stores. Inevitably some staff slipped up, and the Coca-Cola cops were there to catch them. In 1932 Coca-Cola sued and, for good measure, sent Guth a claim for $30,000 for finding that Pepsi was served at his stores when a Coca-Cola was ordered. The Cola War had begun.

Coca-Cola hauled more than one hundred Loft employees before the court for questioning, but Guth's canny precautions paid off. The judge accepted that Loft had substituted Pepsi for Coca-Cola but noted that Guth had clearly told staff not to do this. Coca-Cola, the judge ruled, should have informed Loft rather than suing and dismissed the case. Pepsi had headed off Coca-Cola's initial onslaught.

But while Pepsi survived in court, shoppers weren't buying. Even with Guth's numerous stores, the drink was floundering. In response Megargel sued for unpaid royalties, so Guth used $35,000 from Loft's coffers to buy him out. By 1933 Pepsi was heading for a third bankruptcy. Guth tried selling the business to Coca-Cola for $50,000 only to be rebuffed. Shortly after failing to sell Pepsi to Coke, Guth met a bottle merchant who suggested selling the drink in twelve-ounce bottles to set it apart from Coca-Cola's six-and-a-half-ounce containers. After realizing that the difference in cost between making a twelve-ounce soda and a six-and-a-half-ounce one was almost nothing given that the bulk of the liquid was water, he decided to try selling Pepsi-Cola in twelve-ounce bottles, but for the same nickel price that Coke charged for half that amount. In November 1933, he tested the idea in Baltimore and within six months more than one thousand cases of Pepsi were being sold every day. Guth's twice-as-much-for-the-same-price sales pitch was perfect for the Great Depression, offering American families a way to make their money go further. By the end of 1934 Pepsi-Cola was a different company: the floundering failure had morphed into a swaggering upstart that was making big inroads in the cola market. Guth expanded into Canada by setting up a bottling plant in Montreal, and he poached a Coke executive to run it. Coca-Cola fumed.

Other soda companies quickly jumped on the bigger-is-better bandwagon in the wake of Pepsi-Cola's success. After losing its court battle with Coca-Cola, Chero-Cola had renamed itself Chero only to see sales melt away. With its cola in terminal decline, the business relaunched itself as Nehi, offering a range of root beer, grape, and orange sodas. But after watching the success of Pepsi-Cola, Nehi launched a twelve-ounce-for-a-nickel cola that it named Royal Crown Cola. By 1938 this new cola had revived the company's fortunes and Royal Crown, or RC as it was also known, had become the third-biggest cola in America. Hires Root Beer also followed Pepsi's lead, and its switch to twelve-ounce bottles in 1936 saw the company bounce back. Within two years, sales of Hires were back at pre-Depression levels, and the trend toward ever-bigger soda serving sizes had begun.

But while Guth devoted himself to Pepsi-Cola, Loft was falling apart. Its finances were in shreds and in October 1935 Guth decided the answer was to cut wages. The announcement sparked fury among his employees, and Guth had to lock himself inside his own office as a mob of angry workers gathered outside. He eventually escaped with the help of the police. The staff at Loft's chocolate-making plant in Long Island City went on strike, leaving the company without a supply of candy for the crucial holiday season. Eventually Loft's shareholders rebelled and forced Guth to quit. He didn't care; he was more interested in Pepsi-Cola now.

His replacement at Loft, James Carkner, started his new job by reviewing the company's finances to figure out what was going wrong. While poring over the books he spotted the money that Guth had used to bankroll Pepsi-Cola, a company that Loft owned nothing of. Two weeks later Guth found himself being sued for the control of Pepsi-Cola by the candy chain he had treated as his own. Loft had no money to see through its legal action, and there was a real risk that Guth would simply fire Carkner, retake control of Loft, and drop the lawsuit. Loft needed outside help and in its hour of need it turned to the Phoenix Securities Corporation, a Wall Street investment trust that specialized in bringing dead or dying companies back to life.

Phoenix's president Walter Mack was an energetic Harvard graduate with slicked-back hair, and a leading figure in New York City's Republican Party. In 1932 Mack ran for the New York State Senate, but lost after refusing to pay upper Manhattan mobster Dutch Schultz $5,000 to rig the vote. After the election Mack gathered testimonies from voters about gangsters casting multiple votes and kicking people out of the polling stations—testimonies that led to a clean-up of election practices in the city.

After being approached by Carkner, Mack looked over Loft's books. Phoenix had already taken control of a large drugstore chain and figured he could turn Loft into a manufacturer of cheap candy bars to sell in those stores. So he agreed to prop the company up. Pepsi didn't figure in his thinking at all. "A lot of people thought I was awful smart that I helped finance it because I knew what could happen to Pepsi-Cola, but that's not the truth," Mack recalled at the Pepsi-Cola Bottling Association's annual meeting in 1975. "It wasn't till I got really into it and studied Pepsi-Cola that I saw."

Phoenix pumped $400,000 into Loft and bought up shares to keep it in business while it fought for control of Pepsi. In November 1937 Loft won its case and gained control of Pepsi on the grounds that Guth had built the business using its money, facilities, and staff. Guth appealed immediately, and the court decided that in the meantime Guth would stay at Pepsi as general manager while Walter Mack would become its president. As recipes for disharmony go it was a potent one. Guth shoved Mack into a cramped, sweltering office stuck above the chocolate plant's boiler room and banned staff from supplying the Phoenix president with stationery. He also kept the men's room locked so that Mack was forced to use the facilities of a nearby restaurant. "It was like a two-headed monster trying to function while in constant battle with itself," Mack wrote in his biography *No Time Lost*. "We couldn't agree on anything." Luckily for Mack this frosty working atmosphere came to a rapid end in 1938 when it became known that Guth was secretly setting up a rival cola company in Canada called Noxie Kola. Guth was fired, and Mack took charge of a flourishing business with a network of 313 bottlers and annual profits of $4 million.

Under Mack's leadership Pepsi went from strength to strength. He introduced a standard Pepsi bottle to end the Guth-era practice of sticking a Pepsi label on any old bottle that came its way and finally gave the drink a distinctive brand with a new red, white, and blue logo. When it came to promotion, Pepsi's advertising budget couldn't hope to match that of Coca-Cola, so Mack got creative. In 1939 he struck an exclusive deal with Sid Pike, the owner of the patent for the commercial use of skywriting, which had been developed in World War I to allow military planes to communicate with troops on the ground. For years after, Pepsi took its message into the heavens, drawing the words "Drink Pepsi-Cola" in fluffy, mile-high and mile-wide letters. By 1947 Pike's planes had carried out more than six thousand sorties in the United States, Canada, Mexico, and Cuba. Each of these giant ads cost the company just fifty dollars.

Pepsi also broke the model on the radio. The 1930s saw a boom in radio ownership as the number of American homes with a set soared from 40 percent at the start of the decade to nearly 90 percent at its end. Coca-Cola got into radio advertising early, running its first radio spots in 1927, but struggled to find a way to translate Lee's effective print promotions to the new medium. Even after more than a decade on the air the company was still scratching its head about how to sell itself over the airwaves, with Coke executive Ralph Hayes lamenting in 1938, "For whatever reasons, our several radio experiments, up to now, have been less than satisfactory or successful. To date, it has probably been our least effective medium, considering the expenditures involved."

The following year Pepsi showed them how to do it with a campaign that not only sold its drink but altered the way radio advertising was done. The campaign started when two songwriters, Alan Kent and Austen Croom-Johnson, wrote a song for the company called "Pepsi-Cola Hits the Spot," based on the tune of "Do Ye Ken John Peel." The ditty reinforced Pepsi's value-for-money selling point with the refrain: "Pepsi-Cola hits the spot, 12 full ounces, that's a lot, twice as much for a nickel, too, Pepsi-Cola is the drink for you." Mack decided the song should run on the radio by itself. His advertising agency was horrified. At the time radio advertisements were long, rambling affairs that, like a second-rate politician's speech, tended to drone on and on. Even the shortest lasted at least five minutes. So when Pepsi asked radio stations for a thirty-second slot to play their record, the big stations refused to run such a short ad.

Eventually the company got the song aired on a number of small cash-strapped stations, and it became an instant hit with listeners. Soon big stations were clamoring for the chance to play it too. A vinyl recording of the tune sold more than one hundred thousand copies and in 1941 alone it was played on the radio more than three hundred thousand times, often without Pepsi paying a cent. Ten years after its 1939 debut, "Pepsi-Cola Hits the Spot" was still being played on air, and other radio advertisers had followed Pepsi's lead and started running shorter, snappier ads. "When I listen to some of the jingles that come pouring forth, I'm not so sure that I started such a good thing," Mack reflected years later in his 1982 biography.

Off the air, Pepsi's promotional work was scrappier, reflecting its status as an upstart with everything to gain and little to lose. While Coca-Cola ads tended to be chaste, Pepsi was risqué. One of its ads showed a man leering into the cleavage of a young woman holding a Pepsi bottle alongside the words "Mmmmmm—it looks good." It attempted to buy the rights to Popeye so that the sailor man would now get his powers from Pepsi-Cola rather than spinach. After that ploy failed, Pepsi invented the Pepsi-Cola Cops, a Popeye-inspired newspaper comic strip about two policemen—Pepsi and Pete—who always save the day after guzzling down Pepsi. The pair's cartoons ran in more than two hundred newspapers across America, and they became two of the country's best-known advertising characters. By the time the crime-fighting duo made their debut in 1939, Pepsi-Cola had divorced itself from Loft and increased its earnings by 39 percent on the previous year.

Coca-Cola's response to its emerging rival was to drag it into the courts. In 1938 Coca-Cola sued Pepsi for trademark infringement. But in light of a similar case it brought against Roxa-Cola that backfired when the judge supported its rival, Coke's legal team felt it was too risky to challenge Pepsi in the United States, so it sued in Canada.

Coca-Cola won its Canadian case but Guth—who was still Pepsi's general manager at the time—responded with not only an appeal but lawsuits in the United States claiming that since coca and cola were generic terms the Coca-Cola trademark was invalid. When Pepsi won its appeal to the Supreme Court of Canada, Coca-Cola appealed by taking the case to the Privy Council in London, the highest court of appeal in the British Empire. The legal stakes were getting precariously high. If Pepsi lost in London it would have to change its name, and all the breakthroughs it had made in the late 1930s would have been for nothing. If Coca-Cola lost against Pepsi in America, it could be forced to ditch its fifty-year-old brand. The cola kings were preparing for a final showdown, a legal fight that could only end in destruction for one or other. But on the other side of the Atlantic Ocean, an altogether bigger fight was brewing. The world and soda were about to go to war.

6

Was Ist Cola-Cola?

While Coca-Cola spent much of the days of Prohibition and Depression cementing its place in American life, it had not been idle elsewhere. The Atlanta soda giant had long harbored global ambitions and had started its slow expansion beyond the United States in 1906 with operations in Cuba and Puerto Rico. But, Canada aside, progress had been patchy, and nowhere was its international expansion more troublesome than in Europe.

The continent might have been the place where the secret of carbonation was cracked, but Europeans hadn't fallen for fizzy pop with the same enthusiasm as their American cousins. Soda fountains were a rare sight in Europe, and carbonated drinks almost exclusively came in bottles. What's more, little had changed in the way soda was made and promoted in Europe since the nineteenth century. Most of the fizz on sale in Europe was produced in small factories that still relied on horse-drawn carts for distribution, an approach that restricted their sales to local areas or regions. Instead of replicating Coca-Cola's use of franchising to expand, European soda makers tended to build their businesses by opening new factories, an expensive approach that resulted in slower expansion.

The British soda maker Ben Shaws was typical. Founded in the Yorkshire textile town of Huddersfield in 1871, the company started out bottling mineral water from the Pennine hills before adding flavored sodas such as lemonade and cream soda to its range shortly after. Fifty years later, it was still working out of the same factory and only just starting to think about replacing its trusty horses with motorized trucks. It would take until 1959 before the company started to reach beyond its Yorkshire base after building Europe's first soda canning plant.

There were a few exceptions. Schweppes, the grandfather of the soda industry, was doing brisk business in Britain and beyond with its tonic and mineral waters, which it continued to market as the refined fizz of choice for the upper classes. At the other end of the social scale was Tizer, a distinctive fruity British pop with a hint of carrot. Invented in 1924 by the Manchester-based mineral water businessman Fred Pickup, Tizer became a hit with children, and by 1936 Pickup's company had opened a network of factories across England and Wales to keep the bright red soda flowing.

Another success story was the German citrus soda Sinalco. The drink emerged out of the Nature Cure movement that took Germany by storm in the 1870s with its claim that people were born with the ability to cure all ailments but needed to live wholesome lives to bring out this innate power. One of the leading lights of this Germanic branch of quack medicine was Friedrich Eduard Bilz, a self-proclaimed healer who in 1882 published *Das neue Naturheilverfahren* (The new natural healing), the first encyclopedia of Nature Cure treatments. The book became a runaway success, selling more than two million copies of its various editions by 1917 and turning Bilz into a celebrity.

Bilz used his fame to open Schloss Lößnitz, a luxury sanatorium in the town of Radebeul, near Dresden, that offered Nature Cure remedies to wealthy believers. The treatments revolved around the idea that people needed to be toughened up if their bodies were to drive out disease. Patients walked barefoot through the snow, stood knee-high in baths of cold water, and in the most serious cases, deprived themselves of water and other liquids on the grounds that it would flush out their illness. Eating and drinking healthily was another tenet of Bilz's medical approach, and in 1902 this belief led him to create Bilz-Brause, a soda made from tropical and local fruits and natural mineral water.

Although Bilz created his beverage with the patients at his sanatorium in mind, he decided to sell it more widely, so he teamed up with industrialist Franz Hartmann to bottle the drink for mass consumption. By the end of

1903 the pair had sold ten million liters of Bilz-Brause across Germany, and in 1904 sales reached twenty-five million liters. The success of Bilz-Brause prompted a spate of copycats, so in 1905 Bilz and Hartmann decided the drink needed a more distinctive name and came up with Sinalco, based on the Latin *sine alcohole* (without alcohol). By the start of 1914, Sinalco was being exported all over Europe and could even be found in China, Brazil, Turkey, and the United States. But the outbreak of World War I stopped Sinalco's growth in its tracks by forcing its production to stop. Sinalco returned after the war and, despite the setback of Bilz's death in 1922, could be found in places as far afield as Buenos Aires, Istanbul, Chicago, London, and Warsaw by 1932.

But for all their success Sinalco, Schweppes, and Tizer were working in a continent that was much less partial to soda than Americans. While there are no figures allowing a direct comparison, the pre–World War II sales volumes reported by the bigger European soda makers suggest that carbonated drinks, while not unusual, were consumed far less in Europe than in America. The French continued to quaff their wine, the Germans kept drinking their beer, and the British retained their fondness for tea. What's more, almost no one in Europe had any idea what a cola was. So when Coca-Cola started its push to win over European taste buds it faced not only the challenge of converting a continent to the taste of cola but also a market that had yet to fall in love with soda. It was an expansion fraught with difficulties, and Coca-Cola's first European venture set the tone.

In 1919 the company granted the right to bottle its drink in Paris to an expat American and his French business partner. The pair knew little about bottling and even less about hygiene. They mixed Coca-Cola syrup with unsterilized tap water that they put into bottles and capped with bottle caps they failed to disinfect. The result were fizzy cocktails of bacteria that caused every Parisian who tried the new drink to become violently ill. The incident ruined the name of Coca-Cola in Paris. For years after restaurants and cafés refused to talk to the company's salesmen. One restaurateur was so angered by the poisoning of his customers that he chased the next Coca-Cola salesman who came to his establishment through the streets of Paris while brandishing a butcher's knife.

Despite such failures Robert Woodruff had stepped up Coca-Cola's efforts to conquer the world. In 1926 he created the Coca-Cola Export Corporation, which was charged with giving the world a Coke. On the surface the new business got off to a flying start. Within three years of its creation, Coca-Cola was on sale in seventy-six countries and 15 percent of the company's income came from outside the United States. But the truth was Coca-Cola was struggling to penetrate markets outside Canada, Mexico, and the American colony of Hawaii. Once again Europe was a source of pain. In 1940 all of Coca-Cola's small European operations were racking up significant losses, even though more and more Europeans took to drinking soda during the 1920s and 1930s. All, that is, except one: Germany.

The idea of bringing Coke to the beer-loving nation came from an American named Ray Powers. Born in Brooklyn and raised in Atlanta, Powers first came to Europe in World War I as part of a machine gun battalion. But instead of returning home when the war was over, he decided to stay, convinced big bucks were to be made in postwar Europe. One such business opportunity, he imagined, would be bringing Coca-Cola to the Old World. He knew how big Coke was back home and believed it could be just as big in Europe. So the relentlessly optimistic expat badgered Coca-Cola to give him the bottling rights for Germany. In April 1929 he got the go-ahead and opened Germany's first Coke bottling plant in the industrial city of Essen.

The Essen plant was a primitive operation with basic, hand-powered bottling machines and horse-and-cart deliveries, but it had no trouble meeting demand because there wasn't any. By the end of his first year in the Coke business, Powers had burned through all his money and sold just 5,840 cases of the drink. Undeterred, Powers persuaded Woodruff to sink another $10,000 into the business. Sales doubled but business remained dismal. Yet Powers, full of puppy dog enthusiasm, remained as hopeful as when he started. It was just going to take a bit more time, that's all, he told Woodruff in a 1930 letter. Oh, and don't worry about that Adolf Hitler guy either: "If Hitler comes to power he may bring German signers of the Treaty of Versailles before a court martial and actually some heads may fall . . . but I do not believe that he stands for disorder, lawless violence or arbitrary repudiation of the documents German statesmen have signed."

Powers was more worried about the German love affair with beer than the Nazis. He knew it was vital for people to have a cold rather than warm Coca-Cola when they tried it for the first time. But the only outlets with refrigeration were the taverns owned by the German breweries, which also owned the nation's ice plants, and they didn't want this nonalcoholic beverage taking up valuable space in their iceboxes. Soft drinks, as far as Germans were concerned, were to be consumed warm and stored under the bar or in the cellar.

To convince bar owners to take the drink and keep it cold, Powers invented a special briefcase for his salesmen. The case contained a tin box filled with ice and Coca-Cola bottles so that when bar owners were introduced to the beverage it would be at the ideal temperature. The unlucky salesmen who had to lug this heavy case around with them called it the *Seufzertasche*—"the case of many sighs."

Powers also produced a flyer called *"Was ist Coca-Cola?"* to introduce Germans to the drink. "We had millions and millions of these prospectus. An unbelievable amount," Max Keith, who joined Coca-Cola Germany in November 1933 as an assistant manager, told Coca-Cola's archivists several years later. "We went to restaurants on weekends because on Saturdays and Sundays they had the highest frequentation. We put this prospectus on every table. Sometimes the owner ran after us and took the prospectus off the table or asked the waiters to take them off, but we went back again and again. So that way people finally knew the name Coca-Cola and knew what it meant."

By the time Keith joined the company, Powers's leafleting campaign was paying off. Sales pushed through the one-hundred-thousand-cases mark in 1933 and kept rising, its growth greased with the economic boom that followed the Nazi Party's seizure of power. In 1936 sales passed the million-cases-a-year mark, lifted by sales from the Berlin Olympics and ads that—in stark contrast to the drink's embrace of temperance in America— appealed directly to beer drinkers with the words *"Plagt dich der katzenjammer? Eiskaltes Coca-Cola hilft"* ("Suffering from a hangover? Ice-cold Coca-Cola helps").

But in an increasingly xenophobic Germany, success soon sparked trouble. The Nazi dictatorship ordered the company to declare its caffeine content on its bottles as part of Hitler's puritan drive to wean Germans off tobacco, alcohol, and caffeine. Then came the leaflets created by Karl Flach. Born in Bonn in 1905, Flach first discovered Coca-Cola in 1929 while traveling in America and its popularity stuck in his mind. So in 1931 when he became the owner of Blumhoffer Nachfolger, a Cologne-based lemonade maker, he launched a cola of his own: Afri-Cola. To sell the drink Flach raided his American inspiration's best ideas. He adopted the franchise bottling model that had powered Coca-Cola's American growth and promoted Afri-Cola as a hangover cure. But he also sought to win over customers by emphasizing Afri-Cola's Germanic origins with the slogan: "Always refreshing, good and German."

This mix of nationalism and mimicry paid off. Soon Afri-Cola was doing enough business to keep Powers and his team looking over their shoulders. In 1936, while locked in this head-to-head struggle for cola dominance, Flach joined a group of businessmen on a tour of American companies organized by the German Labor Front, the Nazi trade union that replaced the country's independent unions after Hitler took power. One of the stops on this US tour was the Coca-Cola bottling plant in New York City. While Flach was being shown around the plant, a bunch of bottle caps caught his eye. Unlike the usual Coca-Cola bottle caps, these had Hebrew writing on them, as they were intended to reassure New York's Jewish population that Coca-Cola was kosher. But Flach saw an opportunity, and he slipped some into his bag.

On returning to Germany with the caps he wrote a leaflet warning the German people that Coca-Cola was a Jewish company. He distributed this leaflet to leading Nazi Party members, government officers, and the general public together with a photograph of the kosher bottle caps he collected in New York. The leaflet told how this suspect American business spent more than 4 million reichsmarks forcing its way into Germany in a "loud and arrogant manner," adding that it would be miraculous if there wasn't Jewish money behind such an expensive venture.

The leaflet ended with a call for all Germans to do their duty by refusing to drink this American-Jewish beverage. The accusations may have been false but it was dynamite in Nazi Germany. Throughout 1936 the

Nazis had been attacking Germany's Jews, banning them from politics and teaching, and revoking citizenship rights for anyone of Jewish descent. "They claimed we were an American-Jewish company, because to many of the Nazi people Americans and Jews were just identical," said Keith. "Consequently, our salesmen had also quite a few battles in the taverns with party members."

But while Coca-Cola salesmen ended up brawling with Nazi supporters in German bars, Flach's leaflet didn't spark the public backlash against Coca-Cola that Flach had hoped, and the Nazi state paid little attention to the claims. The incident did, however, underline how much things had changed in Germany since Powers's initial dismissive attitude toward Hitler and his followers. As 1938 ended, Coca-Cola Germany was selling millions of cases every year but Powers was thinking about getting out of Germany. He thought about decamping with his wife and two children to Paris to start again, but that would mean leaving his Coca-Cola fortune behind because the Nazis had banned people from taking money out of the country. The fifty-six-year-old was still thinking about what to do when on Thursday, November 24, 1938, a large truck collided with his car in Berlin. Seriously injured, Powers spent the next three weeks in the hospital fighting for his life before dying on December 13. That same day the Nazis opened the Neuengamme concentration camp.

Keith inherited control of the business, but while sales were set to hit the five million cases mark in 1939, the threat of war loomed large. On September 1, 1939, the inevitable finally happened when Hitler's forces invaded Poland. Two days later the British and French declared war on Germany, and World War II had begun. The British imposed a naval blockade to prevent goods and raw materials from reaching Germany, cutting off Keith's supply of Coca-Cola concentrate from the United States. Eager to keep the Coca-Cola flowing, the company looked for ways to get around the British blockade. It looked at flying its concentrate into Switzerland, toyed with the idea of bringing it through Russia, and explored the possibility of smuggling it in via Romania. Eventually fears of a British backlash that could see the company shut out of Canada, Australia, and beyond prevailed, and the company gave up its hunt for a backdoor route into Germany.

Britain's preparations for battle also hit Coke operations in the United Kingdom. In October 1939 the British froze sugar use by businesses at 1938 levels and told soft drink manufacturers to start using other sweeteners such as saccharin rather than sugar. As war progressed British restrictions on sugar got tighter, eventually forcing Coca-Cola to stop producing its drink in the country and Schweppes to take its popular tonic water off the market due to sugar and quinine rationing.

On May 10, 1940, after months of no direct conflict except at sea, the Nazi Blitzkrieg began. German tanks and troops swarmed west, marching into the Netherlands and Belgium as they raced to conquer France. As the German assault smashed through the Belgian forces with ease, Carl West, the head of Coca-Cola in Brussels, gathered his workers and asked if they would join him in fleeing to France. West's homeland of Norway had already been conquered by the Nazis, and he had no intention of sharing the fate of his countrymen.

West's employees agreed to go with him to Paris. They loaded trucks with their belongings, Coca-Cola syrup, and their families before racing out of Brussels as news of the Netherlands' surrender was announced on the radio. Two days later Brussels fell too. The Coca-Cola convoy reached France, but by then the Germans had punched through the French defenses. So they turned west, heading for the coast, hoping to cross the English Channel and reach Britain. By the time they got to Boulogne, however, it was too late. The convoy spent two terrifying days trapped in the heat of the Battle of Boulogne as machine-gun fire peppered their trucks with holes and the Luftwaffe, the German air force, dropped bombs around them. When the fighting subsided they had, somehow, all survived but most of their cargo was lost along with all hope of escape. They gathered up what was left and began the long, ominous journey back to Brussels to face life under the Nazis.

Another fleeing soda man was Guy Linay, the manager of the French Schweppes plant in the village of Gonesse just outside Paris. As the Nazi forces closed in on the French capital in June 1940, he and his family fled south. They had more luck than Coca-Cola's Belgian team, reaching the relative safety of the unoccupied zone of Vichy France, where he enlisted with the French Resistance. Once France had fallen, Hitler turned his attention to Britain, ordering the Luftwaffe to unleash a bombing campaign that flattened the cities of Plymouth and Coventry and turned much of London into burned-out rubble.

It was into this mix of rationing, air raids, and blackened debris that the former US presidential candidate Wendell Willkie flew in early 1941 on a mission to represent Pepsi-Cola. Willkie owed Pepsi a favor. Back in the summer of 1940 when the corporate lawyer had been seeking the Republican nomination, every pollster and pundit had written him off. By the time the Republicans gathered in Philadelphia to make their choice that June, he was 18 percentage points behind the favorite Thomas Dewey. Then, as the third round of voting began, Walter Mack of Pepsi-Cola came to the rescue.

The Pepsi president had a grudge against Dewey, who had taken the credit for exposing the New York City vote-rigging that Mack had worked to uncover. Now it was payback time. Knowing that many Willkie supporters wouldn't be heard because votes were counted by state rather than locality, Mack demanded a recount in which every local delegate had to name their choice. The recount revealed that Willkie was more popular than anyone had thought and as the rounds of voting continued, more and more people sided with the underdog. In the final ballot he pulled ahead of Dewey and won the presidential nomination.

Willkie lost his battle for the White House to Franklin Roosevelt, but he was eager to return the favor when Mack asked him for help in fighting Coca-Cola in the trademark case that now rested on the decision of Britain's Privy Council. Unlike Coke, Pepsi had only the smallest presence in Britain and no legal representatives to call on in the country. The war also meant that Pepsi couldn't send its own lawyers to the country. So Mack asked Willkie if he could use his influence to travel to Britain and defend Pepsi. After getting over the initial shock of being asked to go to a war zone, Willkie agreed. The former Republican candidate arranged a goodwill mission to Britain designed to reassure the war-torn country that America remained supportive of its fight against the Nazis even though it was staying neutral. While his trip proved to be a much-needed morale boost for the beleaguered nation, the real goal was to help Pepsi beat Coke.

In March 1942 the British lords who watched Willkie and the Coca-Cola lawyers joust over trademark law reached a verdict based almost entirely on looking up the words "cola" and "kola" in several dictionaries. The dictionaries, the lords reported, said cola and kola was the name of an African tree and so could not be trademarked. Their decision meant Pepsi was free to use the word cola in its name throughout the British Empire. Coca-Cola's ten-year battle to banish its New York rival ended there. After the decision Woodruff met Mack in private and hashed out a deal on a hotel napkin that recognized Pepsi-Cola's trademark and ended all litigation between the cola rivals.

As peace broke out in the Cola War, the real world war was getting more, not less, intense. In the summer of 1941 the Nazis had turned on the Soviet Union, sparking what remains the largest military confrontation in human history, and in December that year the Japanese attack on Pearl Harbor finally forced the United States into battle. With war intensifying and widespread raw material shortages, the British stepped up their efforts to make everything stretch further, combing the country for ways to save on gas, labor, and sugar. In summer 1941 the British Ministry of Food decided to take control of the nation's soft drink businesses on the grounds that the industry was "not sufficiently important in war-time to justify the use of so large a proportion of the national resources in its production."

The result was the Soft Drink Consolidation Scheme, and its plan was drastic. By its end 256 soft drink plants had been forcibly closed, and Britain's soda business was using just a fifth of the sugar it had been consuming before the outbreak of war. More than nine thousand employees were moved into more vital work and every soft drink brand in Britain had been temporarily abolished, replaced with generic sodas made to government recipes. When it came into effect in February 1943, Schweppes and Tizer ceased to exist.

Unable to produce its branded products, Schweppes resorted to running ads to remind people that they would once again be able to enjoy the company's tonic with their gin when the war was over. Other British soda companies adopted the same approach, including Pepsi, which ran ads in British newspapers explaining that "the time will come when there will again be Pepsi-Cola for everyone." But while Britain's brands submitted to the pressure of helping the war effort, the Ministry of Food's request that Coca-Cola and Pepsi-Cola join forces to produce a generic "American Cola" was quickly shelved when the bitter rivals decided they would rather stop making their drinks than work together.

America's approach to wartime soft drinks could not have been more different. Instead of curbing carbonated drinks to save resources, the United States militarized soda. While the country remained neutral in the early years of the war, by 1941 there was a growing sense that it was bound to get sucked into the conflict. This worried Ben Oehlert, Coca-Cola's Washington lobbyist, for war meant sugar rationing, and limited sugar meant less Coca-Cola. What the company needed, he felt, was a strategy, a way of persuading the government that carbonated soft drinks were not an inconsequential commodity but a vital part of the war effort.

Oehlert's colleagues were, to say the least, skeptical. Sure, they believed in the greatness of Coca-Cola, but telling the government that fizzy pop was crucial in wartime seemed like a good way to get laughed out of Washington. Despite the dismissive attitude of his colleagues, Oehlert continued to develop his plan for war. Then in spring 1941 Eddie Gilmore, an American reporter for the Associated Press in London, sent the company an urgent telegram: "We, members of the Associated Press, can not get Coca-Cola anymore. Terrible situation for Americans covering Battle of Britain. Know you can help."

The telegram turned heads within Coca-Cola. Here was a reporter in a war zone dreaming about drinking Coca-Cola while the Luftwaffe dropped bombs around him. Maybe there was something to Oehlert's vision after all, they thought. Shortly after came an order for seventeen thousand Coca-Cola bottles from the US Army in Iceland. (The British had invaded the island nation early in the war to keep it out of Nazi hands, and America had just taken over the task of protecting it.) The idea of the army seeing Coca-Cola as part of the supplies its troops needed lent even more weight to Oehlert's plan.

By November 1941 Oehlert's vision of soda as a wartime necessity had gained enough momentum for James Farley, the chairman of the Coca-

Cola Export Corporation, to float the idea in a speech to the annual convention of the American Bottlers of Carbonated Beverages. Farley was a former Washington man himself. He served as postmaster general under Roosevelt before resigning in protest over the president's plan to seek an unprecedented third term in the White House. Now he was Coca-Cola's global cheerleader. Wars, he told the bottlers, are won "not merely with guns but with butter" too. Civilian morale, he argued, can make the difference between victory and defeat, and that means soda matters. "With respect to carbonated beverages there is a natural tendency, at first thought, to classify them among the more easily curtailable items," he explained, but the truth is carbonated drinks are "an affirmative and powerful aid in the defense effort on the military, naval, financial and industrial fronts."

It was not so much a speech as a manifesto that elevated soda from mere belly wash to the very lifeblood of the war effort. So when America was finally dragged into the war by the Japanese and plans to ration sugar came into effect, the company sprang into action, hoping to convince Washington to see soda not as a disposable luxury but as a liquid morale booster. It pressed the case with officials, published pseudoscientific studies claiming that Coca-Cola breaks could boost production at munitions factories, and got one of its executives appointed to the beverage and tobacco division of the War Production Board. But Washington was unmoved. Sugar would be rationed at 80 percent of 1940 levels and the company's sugar stockpile would be bought by the government at cost and that was that. Soon Coca-Cola was in short supply across the United States. But just as it looked as if Oehlert's plan had fallen flat, Woodruff made a patriotic pledge that took everyone by surprise: "We will see that every man in uniform gets a bottle of Coca-Cola for five cents, wherever he is and whatever it costs our company."

Coca-Cola had spotted a loophole in the sugar rationing policy. While the restrictions on sugar use applied to domestic goods, it did not apply to products for military consumption. In other words Coca-Cola could supply the troops with as much Coke as they could drink without affecting their sugar ration. Using this loophole, Woodruff and Oehlert developed a strategy that would cost the company millions and provide it with no end of logistical challenges, but would also take a popular soda and turn it into a liquid as representative of America and its ideals as the Statue of Liberty or the Stars and Stripes. Within weeks of Woodruff's announcement, Coca-Cola bottlers were stepping up rather than winding down production to meet the demand from American troops. The bottler for Elizabethtown, Kentucky, went from producing 100,000 Cokes a year in 1940 to 750,000 in 1944 to quench the thirst of the thousands of troops who were passing through Fort Knox. Boats laden with bottles of Coca-Cola departed from US ports to deliver a taste of home to military stations all over the world, including the Philippine island of Mindanao, where the ill-equipped and outnumbered US troops turned the empty bottles into Molotov cocktails as they fought the advancing Japanese army in April 1942.

By September 1942 supplying the troops with Coca-Cola had become US Army policy, and governments around the world were being pressed to help ensure that the drink made it to the troops. "I have the honor to inform you, in connection with the visit of Mr Patterson of Coca-Cola, that the policy of the U.S. War Department is to endeavor to arrange that this refreshing drink be made available to U.S. troops wherever stationed," America's military attaché in South Africa told the British dominion's minister of commerce. "There are various U.S. troops now stationed at places for which South Africa is the logical distribution center, and Mr Patterson is endeavoring to complete the necessary arrangements to have Coca-Cola made available to them. Any assistance your department can give in furtherance of this will be deeply appreciated, both by myself and by troops concerned."

The US military embrace of Coca-Cola deepened further in May 1943 when the Allies finally drove the Axis powers out of North Africa under the leadership of General Dwight Eisenhower, the supreme commander of the Allied forces in the region. In the wake of the victory, Eisenhower, himself a devoted Coca-Cola drinker, asked his troops what they would like more of. "Coca-Cola!" they replied. But rather than ask for thousands of bottles of Coca-Colas to be transported to North Africa, Eisenhower went one better. He asked not for ready-made drinks but for the equipment and workers to set up ten bottling plants across North Africa that could keep the cola flowing to the front line. The Coca-Cola men sent out to build and operate these plants were given the status of technical observers, or TOs, a specially created rank equal in status to that of an army officer.

Al Thomforde was one of the first TOs. Originally from the Coca-Cola bottler in Hartford, Connecticut, he made an arduous trip on freezing cold planes from New York to Newfoundland to Scotland before traveling down to North Africa to get the Coca-Cola flowing. On arrival he found the equipment, bottles, and syrup had ended up scattered across North Africa. He spent weeks hunting for the mislaid parts before working with Italian prisoners of war to open the first of Eisenhower's plants in Casablanca. Soon US commanders across the world were ordering Coca-Cola plants for their troops. Coca-Cola even started developing special Coke dispensers that troops fighting in the jungles of the Pacific and living on submarines could use. And as the Allied forces advanced, the Coca-Cola plants followed. When the Allies fought their way up the leg of Italy, the Coca-Cola TOs were there, handing out Cokes to soldiers as they fought in the Battle of Monte Cassino and elsewhere.

But this was no mere publicity stunt that had got out of hand, because for the troops Coca-Cola was everything Oehlert claimed it was and more. "Yesterday was a red letter day," one lieutenant wrote to his mother back in Texas. "The party, your two letters and then on top of it all, I got six bottles of Coca-Cola. They were a present from a friend of mine in the air corp and are the first that I have had since we left the States. I haven't made up my mind whether to hoard them or to drink them. . . . It is surprising what just a little thing like a Coca-Cola means to a man in the army over here."

Another wrote to his mother in Berkeley, California, to tell her about how he spied a sailor carrying a Coke bottle in his pocket: "After eyeing it till I could stand it no longer I asked him if I might buy it from him. I explained that I had not had one since I left the States. Whereupon he was so benevolent as to give it to me." The lieutenant spent the rest of the day hiding it from his fellow sailors, eventually sneaking out of the crew's mess with his precious bottle wrapped in a towel. "I then crept out on the transom in the wardroom and tasted for the first time since I left the States [the] 'Nectar of the Gods.' It was celestial bliss."

For many it became a symbol of what they were fighting for. A group of sailors from the US fleet in the Mediterranean wrote to Coca-Cola expressing their hope that Coke would reach them soon before adding: "If anyone asked us what we are fighting for, we think half of us would answer, 'the right to buy Coca-Cola again.'" After the war, the fighter pilot Robert Scott wrote in his memoirs *God Is My Co-Pilot*, "I don't know exactly what democracy is, or the real, common-sense meaning of a republic. But as we used to talk things over in China, we all used to agree that we were fighting for The American Girl. She to us was America, democracy, Coca-Cola, hamburgers, clean places to sleep, or the American way of life."

Even US soldiers taken prisoner found solace in their darkest hour in Coca-Cola. One GI told how the Germans put him through a six-week forced march with barely any food. As the seemingly endless trek continued, he found himself losing hope. Then, as they forced him on through a German town, he caught sight of a fading and peeling advertisement for Coca-Cola. "Memories started coming back to me, of home, of the drugstore where my girlfriend (later my wife) and I used to sit and plan our lives together," he later wrote to the company. "I kept thinking of that Coke sign and what it stood for, of home, of the darling wife and child that were waiting for me, of all the good times and wonderful things that were ahead of me, if only I could get out of this mess alive. Right then and there I said to myself 'I will get out alive!' and a new feeling of hope and strength seemed to come over me."

Pepsi-Cola could only look on with envy. Its complaints to the Pentagon about the army giving its bigger rival a monopoly were dismissed, and it found its World War II operations confined to the home front. To show it was doing its bit, the company opened Pepsi-Cola Centers for Service Men and Women in New York, San Francisco, and Washington, DC. These centers were billed as a home away from home for soldiers, offering free Pepsi, showers, and cheap meals. It also provided a recording studio where GIs could record voice messages to their loved ones that were impressed onto vinyl records before being posted for free to their families. More than three million of these "voice letters" would be recorded by the end of the war.

Pepsi also did its best to hold onto the gains it had made in the late 1930s by doing everything it could to find a way to circumvent the sugar ration. An initial plan to keep its bottlers in business using the 86,000-ton sugar stockpile Pepsi had built up at its Long Island City plant ended when the government requisitioned 40,000 tons of its supplies. Mack then ordered the purchase of a 77,000-acre sugar plantation in Cuba to supply the company, only to find the US government would count any imported sugar as part of Pepsi's ration. Figuring that he could instead sell the sugar on the world market, Mack pressed ahead. After the purchase, he learned that the plantation workers lacked access to fresh water, and he sent engineers to Cuba to drill water wells. Two months later the Cuban government turned up, demanding millions in unpaid taxes. Confused by the mysterious bill, Mack headed to Cuba, where the tax official he met explained that Pepsi's policy of improving the conditions for the plantation workers could encourage unrest among those who worked on other plantations, so if somehow the wells were sealed off, maybe the tax bill would vanish too. "I could have hit that little bastard right then and there, but what good would it have done?" he remembered in his biography. Unwilling to pay the extortionate tax bill or to seal the well, Mack sold off the plantation.

Mack then got wind that there was a surplus of sugar in Mexico. He struck a deal with the Mexican sugar cooperative to buy their excess sugar and opened a factory in Monterrey, where the sugar could be turned into a syrup called El Masco that could then be imported and used by Pepsi bottlers to make the Pepsi-Cola. With El Masco, Pepsi was walking along a legal tightrope. Exporting sugar out of Mexico was illegal, and importing sugar to the United States would count toward the company's limited sugar ration. But El Masco wasn't sugar, so it evaded the letter, if not the spirit, of both Mexican and American law. El Masco saved Pepsi, riding to the rescue just as the United States cut back its sugar rations to a level that would have forced a large number of Pepsi bottlers out of business.

Coca-Cola tried to use its influence to get Washington to block the import of El Masco, possibly in reaction to Mack's successful efforts to get its man on the rationing board removed. A government official questioned Mack, who said that it wasn't sugar he was importing, but if the US government wanted to buy and bring in the sugar Pepsi was using to make it themselves, he would hand it over. The government official checked into it and called back furious. You knew that Mexican law won't allow us to bring in unprocessed sugar, ranted the outwitted official.

Coca-Cola's close ties with the US military also annoyed the British. When US troops gathered in Britain ahead of the Normandy landings, the Americans threw British plans for managing the soft drink industry into chaos. The Americans insisted that the British reopen bottling plants that they had closed so that the Americans could pump out Coca-Cola for the US troops. British officials spent weeks delaying their plans to mothball soft drink factories as they tried to find out where the US troops would be so that they did not shut down plants that would be needed later. The final straw came when the Americans asked that the British provide trucks to ferry their empty Coca-Cola bottles from their bases back to the factories for refilling.

On hearing the request, Ministry of Food official F. J. H. Corbyn blew his top. "This to my mind is a preposterous and retrograde proposal," he spat. "How on Earth can we go to the Ministry of War Transport and ask for extra transport for this traffic?" The next day he wrote back to the British official who had forwarded the American request to him: "It would be a gross waste of transport which we should not be able to justify to the Ministry of War Transport. If the Quartermaster Depots of the U.S. Army cannot or will not accept the responsibility of getting back their empties then I am afraid that so far as we are concerned the only way of describing the situation is in the Trans-Atlantic idiom 'It's just too bad.' We do feel that these people should be realistic on a matter of this description in the fifth year of war when we are having all kinds of transport difficulties and are having very great difficulty even to secure transport for most essential items."

The Nazi press chief Otto Dietrich also picked up on the US Army's obsession with Coca-Cola, telling the German people that "America never contributed anything to world civilization but chewing gum and Coca-Cola." But while he painted Coca-Cola as a symbol of America, Coca-Cola was still very much alive in Nazi Germany.

The outbreak of war had left Max Keith isolated. The German Coke chief could no longer communicate with the Atlanta head office, and supplies of the Coca-Cola concentrate that were needed to make the drink had dried up. To add to his woes the Nazis issued a decree in January 1940 allowing the government to seize control of any "enemy-owned" business. Keith needed solutions and fast.

The first problem he tackled was the drink. With no Coca-Cola left to sell he began looking for a new drink to produce, but with ingredients in short supply there wasn't much to work with. The lack of materials had already resulted in Sinalco ceasing production, but Keith was determined to keep the business going. He eventually came up with a soda made out of fruit waste that would otherwise end up in trash heaps, such as the apple pulp from cider presses. A drink made from "the leftovers of the leftovers" as he later called it. Coca-Cola Germany named it Fanta, and it saved the business. In 1940 the company sold 186,000 cases of Fanta. The next year 1,268,000, and sales kept rising, pushing toward three million cases a year in 1943.

With a new drink in place and the business saved, Keith persuaded the Nazi authorities to put him in charge of every Coca-Cola operation in occupied Europe. Keith used his new position as the Coca-Cola chief of the Third Reich to keep Coca-Cola's European operations alive. He spread Fanta across Europe, saving the Coca-Cola branches that were on the verge of shutting down due to a lack of Coca-Cola syrup. He also used his position to protect Coca-Cola employees from the Nazis—including Carl West, the Coca-Cola Belgium boss who had unsuccessfully tried to escape the German army back in May 1940. "One of Carl West's employees in Brussels went to the occupation authorities saying that West hoarded sugar, which actually should be reported to the food office for distribution," said Keith. "He was in a bad spot and I had to go there and see that it was straightened out. Fortunately I could do it. Then there were many other instances of that sort, because disloyalty during war time was quite a regular occurrence."

Schweppes's surviving factories were up to similar tricks in occupied France. After the manager of the company's plant in Gonesse fled south to join the Resistance, the task of running the business fell to Arthur Corthals, the factory's Belgium-born accountant. Shortly after conquering France, the Germans issued orders for all supplies of fruit juice to be handed over. Eager not to help the occupiers, Corthals rented space in a small store, gathered up the fifteen thousand cans of fruit juice stored on the Schweppes premises, and hid them beneath sacks of potatoes. When the Nazis questioned him about the juice, he said it had fermented so he threw it away. He then started selling the canned juice on the black market so he had enough money to buy the equipment he needed to keep the Schweppes plant going.

Back in Germany, Keith also began setting up "siding plants" in response to the British air raids that were devastating Essen and other German cities in early 1942. Based in barns on isolated farms, these back-up plants ensured that Coca-Cola Germany could keep producing Fanta even when its factories were destroyed, as a great many of them were. But in January 1945, as the German army found itself being squeezed by the Allies from all sides, Keith's luck ran out. The general in charge of the Ministry of Commerce summoned him to his office. The general told Keith he must nationalize the company and drop the Coca-Cola name. Failure to do so, the general added, would result in him being sent to a concentration camp. Frightened, Keith contacted a friendly official in the Ministry of Justice, but he refused to help for fear of also being imprisoned. Unwilling to bow down, Keith braced himself for the worst, only to be saved when an Allied bomb hit the ministry and took out the general. Against the odds, Coca-Cola Germany had survived yet again.

Three months later on April 10, 1945, the Allied forces captured Essen. A few weeks later Hitler committed suicide and Germany surrendered. Japan followed suit in August. The war was over and the spoils of war were Coca-Cola's to reap.

7

Cola-Colonization

In the summer of 1971 Coca-Cola unveiled one of the most successful TV ads ever made. It opened with a close-up of a fresh-faced young woman shrouded in golden sunlight gently mouthing the words "I'd like to buy the world a home and furnish it with love," and ended with a helicopter panorama of two hundred teenagers from across the world standing on an Italian hilltop, Coca-Cola bottles in hand, singing, in perfect harmony, "I'd like to buy the world a Coke and keep it company."

The ad's feel-good message of peace, love, and Coca-Cola offered a vision of hope in a turbulent world. War was raging in Vietnam, America's oil wells were running dry, and the news was filled with nightmarish visions of nuclear and ecological apocalypse, but Coke's mawkish appeal for sales offered an alternative—a happy world where the answers to the complexities of Cold War geopolitics could be found in a bottle of soda pop. Naive maybe, but convincing enough for millions to buy into its message. Thousands of thankful letters poured into Coca-Cola's Atlanta headquarters, and the vinyl record of the advertising jingle soared to the upper reaches of the Billboard Hot 100 chart. As Bill Backer, the McCann-Erickson ad man who created the ad, told the Coca-Cola Company's YouTube channel in 2011, "It was a product saying we could be a little social catalyst that can bring people together."

Thirty years earlier the idea of Coca-Cola presenting itself as some kind of international glue uniting people in a divided world would have been laughable. After all, hardly anyone outside North America had heard of the drink, let alone tasted it. But a lot had changed since Coca-Cola boss Robert Woodruff promised to do whatever it took to get Coke into the hands of the US troops fighting World War II.

As much by accident as by design, Woodruff's expensive gesture paved the way for Coca-Cola to conquer the world. When the conflict ended, the wartime bottling plants the company built with Pentagon dollars stood amid the ruins of Europe and Asia, poised to unleash a flood of Coca-Cola on an unsuspecting world. More important, the American GIs with their Coca-Colas had made a lasting impression on the minds of millions. In a Europe scarred by war and malnourished by food shortages, the sight of the well-fed, smiling, handsome American heroes with their supplies of cigarettes and Coke were Hollywood brought to life. Women swooned. Children aspired to be them.

Austrians looked on in envy and admiration at the US occupiers with their daily rations of ice cream and sprawling Coca-Cola plant in Lambach, out of which twenty-four thousand cases of Coke flowed every day just to refresh the American troops, while most of the country's factories lay in ruins. In Germany women gossiped about the sexy American soldiers sipping their colas in the cafés, and in Britain thirty-eight thousand women became GI brides and left for a new life in the New World. And when the troops began heading home, it was like a light going out. "It was so drab when they had gone," mourned one English woman when the US forces departed. "The whole world had been opened up to me and then it was closed down again."

Even in places far removed from the fighting, the sight of the US soldiers and their Coca-Colas left an indelible impression. During the war America sent twenty thousand troops to the British island of Trinidad to protect it from Nazi attack. The sight of the troops with their Cokes and their womanizing ways inspired local calypso singer Lord Invader to respond to what he called an "American social invasion" with a song called "Rum and Coca-Cola." "When the Yankees first went to Trinidad, some of the young girls were more than glad," Lord Invader sang over a sunny calypso melody. "They said that the Yankees treat them nice, and they give them a better price. They buy rum and Coca-Cola, when down Point Cumana. Both mother and daughter, working for the Yankee dollar." The song's dig against swaggering troops and its allusions to prostitution and liquor kept "Rum and Coca-Cola" off US radio, but when the Andrews Sisters reworked it, Lord Invader's calypso protest song became America's biggest-selling record of 1945.

By the time the troops began returning home in earnest, they had helped Coca-Cola become more than a drink. More, even, than a brand. Coca-Cola had become an icon, a symbol of America and freedom. It was not so much a product of the American Dream as the American Dream in liquid form. Sales soared across the world. In 1936 the company sold just over 150,000 gallons of Coke syrup outside North America, but in 1950 it was exporting almost seven million gallons a year. Yet even as the world turned Coca-Cola red, the company found not everyone was willing to buy into its soda pop dream, especially not America's defeated wartime enemy Japan.

Coke landed in Japan in 1946 to supply the US occupation forces, but the company's hopes of using this as the first step in its ultimate goal of refreshing the former Axis power were quickly quashed. Japan's government didn't want this American beverage conquering the nation's taste buds, so it made it a fineable offense for Japanese nationals to buy so much as a single bottle of Coca-Cola. The ban was still in force in 1952, when the US military left Japan.

With no troops to sell to and no access to Japanese consumers, Coke needed the law to change if it was to survive in Japan. But Coca-Cola's attempts to persuade the Japanese government to let it in prompted a powerful counteroffensive by Japan's beverage companies. This anti-Coke coalition brought together thousands of tiny domestic soda firms, but at its core were Japan's biggest brewers: Asahi, Kirin, and Sapporo. All three had thriving soft drink divisions, not least Asahi, which owned Japan's number-one soda: Mitsuya Cider, a clear, lemonade-like nonalcoholic fizz.

Mitsuya Cider's origins can be traced back to the tenth century, when, according to legend, Minamoto Mitsunaka—the Lord of Settsu—attended the Sumiyoshi Grand Shrine in Osaka. After consulting the shrine's oracles,

Minamoto decided he would fire a *kabura-ya*, a special type of arrow used in prebattle rituals that made a whistling sound as it cut through the air, and set up his home wherever it landed. The arrow whizzed through the air, cleared the Satsuki Yama mountain, and came down in a lake surrounded by mountains. Minamoto followed the arrow's path, and on reaching the lake discovered that it had struck Kuzuryū, a nine-headed dragon that lived in the water. The warrior cut off the dragon's heads, and as the beast writhed in agony, it smashed through the mountains, revealing a hot spring of carbonated water. Victorious, Minamoto established his castle by the lake in what is now part of the city of Kawanishi.

While the dragon was a myth, the Hirano spring it supposedly exposed wasn't. Over the centuries the spring became a popular destination for bathers hoping to reap health benefits from its unusual waters. While its attractions as a spa resort were strong enough to support numerous hotels, interest in drinking the water of Hirano only caught on in the late 1800s, when Japan's push for modernization led the country to embrace more ideas from overseas, including the concept of imbibing carbonated water for health reasons. In 1884 a group of Japanese businessmen, inspired by this European custom, formed the Imperial Mineral Water Company and built Japan's first soft drink factory to bottle the spring's legendary water. As well as selling the water under the name Hirano-sui, the company also launched Mitsuya Cider, which combined the naturally carbonated spring water with a sweet syrup to create Japan's first branded soda. Other homegrown sodas followed, among them the lemony Ribbon Citron, which launched in 1909 and eventually ended up in Sapporo's hands, and 1928's Kirin Lemon.

By the early 1950s these three brands and their owners dominated the Japanese soda market, and they didn't want Coca-Cola crashing their pop party. So when, after intensive lobbying, Coca-Cola convinced the Japanese legislature to consider lifting the Coke ban in 1953, the trio used their considerable influence to ensure the measure was shot down in flames. With hope of removing the ban gone, Coca-Cola Japan crumbled. By 1956 Coke Japan had shriveled to a single bottling plant in Yokohama and six employees. It needed a white knight and eventually found one in Mitsubishi, the Japanese industrial giant that supplied equipment to its bottling plant.

Mitsubishi persuaded the Japanese government to relax the controls on Coca-Cola so that it could be sold to civilians in designated shops. But even this concession came with plenty of strings attached, including a ban on advertising, limits on the amount of Coke that could be produced each year, and a minimum price that ensured Coca-Cola would be significantly more expensive than any Japanese-made drink. Restrictive as these rules were, it was a start, and in 1960 Mitsubishi and Coca-Cola finished the job by fracturing the anti-Coke forces. Kirin belonged to the Mitsubishi *keiretsu*, a complex web of independent corporations bound together by tradition, shareholdings, and business relationships. Mitsubishi used its position as the head of the *keiretsu* to broker a deal. Kirin would drop its opposition to Coca-Cola in return for the right to bottle the drink in Japan.

The deal, signed in August 1960, shattered the Japanese anti-Coke coalition. By the year's end the last restrictions on Coca-Cola had fallen. Unshackled at last, Coca-Cola quickly confirmed the fears of Japan's domestic soft drink industry by stomping over local rivals like a carbonated Godzilla. By 1965 Coke sales in Japan passed the 480 million bottles a year mark and Mitsuya Cider was displaced as Japan's favorite soda after almost eighty years at the top. More than five hundred of the thirty-five hundred Japanese soft drink manufacturers that existed before the restrictions were lifted were gone by 1968, a figure the country's soft drink association blamed entirely on Coca-Cola. Ten years later, Coke was so big in Japan that the country accounted for 18 percent of the company's global profits, enough for Coca-Cola president Paul Austin to wonder how he could maintain growth when he was "fresh out of Japans."

For Japanese nationalists, Coca-Cola's runaway success symbolized all that was wrong with post-war Japan. Yukio Mishima, the Nobel Prize–nominated author who advocated a return to the ways of imperial Japan and the samurai, was among those horrified by Coca-Cola's rise. In his *Sea of Fertility* tetralogy of novels, Mishima painted a vivid picture of a nation in decline, and in the concluding book, *The Decay of the Angel*, he cast Coca-Cola as a symbol of Japan's downfall. When the main character Shigekuni Honda visits Komagoé Beach, he finds sands covered in "empty Coca-Cola bottles, food cans, paint cans, nonperishable plastic bags, detergent boxes, bricks, bones." In the former imperial capital of Kyoto, Honda encounters "a clutter of all the dreary details of new construction, to be seen throughout Japan: raw building materials and blue-tiled roofs, television towers and power lines, Coca-Cola advertisements and drive-in snack bars."

On completing *The Decay of the Angel*, Mishima decided to stage a coup to restore the emperor's powers. On the morning of November 25, 1970 he and four loyal followers headed from his suburban home in a Toyota Corona to the military headquarters in Ichigaya for a seemingly innocent meeting with the army general. On reaching the general's office they took him hostage and barricaded the doors, and Mishima headed for the balcony to deliver a speech to the troops assembled below, hoping to inspire a revolution. The soldiers merely laughed at the pompous novelist, so he retreated inside and, in keeping with his belief in the customs of the samurai, committed ritual suicide by slicing open his own abdomen with a dagger before being clumsily beheaded by one of his followers. If it was a choice between a Japan of Coca-Cola and a Japan of Mishima's beloved samurai, the Japanese clearly preferred the Real Thing.

It wasn't just right-wing nationalists who saw Coca-Cola as a threat. In the ideological clash of the Cold War between the free and Communist worlds, a brand as synonymous with America as Coca-Cola became a target for Communists everywhere. When Mao Tse-tung took over China in October 1949, he banned Coca-Cola from the country. The Soviets refused to let Coca-Cola through the Iron Curtain and ordered Cominform, the Kremlin-controlled agency that coordinated Europe's Communist parties, to stoke opposition to the American drink. As Communist sentiment against Coca-Cola hardened, the company found its operations under fire across Europe. In Italy the Communist paper *L'Unità* claimed that the drink would turn children's hair white. In Vienna Communist activists turned words into action by tracking down the local Coca-Cola boss, pulling him from his car, and beating him in the street.

The French Communist party went even further than its Austrian and Italian peers. It forged an unlikely but highly effective alliance with the country's winemakers and launched a campaign to drive Coke out of France. The winemakers were more concerned about protecting their profits than about Marxism, but in Coca-Cola they and the Communists found a common enemy. By late 1949 their anti-Coke movement had won over the French media and political establishment. The weekly news magazine *Paris Match* reported that "the foreboding noises of the tom-tom of Coca-Cola are already being heard in France." The daily newspaper *Le Monde* called the drink a threat to French civilization. And the Communist newspaper *L'Humanité* summed up the nation's fears with the rhetorical question: "Are we being Coca-Colonized?" Across Paris, Coca-Cola ads were vandalized with graffiti of skull and crossbones signs, while customs officials repeatedly refused to let Coca-Cola import the ingredients it needed to make its drink.

To try to calm the situation, Coca-Cola sent in Alexander Makinsky. Born into a Russian aristocrat family in 1900 and raised by a British nanny in the city of Baku on the shore of the Caspian Sea, Makinsky grew up surrounded by wealth and power. When the Communists took over Russia, he fled to America and became an international political representative for the Rockefeller Foundation. A lover of intrigue and the machinations of power, Makinsky networked his way around the world sipping champagne with presidents and using his aristocratic charm and high-powered connections to steer decision makers around to his employers' way of thinking. In 1946, as Coca-Cola began its rapid global expansion, the company realized it needed to be better plugged into world politics if it was going to deal with the challenges of operating internationally, and it recruited the tall, elegant Russian to be its eyes, ears, and voice in the smoky corridors of power.

But even Coke's corporate diplomat found the French situation hard going. The French government, he reported back to Atlanta, has a "personal grudge against us," and his fears only deepened in late 1949 when the French authorities charged Coca-Cola with breaking the country's health laws by adding phosphoric acid to the drink. The charge, Makinsky noted, was one that may well be upheld in court.

Europe's concerns about phosphoric acid as an additive had been needling Coke since the end of the war. The health laws of many European countries appeared to outlaw its use, and Coca-Cola spent much of the postwar years smoothing over the issue in Belgium, Switzerland, and

Britain. But the intransigent attitudes encountered by Makinsky in Paris suggested that France would not bend so easily.

In December 1949, as Coca-Cola mulled over how to deal with this latest attack, the Communists and winemakers turned up the heat by introducing two separate bills in the National Assembly that were designed to banish Coca-Cola from France for good. The Communist party's proposal was the cruder of the two—a simple demand for a ban to protect French businesses. The winemakers' man in the assembly—Paul Boulet, the mayor of Montpellier—offered a more politically astute proposal that would empower the French health minister to ban soft drinks made from vegetable extracts to protect public health. Boulet's proposal never mentioned Coke by name, but there was no mistaking the target.

The following February the assembly rejected the Communist proposal but passed Boulet's alternative. The prospect of a complete ban from France and its territories, which still included Algeria at this time, seemed uncomfortably close to actually happening. With time running out and the French unwilling to listen, Coke called in the big guns from Washington. Makinsky pressed the State Department to act and it sent David Bruce, the US ambassador to France, to meet with French premier Georges Bidault. Bruce warned the French leader that America would respond to unwarranted discrimination against its products. Coca-Cola also alerted the American public to the situation, with James Farley, the former postmaster general turned Coca-Cola Export Corporation chairman, using a press conference to make the matter a question of national pride. "Coca-Cola was not injurious to the health of American soldiers who liberated France from the Nazis so that the Communist deputies could be in session today," he told the assembled reporters who dutiful recounted the line to their readers the next day. Farley's dig rallied America to the cause of Coca-Cola and unleashed an anti-French backlash.

Politicians and media commentators called France's proposed ban an affront to America and talked of banning French perfume in retaliation. Others demanded an end to Marshall Plan aid for France and labeled the French as snobs. Eugene Cox, the Democratic representative for Georgia, announced he would no longer eat French dressing—clearly unaware that

Soda fountain equipment on display at the 1876 Centennial Exposition in Philadelphia, where Charles Hires launched his pioneering root beer.

The man who tickled our taste buds: John Pemberton, the inventor of Coca-Cola. *Courtesy of the Coca-Cola Company*

An artist's impression of Jacobs' Pharmacy in Atlanta, the first place in the world to sell Coca-Cola. *Courtesy of the Coca-Cola Company*

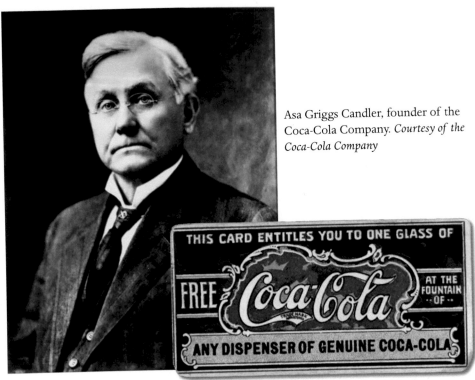

Asa Griggs Candler, founder of the Coca-Cola Company. *Courtesy of the Coca-Cola Company*

The world's first promotional coupon, the marketing trick that turned Coca-Cola into a runaway success. *Courtesy of the Coca-Cola Company*

The 1904 St. Louis World's Fair, the $50 million extravaganza that exposed millions to the fizzing pleasures of Coke, Dr Pepper, and Hires.

An 1890s ad for Coca-Cola, which kept the same nickel price tag until 1951. *Courtesy of the Coca-Cola Company*

New England's homegrown soda Moxie was Coke's big challenger until the 1930s, thanks to outlandish promotional devices such as these Horsemobiles. *Town Archives, New London, NH*

Coke urges people to buy the real thing in this ad from 1914, when it found itself fighting countless cola copycats. *Courtesy of the Coca-Cola Company*

The 1915 prototype of the now famous Coke bottle, created to help the company defend its trademark. *Courtesy of the Coca-Cola Company*

The final version of the Coca-Cola bottle, later dubbed the world's "most perfectly designed package" by Raymond Loewy. *Courtesy of the Coca-Cola Company*

By 1994 the bottle was so famous that Coca-Cola could sell itself with its silhouette alone. *Courtesy of the Coca-Cola Company*

Coca-Cola turned itself into an icon with eye-catching images and concise slogans, such as this 1943 twist on its enduring "The pause that refreshes" theme and, most simply of all, 1946's "Yes." *Courtesy of the Coca-Cola Company*

President of Coca-Cola Robert Winship Woodruff, the man who guided the cola giant from 1923 until his death in 1985. *Courtesy of the Coca-Cola Company*

While 1930s America was falling for Coca-Cola, Schweppes was still the premier soda brand in Britain. *Courtesy of the Dr Pepper Museum and Free Enterprise Institute*

"My hat's off to the pause that refreshes"

Coca-Cola made itself part of the holiday season thanks to Haddon Sundblom, who started painting its iconic Santa ads in 1931 (left) and was still creating Coke-loving St. Nicks in 1963 (below). *Courtesy of the Coca-Cola Company*

Ummm...Ahhh...Delicious!

Coca-Cola's holiday advertising took a new twist in 1994 when it introduced its CGI polar bears in a campaign that proved every bit as popular as Sundblom's Santas. *Courtesy of the Coca-Cola Company*

Dr Pepper took a different approach to winning over winter customers with its seasonal reinvention as an alternative to mulled wine. *Courtesy of the Dr Pepper Museum and Free Enterprise Institute*

Like many sodas in the mid-twentieth century, Dr Pepper made its sugar and caffeine into a virtue by promoting itself as an energy booster. *Courtesy of the Dr Pepper Museum and Free Enterprise Institute*

Dr Pepper may have had a loyal following in Texas during the 1950s, when this ad ran, but it would take until the 1970s for the Waco soda to really break out of the Lone Star State. *Courtesy of the Dr Pepper Museum and Free Enterprise Institute*

By the time this 1966 ad arrived, Coca-Cola's position as America's favorite soft drink seemed unassailable . . . *Courtesy of the Coca-Cola Company*

. . . so its competitors got down with the kids, not least 7Up, which embraced 1960s psychedelia with its "Uncola" campaign, featuring out-there artwork such as this creation by Nancy Martell. *Courtesy of the Dr Pepper Museum and Free Enterprise Institute*

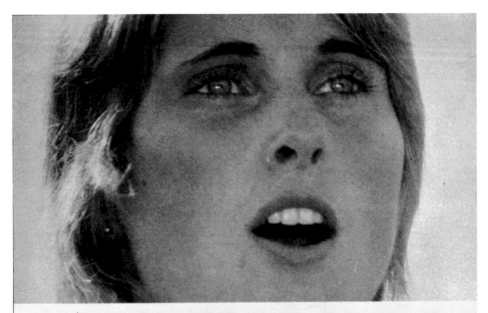

"I'd like to buy the world a Coke"
Trade-mark®

Coca-Cola delivered another iconic advertising moment (and a hit single) with this 1971 TV appeal for world harmony. *Courtesy of the Coca-Cola Company*

Coca-Cola reaches out to the world with this 1940 ad. *Courtesy of the Coca-Cola Company*

But winning over the world wasn't always easy; Coke faced tight government restrictions in Japan and attempts to get it in banned from France to protect the country's wine industry. *Courtesy of the Coca-Cola Company*

Communist Czechoslovakia's Kofola—the Warsaw Pact's answer to Coke. While it fell out of favor at the end of the Cold War, it made a comeback following a relaunch in the early 2000s.

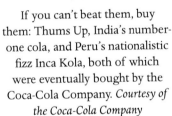

If you can't beat them, buy them: Thums Up, India's number-one cola, and Peru's nationalistic fizz Inca Kola, both of which were eventually bought by the Coca-Cola Company. *Courtesy of the Coca-Cola Company*

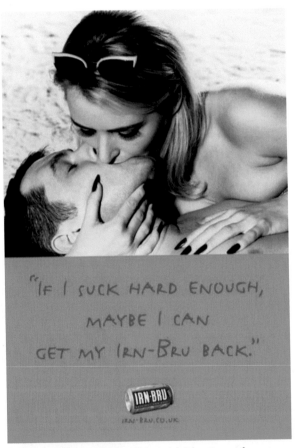

"If I suck hard enough, maybe I can get my Irn-Bru back."

IRN-BRU
IRN-BRU.CO.UK

Irn-Bru made itself part of Scottish identity with tongue-in-cheek ads like this one.

Smash and grab: Irn-Bru's
2001 TV ad "Electric Lady."

"You kin get Schweppes over in Lone Pine, stranger!"

ABOVE you see a heart-warming photo of Schweppesman meeting Schweppesfan.

At right, gazing thirstily towards Lone Pine, is the Schweppesman, Commander Edward Whitehead, President of Schweppes, U.S.A.

At left is Allen MacConnell, devoted Schweppesfan, who picks up a case of the stuff on every shopping trip.

Everywhere the Schweppesman travels in our country these days he meets constituents. Admirers of Gin-and-Schweppes Tonic. Devotees of Vodka-and-Schweppes. And purists, who drink Schweppes *straight*.

No wonder Schweppes has taken the U.S.A. by storm. Only Schweppes gives a drink Schweppervescence — little bubbles that last your whole drink through. *Curiously refreshing!*

Yes, you can get Schweppes in Lone Pine these days. And in Peoria and Palm Beach and everywhere else from sea to shining sea. So get the real stuff — insist on the authentic Schweppes Tonic.

Few non-American sodas have made an impact in the United States, but Schweppes did, thanks in large part to its twenty-year advertising campaign starring British Royal Air Force wing commander Edward Whitehead. *Courtesy of the Dr Pepper Museum and Free Enterprise Institute*

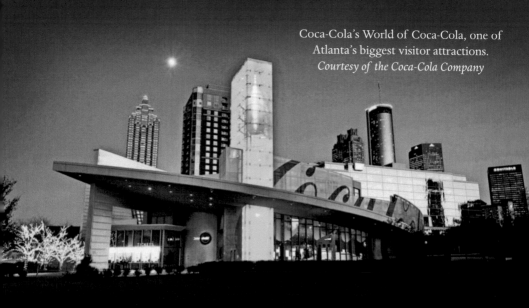

Coca-Cola's World of Coca-Cola, one of Atlanta's biggest visitor attractions. *Courtesy of the Coca-Cola Company*

The "secret vault" exhibit in the World of Coca-Cola shows how the mystery of the drink's formula still captures the imagination today. *Courtesy of the Coca-Cola Company*

Boldly going where no soda has gone before: Coca-Cola's space can. *Courtesy of the Coca-Cola Company*

Pepsi gate-crashed Coca-Cola's attempt to become the first soda in space with its own zero-gravity can.

The Nanny

You only thought you lived in the land of the free.

Bye Bye Venti
Nanny Bloomberg has taken his strange obsession with what you eat one step further. He now wants to make it illegal to serve "sugary drinks" bigger than 16 oz. What's next? Limits on the width of a pizza slice, size of a hamburger or amount of cream cheese on your bagel?

New Yorkers need a Mayor, not a Nanny.
Find out more at ConsumerFreedom.com

The fight over soda and obesity gets personal in this ad from the Center for Consumer Freedom criticizing New York mayor Michael Bloomberg's plan to restrict soda serving sizes.

Slow Cow, Canada's chilled-out answer to the rise of energy drinks.

Antonio Ramos and Caroline Mak, the founders of Brooklyn Soda Works—part of the growing craft soda movement. *Portrait by Chantal Martineau*

no one in France would recognize the American condiment as having anything to do with their cuisine. Soon French wine sales were falling, and the French ambassador was complaining about anti-French attitudes. With a tit-for-tat trade war looming, the fire behind the campaign to rid France of Coca-Cola went out. The French Senate unanimously rejected Boulet's bill, and when the National Assembly forced it into law regardless, the country's Ministry of Agriculture refused to use its new powers against the drink. When the phosphoric acid case finally reached the courts in 1953 the judge ruled in Coke's favor, and the last ember of French political resistance was extinguished.

Not that the French converted to drinking Coca-Cola as enthusiastically as the Japanese. The French still preferred wine, and Coca-Cola also faced an unexpected challenge from an upstart soda called Orangina, which was making rapid inroads with the nation's youth. Created in 1933, Orangina was the brainchild of Dr. Agustin Trigo Mirallès, a Spanish pharmacist who lived in Valencia and had briefly served as mayor of the coastal city a couple of years earlier. It was an unusual soda, a lightly carbonated combination of orange, grapefruit, lemon, and mandarin flavors that came complete with the pulp from the squeezed oranges used to create it. The soda's bulging bottle also departed from the norm thanks to its stopper, which was a vial of essential oils that drinkers were supposed to pour into the liquid to complete the taste. Mirallès named his beverage Orangina Soda Naranjina, and in the fall of 1935 he made the fateful decision to attend a trade fair in the French city of Marseille to tout his unusual sparkling drink.

Léon Béton, a French Algerian essential oils merchant from the town of Boufarik, was among those who sampled the Spaniard's drink at the fair. Béton was so impressed by the drink that two years later he bought the rights to the beverage, by which time the Spanish Civil War had ended Mirallès's own hopes of building its sales in Spain. Béton shortened the name to Orangina, ditched the vial stopper, and set to work trying to establish it in Algeria, only for his plans to be upended by the outbreak of World War II. Orangina vanished from stores during the war, but Béton's dreams of soda success endured and in 1947 his son Jean-Claude relaunched the business. After establishing the drink in Algeria, Morocco, and Tunisia,

Jean-Claude turned his attentions to taking Orangina out of the French colonies and into France itself.

To stand out in the French market, Jean-Claude created a unique pear-shaped bottle with a pebbly surface designed to mimic the bumps of orange peel. He then began hiring students to conspicuously drink Orangina at the outdoor tables of French cafés so that others would notice the eye-catching bottle and think about trying it themselves. In 1953, two years after its arrival in France, the final piece of Orangina's marketing jigsaw fell into place when he met Bernard Villemot, a painter who would do for Orangina what Archie Lee had done for Coca-Cola. Villemot created poster artwork that used a stylized swirl of orange peel, the pear-shaped bottle design, and bright summery colors to carve out a distinctive and attention-grabbing image for the soda. The vivid posters, unique bottle, and fake customers turned Orangina into a hit. By 1957 the company was moving fifty million bottles a year and the drink had become the number-two soda brand in France after Coca-Cola. By the mid-1970s Orangina was an international success that was chalking up sales of five hundred million bottles every year, even though it never replicated its European success on the other side of the Atlantic.

But if Orangina and the governments of France and Japan couldn't stop the global march of Coca-Cola, maybe Pepsi could. Pepsi had entered the postwar years on the back foot; the US military had built Coca-Cola the basis for a global empire, but all Pepsi got from the Pentagon was a lone bottling plant on the remote Pacific island of Guam. If Pepsi hoped to rival Coca-Cola on the world stage, it needed to catch up fast. To make up for lost time, Pepsi began striking deals with large local companies that could launch Pepsi in their home nations with a bang. In Britain it teamed up with Schweppes, agreeing to sell the British company's quinine water in the United States in exchange for access to its extensive distribution net-work in the United Kingdom. In France Pepsi found an ally in the bottled water firm Perrier. In the Netherlands Pepsi joined forces with the beer giant Heineken, and in Venezuela it forged a relationship with the powerful D. Cisneros & Cia conglomerate, which had interests in everything from car manufacturing to television stations. Between 1945 and 1950 Pepsi established operations in thirty-seven new countries, and soon the two American cola superpowers were engaged in a sprawling corporate war for market share across the world.

The battle was fierce. In the Philippines, one of the world's biggest consumers of carbonated drinks, Pepsi and Coke fought a war of attrition across the archipelago's seven thousand islands. They plastered the country in advertising and jostled for the business of even the smallest stores in the hope of gaining the edge over their rival. Dirty tactics followed too, with both companies hoarding each other's returnable bottles, filling fields with their enemy's glassware in the hope of forcing them to invest in new containers rather than more advertising. Coca-Cola even donated $35,000 to a nutrition center founded by Imelda Marcos, the wife of Philippines dictator Ferdinand Marcos, to improve its links with the authorities. But the donation was in vain. By the start of the 1980s Coca-Cola was on the retreat in the Philippines. Its local bottler was more interested in the profits he was making from San Miguel beer than in distributing Coca-Cola, and by 1981 Pepsi was outselling Coke two to one.

Coca-Cola responded with a fight led by Neville Isdell, a Northern Irish Coke executive who would go on to become the company's president. Isdell treated the contest as a war. He christened his sales team the "Tiger Force" after the song "Eye of the Tiger" from the movie *Rocky* and began holding company sales meetings that involved antics more befitting of banana republic dictators than a soft drink company boss. To fire up his sales force, Isdell would smash Pepsi bottles and dress up as a Filipino general—and on one occasion he arrived at a sales conference on a tank. The theatrics did the trick, instilling the message that this was not just about selling soda but a war against a deadly rival. Within two years Isdell's Filipino sales army had turned the tables, spreading Coca-Cola signs in every corner of the country and winning the business of thousands of tiny local stores until Coke was selling twice as much as Pepsi. The discovery that Pepsi's local bottler had been cooking the books to inflate its profits, a scandal that forced the company to write down millions, helped too.

The Philippines was no isolated case. Across the world Coca-Cola and Pepsi piled into countries to slug it out for fizzy drink dominance. No market seemed too small or too poor. From Tristan da Cunha, the most remote inhabited archipelago in the world, to poverty-stricken Cambodia, the cola giants raced to claim cola-free nations as part of their global empire. But while the Communists of France saw such expansion as a program of Coca-colonization that would turn the world American, for many poor, small, or unstable countries the arrival of Coke or Pepsi marked the first time a major foreign consumer company had bothered to invest in them. And when the cola superpowers arrived in these virgin territories they not only changed national drinking habits but altered the economic reality for millions.

In Morocco one study estimated that in 1999 Coca-Cola's activities were directly and indirectly responsible for generating more than 65,000 jobs and 0.7 percent of the country's gross domestic product. In China an estimated 414,000 people had work due to Coca-Cola and the businesses that were part of its networks. But the cola giants didn't just bring jobs and tax revenues; they also introduced new business practices that accelerated the development of domestic businesses.

In post-Soviet Russia, Coke's legal team helped the authorities write the laws recognizing private ownership of land, paving the way not only for the Moscow bottling plant the beverage company wanted to open but also for the operations of countless other Russian businesses. When Coca-Cola entered Romania shortly after the Communist dictator Nicolae Ceaușescu was overthrown, Romanian companies quickly grasped how to become more successful by learning from Coke's advertising and quality control practices. The company's free and regular deliveries to retailers—a practice unheard-of in Communist times—also helped countless small stores to grow. "In Romania they set the standard," says Douglas Woodward, an economics professor at the University of South Carolina, who studied the impact of Coca-Cola's investment in several countries around the world. "Coca-Cola is impatient. They didn't want to wait for these companies to learn about on-time deliveries and quality control, so they set out to make these companies more competitive and help them grow. Early on, they help these economies get on their feet and really have a strong demonstrative effect for how capitalism works and how it's done. You can't quantify that, but it's certainly part of their impact."

A similar effect can be seen in Africa too, he adds: "In South Africa there are millions of little businesses and no one is more in touch with them than Coca-Cola. They are in contact with these small-scale shops every day. The company has a huge influence in terms of making these businesses more competitive. When you work with Coca-Cola if you're an African business you tend to do better."

This was no philanthropic mission, of course. Pepsi and Coke were locked in a global war for profit where the prize was billions of dollars of revenue, but their intense rivalry meant they were often the first consumer products to enter developing countries. So intense was this desire to get nations drinking their cola rather than their rival's that Pepsi and Coca-Cola even smashed through the trade firewalls of the Communist world.

In 1959 the Cold War looked dangerously close to turning hot. Fidel Castro's revolution in Cuba had installed a Communist regime on the doorstep of the United States. The USSR had the upper hand in the space race thanks to the 1957 launch of the *Sputnik 1* satellite, and in Berlin tensions between east and west were rising over the number of East Germans fleeing to West Berlin. The idea that the Soviets, rather than the Americans, would emerge victorious from the Cold War seemed a distinct possibility. Keen to ease the tension and reach out to the Soviet people, the US government organized an exhibition in Moscow to showcase life in America. The exhibition's organizers felt Coca-Cola should be there, but when they asked the Atlanta company to get involved it refused, possibly wary of the reception it might face in Moscow given how the Kremlin had sought to demonize its product around the world.

So the organizers invited Pepsi instead. Donald Kendall, the head of Pepsi's international operations, leapt at the chance, but his cost-conscious bosses were less than keen. Handing out free Pepsi to hundreds of thousands of Muscovites would cost a fortune, and since the USSR wouldn't let Pepsi enter the country, what was the point? When the former US Navy airman insisted on going ahead, his superiors said fine, just don't expect to have a job if you come back with nothing to show for this massive waste of time and money. By the time Kendall got to Moscow, he knew he needed to pull a rabbit out of the hat if he was going to save his neck, so when he was introduced to Vice President Richard Nixon at a US embassy reception ahead of the exhibition's July 24 opening day, he asked Nixon if he would do him a favor.

Kendall explained that he had risked his job to bring Pepsi to Moscow, and asked Nixon whether he could get Soviet leader Nikita Khrushchev to visit the Pepsi kiosk. Nixon agreed to help. The next day, as the vice president wandered the exhibition hall with Khrushchev, he steered the Soviet premier to the Pepsi-Cola stand. Kendall handed the Soviet leader two Pepsis. The first was a Pepsi made in the United States, he told the Communist leader; the second was one made in the USSR for this exhibition. Khrushchev tried both and inevitably declared the Soviet-made Pepsi to be superior before ordering a second Communist cola as they were bathed in camera flashes. Nixon and Khrushchev went on to have their famous Kitchen Debate, where they argued over the merits of the American and Soviet economic systems, but Kendall had his career-rescuing big win. The next day newspapers across the world carried photos of the Communist leader sipping Pepsi. It was the start of an alliance between Nixon and Pepsi that would take the vice president into the Oval Office and Pepsi into the USSR.

Toward the end of 1959, Coca-Cola boss Robert Woodruff invited Nixon to stay with him at his twenty-eight-thousand-acre Ichauway Plantation in Baker County, Georgia. Nixon already looked like a shoo-in for the Republican presidential nomination for the 1960 election, and the visit was the chance for the wealthy corporate leader and the potential president to forge a closer relationship. The meeting went badly. Woodruff loved hunting and was unimpressed by Nixon's lack of shooting prowess. He later confided in colleagues that he didn't like Nixon because he lacked a sense of humor. And when the vice president wrote to thank the Coke boss for his hospitality and "the generous supply of home-grown sorghum," he received a grumpy rebuke from the cola king: "That is home-grown Georgia cane syrup, not sorghum. There is a very great difference between our syrup and sorghum, which is generally a heavy bitter-sweet substance." Nixon went on to lose his bid for the Oval Office, and in 1962 he also lost his campaign to become governor of California. With his political career seemingly over, he returned to practicing law, and he asked Coca-Cola for a job in their legal department. Given his unsuccessful December 1959 stay with Woodruff, he shouldn't have been too surprised when the answer was a firm no.

But while the political world and Coca-Cola had written Nixon off, Kendall hadn't. After becoming the chief executive of Pepsi in 1963, Kendall arranged for Nixon to join the law firm Mudge, Stern, Baldwin & Todd to oversee Pepsi's legal affairs around the world. The $250,000-a-year job came with few strings attached. Nixon could decide his own schedule within reason and his role as a legal ambassador for Pepsi offered plenty of scope for touring the world, meeting foreign leaders, and looking presidential. Nixon used the freedom and international globetrotting his Pepsi job gave him to rebuild his political career, and in 1968 he staged the most remarkable comeback in American political history by becoming the thirty-seventh president of the United States. Soon after Nixon entered the Oval Office, the Coca-Cola vending machines in the White House were removed and replaced with Pepsi machines. The White House pass that President Lyndon Johnson had given Woodruff was also revoked. After years of Coca-Cola-drinking presidents, Pepsi finally had its own man in office.

Kendall's support for Nixon paid off in December 1971 when the Pepsi chief was invited to go to Moscow as part of a US business delegation to discuss American and Soviet trade. During the trip he chatted with Soviet premier Alexei Kosygin and used it as an opportunity to show off a radio in the shape of a Pepsi can that he had pretuned to a Soviet radio station. Kosygin found the promotional radio amusing, and he invited Kendall to join him at his table at that evening's dinner. Over dinner the fishing-obsessed Pepsi chief reeled in the Soviet leader, telling him: "You will never get any real trade going until we start dealing in consumer goods." Kosygin, probably thinking it might be beneficial to help Nixon's pal, replied by suggesting that he bring Pepsi to the Soviet Union in exchange for Russian vodka and wine to be sold in the United States. They shook hands on the deal. In November 1972, after ten months of talks between Pepsi and the Soviet trade ministry, a deal to make Pepsi the first American consumer product to go on sale in the USSR was signed. While Kendall denied that Nixon intervened directly in the talks, he conceded that his friendship with the president did help.

On May 28, 1974, Pepsi went on sale in the port city of Novorossiysk, on the Black Sea, where the Soviet trade agency Sojuzplodoimport had opened a bottling plant to produce the cola. Crowds flocked to the store that was selling the first Pepsis to get a taste of the American soda, even though it cost significantly more than a beer. Back in America, Stolichnaya vodka went on sale courtesy of Pepsi. Coca-Cola found itself frozen out and unable to follow suit, as Pepsi's deal gave it a ten-year monopoly on cola drinks in the Soviet Union. To save face, Coke agreed to share its expertise in water purification and in cultivating fruit with the Soviets in exchange for Lada cars, only to find that the vehicles were so poorly made that Coca-Cola had to ship them to Britain for repair before it could sell them. With Pepsi the clear victor in the race to claim the Soviet Union, Coca-Cola turned its attention to that other Communist colossus, China, and began grooming a president of its own to help pull back the bamboo curtain: a peanut farmer named Jimmy Carter.

Coke first encountered Carter in 1970 when he was seeking the Democratic nomination for governor of Georgia. Woodruff was already supporting Carter's Democratic rival Carl Sanders, but to hedge its bets the company's president Paul Austin donated $2,500 to Carter's campaign. When Carter won the nomination and the election, Austin followed Kendall's lead and started building a close relationship with the potential presidential candidate. As well as giving Carter access to Coca-Cola's fleet of jets, as the company did for all governors of Georgia, Austin used Coke's international network to help Carter develop his foreign policy credentials. Carter later credited Coke's support on the international stage with helping him become more than a provincial candidate for president: "Georgia has a particular advantage over some states in that we have our own built-in State Department in the Coca-Cola Company. They provide me ahead of time with much more penetrating analyses of what the country is, what its problems are, who its leaders are, and when I arrive there, provide me with an introduction to the leaders of that country in every realm of life."

When Carter announced he would run for president, Austin worked to allay the concerns of other leading businessmen about a Carter administration and persuaded many of them to back the Democratic candidate. His

Republican rival, Gerald Ford, ended up with just four corporate support-ers, including PepsiCo. Coke's advertising men also helped turn Carter into presidential material, crafting his public image as a laid-back peanut farmer. As Tony Schwartz, the director who oversaw Carter's TV ads as well as dozens of Coca-Cola commercials, explained, the goal of TV advertising wasn't to explain a point of view but to use images and sounds that made viewers think positively about the product, whether that product was Coke or Carter.

Carter's triumph in the 1976 election ushered in a new Coke-friendly regime at the White House. The Pepsi vending machines installed by Nixon back in 1969 were removed, replaced by Coca-Cola's. Charles Duncan, a former Coca-Cola board member and the second-largest shareholder in the company after Woodruff, became deputy secretary of defense before being promoted to energy secretary in 1979. Carter's administration also made Austin a board member of the National Council for US-China Trade, the perfect battering ram for getting Coke into China.

Since 1973 Coca-Cola had been building ties with the Chinese, as rela-tions between the United States and the Middle Kingdom thawed in the wake of outreach efforts by President Nixon. So in late 1978, as the two nations moved closer to a mutual understanding, Coke struck a deal to make its famous drink the first American consumer product to enter the world's most populous nation since Mao took power. The deal, signed in Beijing on December 13, 1978, handed Coke the exclusive right to sell non-Chinese-made cola in China, starting with imported bottles and cans but to be followed by the construction of bottling plants across the country. The agreement was nominally only to let tourists visiting major cities buy Coca-Cola, but by 1981 the drink was on sale to Chinese citizens in parts of Beijing.

Two days after the Coke deal, the US government and China agreed to normalize diplomatic relations by opening embassies in each other's country. Coca-Cola kept quiet about its own deal for a week, so as not to steal the State Department's thunder. In early 1979 Coke made its trium-phant return to China with the delivery of almost half a million bottles and cans transported into the country via a train from Hong Kong. The drink Mao had called a symbol of "degenerate capitalism" had taken its first step toward quenching the thirst of a billion Chinese. Ian Wilson, the executive in charge of Coca-Cola's Pacific operations, told reporters, "This agreement is more than just a sales contract. I look on it as a symbol of both Chinese pragmatism and the ubiquity of Coca-Cola."

As Coke and Pepsi pushed into China and the Soviet bloc, the Communists' own colas— such as Happiness Cola, the first product to be advertised on Chinese TV, and Kofola, a cola created by Communist Czechoslovakia in 1960 to satisfy its population's interest in American pop—found themselves competing with the genuine articles. But while Coca-Cola and Pepsi looked like large American corporations steamrolling their way around the world, the soda bottling system made it hard to distinguish the boundary between local and foreign. The brands were unquestionably American, but when the organization handling the bottling, marketing, and distribution was a local business or the state, the result was a product that was both global and local at the same time. Was Coca-Cola in China a product of the Communist government or a symbol of America? The truth lay messily in between. It was a setup that helped Pepsi and Coke overcome trade barriers across the world, convincing wary governments that ultimately the soda business they would create would belong to their nation. It also helped the American soda giants distance themselves from criticism about the employment practices of some of their bottlers, by pointing out that these were independent companies and their contracts gave the US corporations no right to intervene in employment disputes. Coca-Cola would use this defense when some of its bottling plant franchisees in Colombia and Guatemala were accused of hiring death squads to murder unionized workers.

Sometimes the challenge came in the places where Coca-Cola and Pepsi *didn't* have bottling operations. Coke and Pepsi might have spread far and wide by the mid-1960s, but neither company had ventured into Israel. So in December 1964 the Tel Aviv–based soft drink company Tempo hit on the idea of applying for the right to bottle the world's favorite soda, only for Coke to say no. Tempo's president Moshe Bornstein asked again. Once again Atlanta said no, arguing that Israel's economy wasn't big enough to enter. Bornstein was suspicious. After all, Coca-Cola was on sale in Ireland

and El Salvador, countries with a similar-sized population to Israel. He figured that the real reason Coca-Cola rejected his request for a bottling franchise had nothing to do with economics and everything to do with politics.

After the formation of Israel, the Arab world had united to do whatever it could to strangle the young Jewish nation and support the Palestinians. In 1948, as part of this campaign against Israel, the Arab League organized the Arab Boycott, a concerted effort to cripple the Israeli economy by getting the Muslim world to boycott companies that operated in Israel. Essentially, businesses were told that if they traded in Israel their access to the millions of people living in the Islamic nations of the Middle East would be cut off. Bornstein believed Coca-Cola wouldn't work with him for fear of falling afoul of the Arab Boycott, so he decided to bring Coke's reluctance to enter Israel to the attention of the world. On April 1, 1966, he held a press conference in which he accused Coca-Cola of turning its back on Israel for fear of upsetting the Arab nations.

Jewish groups in America quickly picked up on Bornstein's accusation. Six days after the Israeli businessman's press conference, the Anti-Defamation League of B'nai B'rith Society called on American Jews to respond by boycotting Coca-Cola. Nathan's Famous, a New York chain of hot dog stands, signed up to the boycott and announced that it would stop serving Coke unless the company changed its policy. The Jewish War Veterans association also announced it was toying with the idea of calling on its members to boycott the beverage. On the afternoon of April 11, 1966, the Jewish-run Mount Sinai Hospital in New York City announced it was no longer going to sell Coca-Cola—although its boycott only lasted until the evening, when hospital director Dr. Martin Steinberg stepped in and blamed the decision on a wayward purchasing official. "We're here to cure people, not to fool around with Coca-Cola," he explained.

But while Mount Sinai Hospital only flirted briefly with backing a Jewish boycott of the drink, the pressure was mounting. Coca-Cola found itself caught between an Arab world determined to punish those that worked with Israel and Jewish groups in America who saw Coke's lack of activity in Israel as a cave-in to Arab aggression. To defuse the problem, Coca-Cola explained that it wouldn't work with Tempo in any case since it had sued the firm for infringing its trademark back in 1963, but it would consider giving the franchise for Israel to another company. Coke found an alternative bottler in Abraham Feinberg, a Jewish New York businessman, and signed a letter of intent as the first step on the road to entering Israel. The move quelled the talk of a Jewish Coke boycott. Morris Abram, president of the American Jewish Committee, said the agreement was "evidence of the company's independence of Arab or other boycott threats."

Yet while the move stopped the Jewish campaign, the Arab League responded by announcing it would discuss Coca-Cola's plan to enter Israel at its next conference in the Syrian capital of Damascus. Coca-Cola now found itself embroiled in the bitter politics of the Middle East and facing a battle to save its lucrative operations in the Arab world. It was a situation that would demonstrate how Coca-Cola's global expansion had become as much about spreading American influence in the world as selling soda.

Together with the US State Department, the company launched an urgent charm offensive to save its Middle Eastern business, only to find the Arab nations were in no mood for talking. Kuwait and Libya made it clear that they couldn't care less about Coca-Cola's fate. While Lebanon's government was sympathetic, it signaled that it wouldn't do anything that its Muslim opponents could use to claim it was being soft on Israel.

Even the Coca-Cola bottlers in the Middle East proved unwilling to help. Saudi Arabian Coca-Cola bottler Sadaqa Kaki told the US government representatives that he saw Coke's Israeli deal as an act of "bad faith" that had let down loyal Arab bottlers. When asked if he might try to persuade the Saudi government to support Coca-Cola, he replied that it was Coca-Cola not his country's leaders that needed to change their minds. The State Department reported back to Coke that Kaki's lack of willingness to help and the fact that the chief of King Faisal's executive office owned the Pepsi plant in Jeddah meant it was likely that Saudi Arabia would support the boycott.

Coca-Cola sent in its corporate diplomat Alexander Makinsky to see if he could negotiate away the boycott, but his reports proved even less reassuring than those from the State Department. Syria, he wrote, was unlikely to be swayed because "the American ambassador is particularly persona non grata, partly because he is a Negro, which the Syrians consider as a deliberate insult, and partly because he is not either tactful or diplomatic." Egypt's government wanted the boycott too. "Coca-Cola is non-essential to Egypt, where it can be easily replaced," Makinsky reported back to Atlanta. "It is irreplaceable, however, to the USA, since it is a powerful instrument of US propaganda, on par with Hollywood films and the Voice of America. . . . If [Egypt has] tolerated us for so many years it is merely because they were afraid the banning of Coca-Cola might be construed as an anti-American move."

The Israeli bottler dispute gave the Egyptians the perfect excuse to kick out Coca-Cola, but Makinsky still regarded Egypt as the company's only hope, as other Arab states tended to follow Egypt's lead. With time running out, Coca-Cola turned its charm offensive on Egypt. Makinsky tried to get Spain, the sole European country that Egypt had warm relations with, to speak out on Coca-Cola's behalf, hoping that his own position as president of Coca-Cola's Spanish subsidiary would be enough to get General Francisco Franco's dictatorship to help. Coca-Cola also offered to build a concentrate plant in Egypt, a move that would bring currency into the country by reducing imports and increasing exports since the facility would also service neighboring nations.

By August 1966 it wasn't just Coke that was facing the heat. Coca-Cola executive Ben Oehlert alerted the State Department that many of the Arab government officials the company had spoken to believed that it was the US government, rather than pressure from the American Jewish groups, that was behind the Israel bottling deal. "I feel sure that the administration would be as anxious as we are to make sure that the Arab nations do not connect our government with the decisions we have made," he wrote. The Arab League had also begun to see their fight with Coca-Cola and Ford, which was also facing a boycott for backing the creation of a car assembly plant in Israel, as a major moment in the Arab clash with the Jewish nation. Rashad Mourad, the Arab League representative in the United States, wrote to Arab governments to let them know that American companies regarded what was happening to Coke and Ford as a test case and that if the two were not blacklisted "it would be the end of the boycott itself."

Coke's efforts in Egypt failed. The country's finance minister told the US embassy in Cairo that the concentrate plant bribe simply wasn't big enough, and when the Arab League met in Kuwait in September 1966 to decide the company's fate it was hardly a surprise when both Coke and Ford were added to the list of boycotted companies. The boycott took two years to come into force, but on August 1, 1968, Coca-Cola was shut out of the Arab market. Pepsi, which had managed to keep well away from the dispute despite having no Israeli bottler, was able to mop up the Middle East cola market, free from its most fearsome rival. Coca-Cola wouldn't make it back into the Arab League states until after the Camp David accords were signed in 1978.

India also proved to be a challenge for Coca-Cola. Coke entered the country in 1950, the same year that India gained independence from Britain, and by the start of the 1970s Coke dominated India's small but potentially enormous soda market, selling more than 700 million bottles of Coca-Cola a year. Pepsi had yet to enter the Indian market; Coke's only competition of note was an orange soda called Gold Spot, produced by a company called Parle Bisleri. The New Delhi soda company started out making cookies for the British military in India during World War II before moving into the fizzy drink business in 1949. Its first drink, Gluco Cola, named after its range of cookies, flopped, so in 1952 it came out with Gold Spot, which gained a sizeable following in New Delhi before starting to expand across the country in 1967.

But as the 1970s progressed, India was gripped by anti-Western sentiment, partly due to longstanding resentment about the injustices of British rule and partly because of America's willingness to supply weapons to Pakistan at a time of conflict in Kashmir and Pakistani suppression of rebels seeking independence for East Pakistan (now Bangladesh). In response to rising nationalism, Indira Gandhi's government introduced a law in 1973 requiring foreign businesses in India to be majority owned by Indian companies or citizens. The law was poorly enforced, but in 1977 the rival Janata Party won a landslide election victory against Gandhi's Indian National Congress. The new government believed that enforcement of the 1973 law should be ramped up, and new industry minister Georges

Fernandes soon took Coca-Cola to task. Fernandes, who once questioned Gandhi's government over the widespread availability of Coca-Cola in Indian cities where there was no clean drinking water, saw the soda company's success against domestic businesses as a prime example of why the "Indianization" of foreign-owned companies was necessary.

The trade unionist turned industry minister told Coca-Cola to comply with the law by ensuring that Indians owned a 60 percent stake in all its operations in the country, and Coca-Cola agreed. But then Fernandes insisted the company must also hand over the secret formula, claiming that without the recipe India's Coca-Cola businesses would be no more than local sales offices. Coca-Cola said never. Fernandes replied that the secret formula was the price for staying in India. That price is too high, the Atlanta firm responded, and pulled out of the country. Coca-Cola wasn't alone in its flight from India. The government's Indianization policy caused thirty-eight other foreign multinational corporations, including IBM, to withdraw. As far as Fernandes was concerned, though, the exit of Coke and other foreign companies was a victory for his campaign to protect India's homegrown industries. To celebrate—and find work for the thousands of now unemployed Coca-Cola workers in India—the government launched a cola of its own, which it named 77 in honor of the year that Gandhi and Coke were defeated. But while 77 launched in a blaze of publicity and to long queues of curious Indians waiting to try it out, the government cola soon floundered.

The following year two new Indian-made colas filled the gap left by Coca-Cola. Parle Bisleri came out with Thums Up, even though the company's boss, Ramesh Chauhan, thought cola wasn't all that nice. "Cola is like beer, or like smoking," he told *Port* magazine in 2011. "It's an acquired taste." Thums Up's rival was Campa Cola. Created by former Coke bottler Pure Drinks, it sought to mimic Coca-Cola as closely as possible, even adopting the same Spencerian handwriting style for its logo. The two Indian sodas quickly developed a rivalry that was an Indian microcosm of Coke and Pepsi's global war, complete with close ties to Indian politics. Thums Up established an early lead by sponsoring a tour of India by the West Indies cricket team and nailing Thums Up signs in stores and stalls across the nation. Within two years of its 1978 launch, Thums Up had started expanding outside India, opening plants in Kuwait, Singapore, Nigeria, and elsewhere. As Campa Cola struggled to catch up, it didn't take long before personal ties between Thums Up's Chauhan and the Janata Party on the one hand and Campa Cola boss Charanjit Singh's position as a prominent member of Gandhi's party on the other turned the Indian cola war political. After Indira Gandhi returned to power in 1980, her son Sanjay attacked Thums Up in the Indian Parliament, questioning its right to advertise itself as a "refreshing cola" when it contained no kola nut. A lawsuit followed, seeking to prevent Thums Up from calling itself a cola, but the court dismissed the claim, ruling that a cola was a carbonated drink with caffeine and that the presence of kola nut didn't matter.

Despite the attacks, Thums Up thrived. In 1991, two years after Pepsi's launch in India, the drink held a 60 percent share of the soda market, a base so strong that when Coca-Cola returned to India it decided to pay $50 million for the rights to Thums Up rather than try to topple it. Today, Thums Up remains India's number-one soft drink, ahead of Sprite, Pepsi and the number-four brand, Coca-Cola—making India, along with Peru and Scotland, one of just three places in the world where neither Pepsi nor Coke rule.

In Peru, Coca-Cola's hopes of becoming the South American nation's favorite soda were thwarted by Inca Kola, a lurid yellow-gold fizz made from a mixture of local flavors, including the herb lemon verbena. The drink was created in 1935 by José Lindley, the son of an English immigrant family that opened a soda company in Lima in 1911. Lindley created the drink to mark the four hundredth anniversary of the Peruvian capital's founding. To promote the drink, Lindley appealed to Peruvian nationalism, pushing the idea that to drink it was a sign of loyalty to the nation. By the 1970s Inca Kola had become as tied up with Peru's national identity as Coca-Cola's was with America's. It pushed itself as "the flavor that unites Peru," a message that plenty of Peruvians agreed with. As one Inca Kola fan told the *New York Times* in 1995 while drinking it with his daughter in a Lima chicken restaurant, "I tell [my daughter]: 'This is our drink, not something invented overseas. It is named for your ancestors, the great Inca warriors.'" Eventually, after years of almost but not quite toppling it as Peru's number-one soda, Coca-Cola resorted to paying an estimated $200 million to gain control of the beverage. When Coke president Doug Ivester toasted the 1999 deal with a glass of Inca Kola, the Peruvian press published photos of the Coca-Cola boss drinking it and hailed the moment as a defeat for the American giant, even as its national soda became part of the American beverage giant's portfolio.

A similar appeal to national pride also lay behind Scotland's preference for Irn-Bru, a vivid rust-colored soda with a taste as unique as Dr Pepper, which one carpet-cleaning company claimed in 2012 caused more persistent carpet stains than red wine or curry. Irn-Bru started life in 1901 as Iron Brew, one of numerous sodas produced by the Glasgow-based soft drinks company A. G. Barr, which opened its doors in 1875 as an offshoot of a cork-cutting business. The company promoted Iron Brew as a strength-giving drink, backed with endorsements from Scottish sportsmen such as champion caber tosser Alex Munro who called it "a grand pick-me-up after a tussle." By the 1950s it had changed its name to Irn-Bru to comply with changes to UK food labeling laws that made it illegal for the drink to be called Iron Brew because it didn't contain iron and wasn't brewed.

While it had long been popular in Scotland, the link between Irn-Bru and Scottish identity really took off in the 1970s, on the back of the rapid growth of the Scottish independence movement. A. G. Barr adopted slogans that played up the drink's Scottishness, such as "Made in Scotland from girders" and, in a reference to the country's love of whiskey, "Scotland's other national drink." By 1975 Irn-Bru had edged ahead of Coca-Cola to become the best-selling soda in Scotland. By the 1990s Irn-Bru was as much a part of Scottishness as Inca Kola was part of being Peruvian, and it was keeping Coca-Cola at bay with a series of brash and often controversial ads that were shot through with sentimental nods to Scotland.

Complaint-inspiring posters showed a photograph of a cow accompanied with the line "When I'm a burger I want to be washed down by Irn-Bru"; a TV ad featured a balaclava-wearing granny on a mobility scooter who rams a shop's Irn-Bru display so that the cans fall into her wire basket before making her escape; and a newspaper ad showed a woman kissing a man next to words, "If I suck hard enough, maybe I can get my Irn-Bru back." In a 1991 TV commercial, the company offered a pastiche of Pepsi and Coca-Cola's all-American advertising to appeal to a rain-swept nation where it was hard to relate to bouncy US teens hanging out on sun-kissed Californian beaches. Over scenes of white-teethed smiling youths and break dancers, the ad's soft rock soundtrack sang, "Wouldn't you know it, it's one of those ads, lots of kids with white teeth and giant shoulder pads, it's not a drink by those crazy Yanks, it's made right here, you know it's tougher than tanks," before ending with a customer getting headbutted by an Irn-Bru vending machine. As Scotland embraced the independence, Irn-Bru became an obvious and highly visible way of buying into Scottishness.

But for all their domestic popularity Irn-Bru, Inca Kola, and Thums Up barely registered outside their home nations, and that they stand out so much as competition for Coke and Pepsi merely underlines just how successful Pepsi and Coca-Cola's race for the global market was. Beginning with a minimal global reach at the start of World War II, the American cola superpowers conquered the world's taste buds. They changed drinking habits, weaned people off local favorites, encouraged the consumption of cold drinks, spread American culture, paved the way for better relations with China and the Soviet Union, boosted economic growth, and helped create US presidents. The age of soda diplomacy might have ended with Ronald Reagan, who in 1976 accused President Ford of having "a foreign policy whose principal accomplishment seems to be our acquisition of the right to sell Pepsi-Cola in Siberia," but when the Cold War ended, Coca-Cola's dream of a world united by Coke had largely come true.

The world had united around cola, usually Coca-Cola, and nothing said it more than the night the Berlin Wall fell—November 9, 1989. As East Germans poured into West Berlin that momentous evening, they were greeted by red Coca-Cola trucks handing out free Cokes. Almost none of the East Germans who crossed the border that night had ever tasted it before, but they all knew what it was, and knowing what it represented, they all wanted one. At the Brandenburg Gate alone, Coca-Cola gave away seventy thousand cans of its drink to joyous East Germans. One witness to the celebrations recalled seeing wide-eyed East Germans getting drunk while stuffing themselves with McDonald's and Coca-Cola at Checkpoint Charlie and being bruised by the twenty-four-can cases of Coke that people were triumphantly carrying around with them.

In the days following the opening of the wall, Coca-Cola dished out more free cases of Coca-Cola to East German visitors, who flocked to the company's West Berlin warehouses in their plastic Trabant autos. As Heinz Wiezorek, the regional manager of Coca-Cola in Germany at the time, recalled in Coke chief Neville Isdell's biography *Inside Coca-Cola*, "There were thousands of cars per day just circling the warehouse, which showed very clearly the hunger they had for Coca-Cola."

Them and the world, Heinz. Them and the world.

8

Racists, Eco-Freaks, and Cancer Rats

As the first shots rang out in the global cola war, back in America Pepsi was on its knees. Pepsi president Walter Mack's cunning Mexican syrup scam during World War II had saved the company from the ravages of wartime rationing, but its hopes of a peacetime recovery were fading fast.

The problem was inflation. After Japan surrendered in 1945, businesses and unions began pushing the federal government to drop wartime controls on prices and wages. Under pressure from all sides, Washington caved. But the sudden removal of these restrictions sent the country into an inflationary spiral. Within months prices and wages skyrocketed, and America felt the pinch of double-digit inflation. Pepsi and other soda companies watched in horror as the rising cost of materials and wages devoured their profits. Larger costs meant smaller profits. Smaller profits meant reduced marketing budgets. Reduced marketing budgets meant fewer sales. Fewer sales meant smaller profits. It was a feedback loop that threatened to drag soda companies into ruin.

For Moxie the spike in inflation was the final straw. The New England soda pop had been in decline for years, crippled by a series of business misjudgments. The advertising cutbacks it made in the 1920s handed the advantage to its competitors. Moxie's paranoia about soda fountains passing off cheaper imitation syrup as its own had caused it to shut itself off from this lucrative market. The company's preference for opening its own bottling plants rather than adopting the franchising approach of Coca-Cola also limited its distribution reach. Moxie was also out of promotional ideas. Thirty years had passed since its eye-catching Horsemobiles with their model horses made their 1917 debut, but rather than finding new ways to drum up interest Moxie continued to flog its aging gasoline steeds. As rising costs bit deep, the company retreated to its New England heartland, disappearing bit by bit from stores and eventually sinking into obscurity as a dimly remembered regional soda catering to a dwindling fan base of diehard Moxie drinkers. That even its most loyal drinkers had to admit its licorice-like aftertaste took some getting used to didn't help either.

As Moxie faded away, Pepsi found itself fighting for survival. It could have increased the price of a Pepsi, but the cost of a soda hadn't changed for the best part of a century. Soda cost a nickel back when John Pemberton cooked up his first batch of Coca-Cola, and it was still five cents in 1947. Americans expected five-cent pop, and any company that increased its price faced losing customers to competitors who held onto the traditional price tag, a risk Royal Crown Cola learned about the hard way. In 1947 Royal Crown upped the price of its cola from five to six cents and watched sales collapse. Within weeks its bottlers had returned to the nickel price point, having concluded that declining profit was better than no profit at all.

Adding to the pressure was Coca-Cola. The Atlanta cola king knew its smaller rivals with their bigger bottles were more vulnerable to rising prices, and Coke decided to stick to its nickel price tag for as long as it could bear, hoping that its competitors would either go bust or be forced to raise their prices before it would.

If Coke's price freeze and cost-sensitive shoppers weren't enough of a problem, Pepsi also had its advertising to consider. Pepsi had turned itself into America's number-two soda with its "twice as much for a nickel too" promotional campaign. Increasing prices would require a complete marketing overhaul, and there was no guarantee the company would develop an equally powerful campaign.

With so much risk attached to a price rise, Mack looked for ways to save money, but options were few. Cutting back on the company's international expansion was out of the question—that would let Coca-Cola storm the world unopposed. So Mack homed in on smaller savings, pruning nonessential costs here and there. One of the victims of the cuts was the Pepsi Scholarship Program, one of several company initiatives that had smashed through the racial barriers of the 1940s.

Mack described himself as "an unrepentant capitalist and a liberal" and had used his position at Pepsi to put his politics into practice. Shortly after taking charge of Pepsi in 1939 he discovered that there wasn't a single black employee at the company's vast plant in Long Island City due to union opposition to mixed-race production lines. Unable to mollify the union, Mack added two black-only production lines. He hated the segregation, but he figured that at least the move would force the union to recognize black workers.

In spring 1940 Mack built on this by hiring Herman Smith, a twenty-eight-year-old African American, to oversee the promotion of Pepsi to black consumers. The appointment made Pepsi one of the few large American corporations with a black person in a senior role. In July Mack went a step further by launching the Job Awards for American Youth, a paid internship program offering college graduates a job at Pepsi for a year. A structured internship program was groundbreaking enough, but Mack's initiative also broke from convention in its commitment to racial and gender equality. The awards were open to black and white students alike, and co-ed colleges were required to submit one male and one female candidate. At a time when less than two thousand of the twelve million African Americans in the United States had a degree, this was radical stuff.

Seven of the thirteen graduates selected that year were women, and two were African Americans: Allen McKellar and Jeanette Maund. The *Weekly Review*, a black newspaper based in Indiana, declared their appointment as Pepsi sales representatives "a forward step by business in giving qualified Negro youths a break." McKellar and Maund were charged with building Pepsi sales in black communities throughout the United States. Training was minimal; no one at Pepsi—or, for that matter, any other large corporation at the time—knew anything about selling to black people. "No one knew anything about it back then," McKellar said in a 2012 talk at Webster

University. "They didn't have any method of going into the black market at that time. We had to come up with our own ideas."

McKellar and Maund traversed the country by train, crisscrossing America to visit Pepsi bottlers and help them reach out to black communities in their area. Much of their work took place in the South, where segregationist Jim Crow laws were in effect. They found themselves rubbing up against racism at every turn. Train conductors would draw the curtains on their windows when coming into stations so that white passengers would not see them and cause trouble because there were black passengers—as opposed to railroad employees—on board. Some of the Pepsi bottlers they came to help struggled to accept the idea of black people teaching them how to improve their sales and tried to get them to clean the plant or make deliveries. Even finding a bed for the night and something to eat was a challenge, since restaurants and hotels would refuse to cater to black customers. For Maund, who grew up in Massachusetts, the racism of the South was a shock. "She couldn't understand why there were segregated fountains—colored and white—restrooms—colored or Negro or whatever they called them," the South Carolina–born McKellar told Stephanie Capparell, author of *The Real Pepsi Challenge*. "Nothing was integrated in the South. Nothing."

The welcome in the black communities they visited couldn't have been more different. They were the pioneers of black equality in corporate America and role models for schoolchildren who hoped for a better future. Stores dumped Coca-Cola for Pepsi, and loyal Coke drinkers switched allegiance in recognition of the company's willingness to reach out to black America. Pepsi rapidly conquered much of the black market, and by 1946 the company had grabbed 45 percent of the cola market among black consumers against Coca-Cola's 36 percent and Royal Crown's 16 percent. The pair had not only blazed a trail in opening up corporate America but also turned Pepsi into the leading cola among African Americans.

Mack kept pushing at the racial boundaries. His wartime Pepsi-Cola Centers for Servicemen were integrated, even though the military remained segregated. The four Pepsi-Cola Junior Clubs that he opened in Queens and Harlem to give teenagers something to do during World War II were also open to all races. Mack's bold commitment to racial equality was a world away from mainstream corporate America, which avoided openly courting black customers for fear of a white backlash. Companies thought nothing of racist advertising such as Hires Root Beer's 1937 ads in *Life* magazine that showed a stereotypical black porter serving a white couple alongside the words: "Yassuh . . . it's genu-wine Hires."

After the war Pepsi stepped up its efforts to win over the black market. In 1945 it launched the Pepsi Scholarship Program, which awarded university scholarships to two students from every state and an extra two scholarships for African Americans in each segregated state. A couple of years later the company hired Ed Boyd, an African American who had been working for the civil rights group the National Urban League, to head up its Negro-Market Team. Under Boyd, the team developed groundbreaking ads that championed black progress as much as they promoted Pepsi. One of the team's most popular campaigns was "Leaders Within Their Own Fields." Launched in 1948, this series of ads in black newspapers profiled successful African American professionals who worked in areas such as science, banking, or business. People such as Ralph Bunche, who worked for the United Nations on the issue of Palestine, and Cornelius Ford, a successful livestock trader and the only black member of the Buffalo Livestock Association. The ads proved so popular that people would call Pepsi's headquarters asking for copies, and black schools would put them on classroom walls to raise their students' aspirations. In fall 1948 Boyd and his team followed this campaign with another groundbreaking ad, showing a happy black family enjoying Pepsi. It was the kind of image soft drink companies used all the time but only with white families. Ronald Brown, the smiling seven-year-old boy reaching up hopefully for a Pepsi in the ad, went on to become the first African American secretary of commerce during Bill Clinton's first term as president.

While Pepsi pushed for equality, Coca-Cola struggled with the issue of race during the 1940s and 1950s. While its boss Robert Woodruff donated generously to black schools and churches and the United Negro College Fund, he and the company erred on the side of caution. In 1950 Woodruff even endorsed Georgia governor Herman Talmadge, a staunch opponent of racial integration who regarded the civil rights movement as a Communist plot. Woodruff toasted the candidate as "the second-greatest governor, sired by the first-greatest governor." If his endorsement of the younger Talmadge upset the civil rights campaigners, his praise for his white supremacist father Eugene was even harder to swallow, given that the elder Talmadge openly admired Adolf Hitler and called black children "the enemy." Woodruff's support for the Talmadges inspired calls for a black boycott of Coca-Cola. By January 1951 Coca-Cola had responded by starting to advertise in African American newspapers.

As the civil rights movement gathered momentum, Woodruff became an increasingly active supporter of the cause. In December 1964 when Atlanta's white business leaders were refusing to buy tickets for a dinner to celebrate Martin Luther King Jr. being awarded the Nobel Peace Prize, Woodruff intervened and used his considerable influence to get the city's businessmen to come out in support of the civil rights leader. And, on hearing of King's assassination, he told Atlanta's mayor to spare no expense on the funeral, offering to cover the city's costs himself if necessary.

While Coke faced calls for boycotts from the black community, Pepsi found itself clashing with white supremacists as the battle over civil rights intensified. In 1965 the company appointed Harvey Russell as its vice president of corporate planning, a move that prompted the Ku Klux Klan to distribute thousands of flyers with a photo of Russell and his wife with the words: "Below, picture of Negro vice president of Pepsi-Cola, at left, and his white wife, in center; Let the Pepsi people know what you think of their vice president and his white wife." Pepsi's African American sales team hit back with an unofficial "Fight the Klan, Drink Pepsi" campaign. By then, however, corporate America was finally catching up with Pepsi's way of thinking.

But back in the late 1940s all of Pepsi's efforts on race equality seemed under threat. To cut costs Mack found himself forced to put the Pepsi Scholarship Program on ice along with plans to expand the Negro-Market Team from four to twelve people. These cutbacks did little to stop the rising tide of price inflation. As the 1950s approached Pepsi watched the gains it had made in the previous decade unravel: by 1949 sales were nosediving, and in 1951 Wall Street analysts were predicting Pepsi would go bust for the third time. With time running out Mack hatched a plan to put Pepsi in cans.

Canning originated in France where, in 1795, the government offered the enormous sum of 12,000 francs to anyone who could devise a superior way for the nation's army to preserve its food supplies. Nicolas Appert, a confectioner from Châlons-sur-Marne, was among those who took up the challenge. He believed that food sealed in airtight glass jars that were then heated in boiling water would not spoil. It took Appert fifteen years to perfect the process, but in January 1810 he claimed the prize after demonstrating the effectiveness of his method by preserving soup, vegetables, meat, and—in one case—an entire sheep in his jars. No one, including Appert, knew why it worked, only that it did. That mystery would only be solved more than fifty years later when Louis Pasteur worked out that the airtight seal kept out microorganisms that caused decay and that the boiling of the can killed the microbes already within the jar.

Word of Appert's innovation soon spread across the English Channel, where a merchant named Peter Durand refined the idea. Seeking an alternative to the heavy and fragile glassware used by Appert, Durand rolled sheet iron into a cylinder before soldering flat discs of iron to the top and bottom to create an airtight container. To prevent rusting, he covered the iron sheets in tinplate. Lighter and more durable than Appert's glass jars, Durand's "tin" can became a favorite of militaries across the world. By the 1850s canned food was on sale to civilians too, and the arrival of the can opener that same decade finally ended the days of needing a hammer and chisel to open the containers.

Food and still liquids were commonly sold in cans by the beginning of the twentieth century, but carbonated drinks, including alcoholic beer, had proved problematic. The challenge was twofold. First, the carbon dioxide gas made the liquid acidic, which caused it to corrode the metal and react with the lining of the can, ruining the taste. Second, while food and still liquids were canned at the same pressure as the outside air, the gas within a carbonated beverage made the pressure inside the can greater than the outside atmosphere. This pressure difference meant that cans of carbonated liquids with inadequate or weak seals would leak or even explode, with the accompanying danger of injury from the sharp ruptured metal.

With fortunate timing, the canning industry finally cracked the problem of storing beer in cans just as Prohibition ended. The brewing industry wasted no time in adopting the new container. Cans offered numerous benefits over glass bottles. They were lighter and required half the space for the same volume of liquid, saving on transport costs. The flat cylinder shape allowed them to affix more eye-catching paper labels that encompassed the entire package rather than just part of the bottle. Cans chilled quicker too, and the contents didn't spoil as quickly. Even better, cans were a "one-way" container designed to be thrown away after use, which meant there was no need to lug empties back to the factory for cleaning and refilling. Nor would customers have to pay the refundable deposits added to the cost of beverages sold in returnable bottles to encourage them to bring them back. By 1941 10 percent of the beer sold in America came in a can.

The success of the beer can caught the eye of ginger ale makers Clicquot Club, and in early 1936, a year after the first beer can landed on the shelves, the company became the first soda firm to join the canning revolution. Clicquot Club used a new type of can, the cone top. Unlike the standard flat-top cans, the conical heads of these containers tapered to a small opening sealed with a standard bottle cap, which made them easier to open and fill. But Clicquot Club's revolution didn't go well. The canning industry might have figured out how to deal with beer, but fizzy drinks were more acidic and more carbonated. Clicquot Club produced one hundred thousand cans of its ginger ale only to face a barrage of complaints from all quarters. Stores and warehouses were far from impressed at the sticky, sugary trail of liquid the leaking cans left behind, let alone the ones that exploded. Even when the cans made it in one piece to shoppers' homes, people found that the ginger ale had reacted with the lining and the taste of the drink was ruined. Before the year was out Clicquot Club had pulled its canned drinks off the shelves.

Clicquot Club's experience made many in the soda business wary of cans, but in 1949 Mack figured that the can's time had come. Cans were stronger and linings better than in 1936, after all. Mack tried to get Pepsi bottlers interested in canning the drink, but the high cost of the equipment needed to produce the unproven container caused them to refuse to help. Mack was a man unused to taking no for an answer, so he had Pepsi build a canning plant of its own, and in February 1950 the first Pepsi cans went on sale in New Rochelle, New York. It was a disaster. Not only did the company's cone-top cans suffer the same leakage and taste problems that had dogged Clicquot Club back in 1936, but Pepsi's independent bottlers were furious that Mack had infringed on their exclusive geographical right to produce the drink. With cans leaking cola, bottlers threatening to sue, and the company heading down the tubes, Pepsi's board decided enough was enough. Less than two weeks after the launch of the Pepsi can, they moved Mack into the chairman's role and installed Al Steele, a former Coca-Cola executive, as president. By September Mack had quit.

Mack still believed the future of soda lay in the can. In 1953 he returned to the soda business in a blaze of publicity by buying Cantrell & Cochrane, the company that had popularized ginger ale in the 1800s. The company launched a range of canned sodas enriched with vitamin C that Mack christened Super Beverages. Mack pushed the can as the beverage container of the future, free from deposits, returns and chipped glass. Cans, the company's ads proclaimed, also cool faster, take up less refrigerator space, and are "super-sanitary" since "as many as 30 people may drink out of the bottle before it comes to you." Despite the hype surrounding the launch of the Super Beverages and some lucrative deals with US military bases, Mack's comeback failed to bring in the big money that he hoped for and leaking cans continued to dog the business. But by the end of 1954, most of canned soda's leakage problems had been fixed, and the likes of Canada Dry, Nehi, Vernor's, and White Rock were busy exploring the potential for canned fizz. A year later Coca-Cola also started some small-scale experiments with canning its cola.

Breweries also got in on the act, hoping to capitalize on the soda industry's slow embrace of cans and the canning facilities they had already built for their beer operations. Among them was the Sheridan Brewery Company of Sheridan, Wyoming, which launched the Can-a-Pop range of soda in July 1953. Can-a-Pop was the first soda to be packaged in easier-to-stack, flat-topped cans as opposed to the cone-top design that Pepsi had used, and the small-town brewery's innovative cans proved an instant hit. Within a month of launch the company was selling sixteen thousand cans of soda a week, enough to convince it to quit the beer business to focus on taking

Can-a-Pop nationwide. Can-a-Pop's success was, however, short-lived. As the 1950s became the 1960s, soda's big players, including Pepsi, were moving into canning en masse, and it didn't take long for Sheridan Brewery to find itself hopelessly outgunned by the superior marketing and distribution of the larger companies. By then the only thing holding back the canned soda revolution that Mack had envisaged back in 1950 was a simple opening mechanism, a problem soon overcome by the invention of the pull tab in 1962. Three years later some 3.8 billion cans of soda were being sold worldwide every year.

This, of course, was all to come when Steele replaced Mack as the boss of Pepsi. The new Pepsi chief was a refugee from Coca-Cola. Born in Nashville, Tennessee, Steele managed a circus before joining Coca-Cola's advertising agency D'Arcy. Impressed by his advertising work, Coca-Cola hired him, and by 1945 he had risen to vice president level. But Steele's flamboyant style clashed with the staid hierarchical culture of Coke and, after a falling out with Woodruff, he found himself sidelined. So when Pepsi's board asked him to come to New York and save the company, he leapt at the chance. Coca-Cola was furious. It expected Steele to quit but not to go to "the imitator," as Coke had begun calling Pepsi internally. It was nothing short of treason as far as Coca-Cola was concerned, and when Steele poached a cabal of Coke's rising stars to join him, his name became as unmentionable at the company's Atlanta headquarters as the word Pepsi.

Steele worked fast to get Pepsi back on track. He shut down the canning operation and, in a push to decentralize operations, created regional offices across the United States, farming out many of the company's national divisions to these offices, including the work of the Negro-Market Team. He standardized the use of the Pepsi logo—now a bottle cap that displayed the words Pepsi-Cola in script within a white middle topped and bottomed with waves of red and blue—and created a team of mobile chemists to roam the nation carrying out spot checks on the company's 650 bottlers to make sure the drink was the same wherever it was purchased. To get the bottlers back on his side after Mack's canning experiment and years of falling sales, he made them a bold promise: "The time has come for you to stop driving around in lousy Fords. I'm going to put you in Cadillacs."

Steele also upped the price of Pepsi and adopted a new advertising theme, "More Bounce to the Ounce," that emphasized Pepsi as a source of energy. It was a theme that plenty of soda companies had embraced before. From Coca-Cola's wartime claims of productivity-boosting Coke breaks to Dr Pepper's pseudoscientific "Drink a Bite to Eat at 10, 2 and 4" claim, soda companies had long pitched themselves as energy replenishing drinks. "More Bounce to the Ounce" tried to do the same, making a virtue of the sugar in Pepsi in TV advertising that showed teenagers doing the jitterbug while singing "Go get Pepsi for the Pepsi bounce" with a stunningly handsome first-time actor named James Dean at center stage. The ad launched Dean's career, but the campaign failed.

It turned out that postwar America didn't want calories. American society was changing fast. The postwar economic boom led to an explosion in car ownership, and as Americans became motorists they left the inner cities and headed for the greenery, space, and peace of the suburbs. To supply their needs came new types of retail environments: shopping malls, supermarkets, drive-in movie theaters, fast-food chains, and gas stations—all offering convenience and copious parking. Main Street with its soda fountains and mom-and-pop stores was left behind as America headed for the highway. By the middle of the 1960s the once ubiquitous soda fountain was in steep decline. Before the war every small town had a soda fountain, but in 1965 only half of them did. In the cities the shift was even more marked. Drugstores dumped the fountains and new fast-food chains like McDonald's nabbed their customers. The birthplace of the American soda industry turned into a relic, the fountains that survived becoming little more than museum pieces. The new American society was one of greater affluence, labor-saving devices, TV dinners, and extra leisure time. Yet it was also a society that constantly fretted about its weight even as its increasingly sedentary lifestyle increased its jean size.

The idea that to be thin was to be beautiful took root in the 1920s and embedded itself deeper in people's minds during the postwar years. This cultural shift in attitudes to attraction could be seen in the changing shape of Psyche, the topless mascot of the mineral water and soda company White Rock. In 1894 the Wisconsin company first adopted Psyche, a mortal of Greek legend who was so beautiful she made the goddess of love, Venus, jealous. Back then its vision of the legendary symbol of beauty had a five-foot-four frame and a 37-27-38 figure, but in 1947, to reflect changing attitudes, Psyche went on a crash diet, shedding two inches from her bust and waist plus a full three inches from her hips. She also grew a couple of inches taller. The trend would continue. By the end of the 1970s, White Rock's Psyche had slimmed down to a twenty-four-inch waist and thirty-four-inch hips.

Pepsi quickly realized that it had misjudged the national mood with its talk of extra calories and did a spectacular u-turn. "More Bounce to the Ounce" was out, replaced by "Pepsi-Cola, The Light Refreshment" in a campaign backed by newspaper ads aimed at weight-watching housewives that declared: "The modern woman owes a lot to today's good sense in diet. She eats light, drinks light, and keeps her youthful figure longer. She looks better, feels better. Men like her better. And so does her insurance company. For her, today's Pepsi-Cola is refreshment made to order."

This was Pepsi as a diet drink, not a calorie-packed soda. The trouble was that nothing had changed but the ads. After seeing Pepsi's change in direction, Coca-Cola ordered its chemists to find out how the Pepsi formula had changed. The results were surprising. Pepsi's formula hadn't changed noticeably. In 1950 Coke's chemists reported that Pepsi averaged 13.67 calories per ounce. In 1953 the newly christened light refreshment had an average of 13.41 calories in every ounce. Coca-Cola averaged 12.7 calories. One Coca-Cola employee tried to find out more by calling a local Pepsi bottler and pretending to be a fat man who hoped Pepsi might help him lose weight. The bottler cheerfully replied that there were just 10 calories per ounce in a Pepsi, providing a lower calorie count than Coca-Cola's scientists were reporting and neatly fudging the fact that it came in twelve-ounce bottles.

While Pepsi's attempt to woo housewives by presenting itself as the lightweight option was largely smoke and mirrors, this and Steele's other reforms did the trick, bringing the company back from the brink of ruin and transforming it, once again, into a fast-growing threat to Coca-Cola. By the middle of the 1950s Pepsi's revival became threatening enough to finally persuade the increasingly conservative Woodruff that Coke would have to be sold in larger bottle sizes if the company was to win over supermarket shoppers looking to buy cola for their entire family. Soon soda companies were locked in a bottle size arms race to win over car-driving housewives who homed in on larger bottles that offered a lower price per ounce.

But the concept of a diet soda was already becoming more than advertising fiction by the time Pepsi relaunched itself with its "Light Refreshment" campaign. Diet soda originated in 1951 when Hyman Kirsch became vice president of the Jewish Sanitarium for Chronic Disease in Brooklyn. Born in the Russian city of Simferopol in 1876, Kirsch moved to America sometime around 1900 and in 1904 founded Kirsch Beverages to produce a range of bottled sodas that included grape, lemon-lime, celery, and black cherry flavors. A year after taking the position at the sanitarium, Kirsch began thinking about how patients with diabetes or cardiovascular problems had to go without soda. He thought it was a shame that they couldn't enjoy a refreshing drink of fizz, and together with his son Morris, he began looking into creating a sugar-free soda for them. The father-son duo asked Kirsch Beverages' chemist Dr. Samuel Epstein to research the world of artificial sweeteners to see what sugar substitutes could be used.

The best-known synthetic sweetener at that time was saccharin, discovered in 1879 by a German chemist who spilled some on his hands before tucking into a piece of bread only to find that it now tasted incredibly sweet. Although it was calorie-free, saccharin's intense sweetness—about three hundred times that of sugar—also came with an unpleasant metallic aftertaste that was nearly impossible to conceal, so Epstein passed over saccharin and continued his search. One chemical laboratory he spoke to told him about a new form of artificial sweetener: cyclamates. Created at the University of Illinois in 1937, cyclamates could be used in two forms—sodium cyclamate and calcium cyclamate—but the result was the same: a sweetener thirty times as sweet as sugar, but with zero calories and a better taste than saccharin. And, in a fluke of timing, cyclamates had just been approved for use in food and drink.

Using the new sweetener, Kirsch and his team developed two sugar-free sodas—a ginger ale and a black cherry flavor. They named the drinks

No-Cal, and they proved popular with the sanitarium patients, but there weren't enough patients to sustain production. So Kirsch decided to sell the range more widely and added root beer and chocolate soda flavors to it. Chocolate sodas had been a big fad in the soda fountains during the late nineteenth century, but while the rest of the United States had lost interest by the mid-1900s they remained popular in New York, especially in the form of the New York or Brooklyn egg cream, a frothy mix of soda water, milk, and chocolate syrup that contains neither egg nor cream. The drink's roots are thought to lie in soda fountain egg creams or early chocolate milkshake recipes of the late 1800s, which often contained egg, cream, and soda water. In the 1920s cost-conscious New York fountain owners took out the egg and swapped cream for milk to save money. The result was the modern-day egg cream, a soda enduring enough among New Yorkers for Lou Reed to write a song about it for his 1996 album *Set the Twilight Reeling*.

Armed with his new flavors, Kirsch started selling No-Cal in stores across the New York City area, pitching it as a sugar-free soda for weight-conscious women. By the end of 1953 Kirsch's innovative diet sodas were racking up sales of more than $5 million a year, and No-Cal could be found in nearly three-quarters of New York grocery stores.

It didn't take long for other soda companies to latch onto the diet drink idea and start releasing their own sugar-free beverages, including Canada Dry, which launched a zero-calorie ginger ale called Glamor in 1954. By 1957 around 120 million bottles of diet soda were being sold in America every year. The wider diet industry wouldn't take off until the 1960s but the soda companies were already laying the groundwork with their no-calorie sodas. Popular as these drinks were in the late 1950s they were but a drop in a soda ocean, but that was all about to change.

In 1958 Royal Crown joined the diet pop bandwagon with Diet-Rite. Initially the company promoted it as a drink for diabetics and sold it in the medical section of drugstores. But in 1961 the company decided to see if it could break Diet-Rite out of its diabetic niche by launching it in Chicago's supermarkets and promoting it as a cola with all the taste but none of the calories. It was a decision that sparked a revolution.

Diet-Rite's new visibility and sales appeal hit the spot with weight-watching Chicagoans, and the following year Royal Crown launched it in stores across America where it was an instant success. Pepsi and Coca-Cola were caught napping. Diet-Rite's national breakthrough made sugar-free soda a big deal. Coke and Pepsi rushed to bring out their own diet drinks. After being warned by its lawyers that calling its sugar-free cola Diet Coca-Cola could undermine the company's valuable trademark, Coke programmed an IBM 1401 computer to spew out a list of 250,000 three- and four-letter words that the company then whittled down to Tab, the diet cola it introduced in April 1963. That same year Pepsi, clearly getting the same advice from its lawyers, launched Patio Diet Cola, only to ignore its lawyers and change the drink's name to Diet Pepsi a year later. Dr Pepper launched Dietetic Dr Pepper before dumping the medical name and opting for Sugar-Free Dr Pepper instead. In 1966 Coke came out with a second diet drink, the citrus-flavored Fresca. Even 7Up, which initially refused point blank to release a diet drink due to its concerns about taste, eventually caved.

In 1965 Americans were drinking ten million pounds of cyclamates and two million pounds of saccharin every year through diet soda, which now accounted for 15 percent of the entire carbonated soft drink market. A liquid reflection of the rise of diet culture, the sugar-free soda boom of the 1960s made the growth of energy drinks in the late 1990s and early 2000s look like nothing more than a ripple in an ocean. Soda, it seemed, was getting healthy, and Royal Crown's Diet-Rite had fended off Coke and Pepsi to remain the leader of the pack.

The rise of the diet sodas shocked the sugar industry. In just three years diet soda had gone from a mere sliver to a chunky wedge of the carbonated soft drinks industry, drawing people away from sugar and toward artificial sweeteners. Soda was big, big business for the sugar producers, and the trend worried them. Artificial sweeteners were cheaper than sugar and less prone to supply shortages, so the soda companies stood to make more money from selling diet drinks than their regular sugar-based fizz. What, the sugar industry wondered, if the growth of diet beverages didn't stop? What if sugared soda became the niche and diet soda the norm? Could the future be sugar free? The sugar industry figured that if that was the future, it'd be damned if it was going to let that happen. As John Hickson, the vice president of the International Sugar Research Foundation, told the *New York Times* in 1969: "A dollar's worth of sugar could be replaced with a dime's worth of [cyclamate]. If anyone can undersell you nine cents out of 10 you'd better find some brickbat you can throw at him."

Big Sugar found its brickbat sitting in the law books. Back in 1958 a New York congressman named James Delaney chaired an investigation into the use of chemicals and insecticides in food and drink. The Democratic representative used the probe to introduce an amendment to the 1938 Food, Drug, and Cosmetic Act that was designed to protect the public from dangerous carcinogens. The measure, known as the Delaney Clause, required the Food and Drug Administration (FDA) to ban the use of chemical additives that had been found "to induce cancer in man, or, after tests, found to induce cancer in animals."

By the time the diet soda boom took off, the Delaney Clause had already rocked the root beer industry to its very foundations. In December 1960 the FDA ordered safrole, the oil of sassafras, to be removed from all food and drink after it was deemed a carcinogen. Safrole had been a core ingredient of root beer for more than a century and now, suddenly, it was gone, and much of root beer's flavor with it. For a drink that had been losing ground to cola, ginger ale, and lemon-lime sodas for years, this very public cancer scare, coupled with the resulting taste change, smacked root beer even further down from its temperance heyday. Root beer eventually staged a minor recovery in the mid-1960s after developing a process for purging the safrole from its ingredients, but the incident almost killed the drink.

The root beer crisis provided a clear demonstration of the power of the Delaney Clause. The sugar industry reasoned that establishing a link between cyclamates and cancer would be the perfect way to snuff out diet soda. So it flung money at studies of the artificial sweetener in the hope of finding something—anything—it could use to invoke the Delaney Clause. In 1969 the sugar industry's $600,000 investment in cyclamate studies hit pay dirt when scientists at Abbott Laboratories plied rats with the sweetener for eighteen months and reported that the rodents had developed cancerous bladder tumors. Big Sugar had found its silver bullet. That the unfortunate rats were pumped with so much cyclamate that a human would need to gulp down more than five hundred Frescas a day to consume an equivalent amount didn't matter. The Delaney Clause might have been well meaning but it was ineptly drafted, making no distinction for potency or risk. If a substance could cause cancer even in unrealistically extreme circumstances, that was enough to invoke a ban.

On learning of the test results, the FDA slapped a ban on cyclamates effective from October 19, 1969. Britain, Finland, and Sweden followed with bans of their own. The resulting cancer scare destroyed the diet soda boom. Coke, Pepsi, Royal Crown, and others were quick to reformulate their diet drinks with less tasty saccharin or a more calorific sugar-saccharin mix, but the damage had been done. Before the ban, diet soda accounted for 19 percent of fizzy drink sales in America. In the wake of the cyclamate ban, diet soda's share of the business collapsed to just 3 percent. Royal Crown watched sales of its Coke- and Pepsi-beating diet drink evaporate.

Subsequent studies would clear cyclamates of their cancer connection, and it remains in use in some parts of the world, but in America the sweetener that sparked the creation of diet soda was gone. The cyclamate ban was just the first hit. In early 1970 another study funded by the Sugar Research Foundation came out, this time linking saccharin to bladder tumors in rats, raising the prospect of a ban of the last remaining artificial sweetener approved for use in food and drink. Again the tests involved rats consuming saccharin at levels that would be equivalent to a human guzzling their way through eight hundred diet sodas a day, but the Delaney Clause didn't deal in gray: substances either caused cancer or they didn't in its world.

Panicked by the prospect of a ban that would effectively abolish diet soda altogether, Coca-Cola chief executive Paul Austin wrote to Robert Finch, the US secretary of health, education and welfare, in April 1970 to plead with him not to ban saccharin. "Action affecting the use of saccharin along the lines of that taken with respect to cyclamate will have implications for this industry far exceeding those which accompanied the cyclamate ban," wrote Austin. "Consumers also have a vital interest in the continued availability of artificially sweetened soft drinks. To deprive diabetics or those with a need to control their caloric intake of a supply of refreshing beverages in the absence of scientifically compelling reasons would be highly prejudicial to that consumer interest."

Finch was sympathetic—he felt the Delaney Clause was too extreme and harbored doubts about whether cyclamates should have been banned—but the law was the law. So he engineered a compromise: saccharin would remain on the market but the levels of the sweetener in any product would be restricted and diet soda would need to carry the warning: "Use of this product may be hazardous to your health. This product contains saccharin, which has been determined to cause cancer in laboratory animals."

The soda industry's fight to save saccharin continued throughout the 1970s. The Sugar Research Foundation continued to bankroll studies linking it to cancer while the beverage industry managed to get Congress to keep delaying the imposition of a ban while it waited for aspartame, a new artificial sweetener, to get approval for human consumption, which it finally got in 1981. The fight over saccharin eventually ended in 2000 when it was discovered that it caused cancer in rats due to a toxicological mechanism that didn't exist in humans. With this finding and a lack of conclusive evidence that saccharin caused cancer in humans, the restrictions were lifted and the warning labels introduced in the early 1970s were finally removed. By then the impractical Delaney Clause was gone as well, reformed in 1996 so that future bans would depend on the level of risk posed by a carcinogen rather than its mere presence.

By the time the sugar producers began their assault on saccharin, however, soda had another enemy. At 1:30 PM on April 22, 1970, a group of hippies and students gathered at Atlanta's Piedmont Park to mark the first ever Earth Day. They had come together at the urging of the *Great Speckled Bird*, the city's weekly countercultural newspaper, and their target was Coca-Cola. In the weeks leading up to the protest, the radical newspaper had called on "ecology freaks, fed up with litter and mountains of undegradable solid waste" to bring empty cans and bottles of Coke, Fresca, Tab, Sprite, and Fanta with them to dump outside the beverage giant's headquarters. "Bring more than you can carry," the paper told its twenty-two thousand readers. "Bring the trash home to the people who make it." After loading a pickup with piles of branded flotsam and jetsam, the protestors took their convoy of garbage through the streets of Atlanta. After a three-mile trek to the Coca-Cola headquarters on North Avenue they dumped the mounds of bottles and cans outside the entrance and, having displayed their displeasure at the company's throwaway containers, walked away, leaving Coke to clean up the mess.

The following year a tiny group of green activists in London called Friends of the Earth did the same to Schweppes, after the company announced that it would only sell its drinks in throwaway bottles in future. The activists spent weeks gathering up empty Schweppes bottles only to find, as the second Earth Day approached, that they were still short of the target of two thousand bottles that they had set for their "Many Happy Returns" stunt. "We had about a week to go and simply couldn't find enough of the damn things, or couldn't find enough hours in the day to collect them," Pete Wilkinson, the activist charged by the group's leader Graham Searle with collecting the bottles, recalled in Robert Lamb's book *Promising the Earth*. "We had to go out and buy loads of Schweppes drinks, which we promptly poured into plastic containers. Graham produced a lot of gin and we drank it with tonic in order to justify our purchase."

On Earth Day 1971 the badly hungover environmentalists drove their collection of two thousand bottles to the headquarters of Schweppes in Uxbridge and dumped them at the entrance in front of a gaggle of newspaper reporters and photographers. The stunt made the group famous, turning it into one of the leading environmental campaign groups in Britain. "Nonreturnable bottles were a step toward the 'out of sight, out of mind' culture we now have and dumping the bottles really helped raise the issue up the agenda in Britain and launch us," says Neil Verlander, spokesperson for Friends of the Earth. "But ultimately Schweppes went ahead anyway."

The green movement was too late. The battle over returnable bottles and cans had already been won, and the supermarkets were the winners. Back in 1947 every bottle of fizzy pop in America was returnable, but in the 1950s the soda industry found itself under pressure from all sides to move away from returns and to adopt throwaway cans and bottles. The success of beer sold in cans and nonreturnable bottles had demonstrated that many consumers were happy to pay a bit more for the convenience of being able to dump the container rather than return it. The canning industry was doing its very best to persuade soda companies to adopt disposable cans. Glassmakers were also keen on throwaway bottles, knowing that a move to nonreturnable bottles would boost their sales. The US military wanted canned soda too. For years US Army bases had been dealing with returnable bottles, but in 1956 the sprawling Fort Greely base in Alaska decided it was tired of losing warehouse space to empty containers that were awkward to stack and left behind broken glass. It announced it was only going to take soda in cans. Keen not to lose the base's business, the local 7Up, Canada Dry, and Coca-Cola bottler obliged and set up a canning plant. Other US military bases followed Fort Greely's example, switching to a can-only policy to reap the benefits of more durable, easier to stack, and disposable containers that were also lighter and faster to cool.

But the strongest pressure of all came from retail and, in particular, the new and increasingly influential supermarkets. Supermarkets didn't want returnable bottles and the hassle of processing deposits and collecting empties. They wanted convenience—one-way containers that shoppers could buy and throw away. To underline the point, supermarkets launched their own sodas in cans and nonreturnable bottles that ate into the sales of established soda brands. As the 1960s began, the tipping point came and the soda industry finally embraced throwaway packaging. By 1965 12 percent of soda sold in America came in disposable containers and by 1970 nonreturnable packaging accounted for 40 percent of the market and an estimated 5 percent of the nation's solid waste. Coca-Cola held out the longest. Even in June 1967 the company was debating how it should respond to the rise of throwaway packaging. "There is a definite feeling on the part of the food chains that soft drinks in returnable bottles are unprofitable, and are stocked only because of consumer demand," Coca-Cola executive Eugene Smith wrote in an internal memo. "We must determine what our overall attitude is to be—stay out of the fastest growing market (convenience packages) or get in with the idea of continuing to dominate every part of the soft drink market. Do you perform in the main arena, or do you become a speciality drink?"

Coca-Cola opted for the main arena. In March 1970, a few weeks before the Earth Day protestors dumped their trash outside its headquarters, the company's chief executive Paul Austin admitted that returnable bottles were on their way out in a speech to a group of Atlanta bankers: "Even though it's far more economical for consumers to buy our products in these returnable packages, some of our dealers—supermarkets and convenience stores—find it more desirable to handle one-way bottles and cans." The environmental movement's objections to soda waste would only grow as glass gave way to plastic bottles formed from polyethylene terephthalate, or PET, a synthetic fiber that not only offered the durability and lightness of cans but was cheaper to make and could be recycled into other products including bags and pants.

But if these battles with environmentalists, racists, sugar producers, and supermarkets suggested soda was an industry under fire, nothing could have been further from the truth, for fizzy pop was going from strength to strength. By the time Al Steele died suddenly from a heart attack in 1959, Pepsi was back in the game and on a mission not just to survive but to do what would have seemed unthinkable only a decade earlier: to topple Coca-Cola. What would follow would be one of the highest-profile marketing struggles ever seen in corporate history: the Cola War, a contest for American taste buds that would captivate the world, pioneer new promotional practices, turn retail space into an invisible battlefield, and flood the country with fizz.

9

A Better Mousetrap

A trumpet blast. Then, over aerial scenes of open roads, the clarion call of jazz starlet Joanie Sommers punctuated by bursts of sassy brass. "Come alive! Come alive!" she sang. "You're in the Pepsi Generation!"

As the brisk jazz soundtrack swept Sommers's buoyant vocal along, TVs across America showed a young and beautiful carefree couple speeding through the countryside on a Honda motorcycle. As they zoomed through the winding roads to the hilltops, a helicopter towed a Pepsi-Cola vending machine through the skies to deliver a bubbly dose of refreshing cola as the carefree couple reached the summit. "Who is the Pepsi Generation?" asked the narrator. "Just about everyone with the young view of things. Active, livelier people with a liking for Pepsi-Cola, the light refreshment with the bold, clean taste. Generous in flavor and sparkle. Pepsi belongs to your generation."

It was fall 1963 and, after years of hunting, Pepsi had found an identity of its own. Ever since it dropped the value-for-money campaigns of the 1930s and 1940s, Pepsi had lacked a distinctive promotional image. Al Steele might have delivered sales of more than $157 million by the end of the 1950s, moved its headquarters to Manhattan, and even sprinkled the drink with the glamour of his wife Joan Crawford, but Pepsi remained the kitchen cola—the drink people served to their guests in glasses while claiming it was Coca-Cola. If Pepsi was ever going to knock Coke off its perch, it needed to be more than just "the other cola." It needed an identity consumers could rally around.

The first step toward the Pepsi Generation came in 1960 when the cola superpower asked its advertising agency BBDO to come up with a new campaign. BBDO homed in on the huge crop of young Americans born in the postwar years. This great demographic bulge was reaching its teens, heading toward the prime soda drinking ages of sixteen to twenty-four. Figuring that this generation was still too young to be loyal to a particular soda, BBDO reached out to them with the slogan "Now it's Pepsi for those who think young!" The slogan didn't set the world on fire, but the idea of capturing the new generation took root at Pepsi. The New York beverage company started to see that maybe, just maybe, Coca-Cola's position as the established market leader could be turned against it. Maybe Coke with its Norman Rockwell nostalgia and homely Santas could be painted as the drink of the status quo and Pepsi recast as the choice of tomorrow.

The Pepsi Generation campaign was the result. It bombarded America with images of Pepsi as the accompaniment to a life of youthful fun and frolics. A drink for happy, hopeful teenagers who played volleyball on the beach, surfed the waves, carved up the ski slopes, and drove motorcycles on mountain back roads. The assertion that Pepsi was for the young at heart, and the subtext that Coca-Cola drinkers were old and tired, resonated with the rise of the new generation. "After the Second World War there was, obviously, the baby boomers but the words baby boomers and the whole notion of that was not obvious at that particular moment," recalled Alan Pottasch, Pepsi's advertising director, in an interview for Yahoo!'s Giants of Advertising series. "As it unfolded, people were searching for a name for this group and the Pepsi Generation campaign broke about that time. So for us to name and claim a whole generation after our product was a rather courageous thing that we weren't sure would take off. . . . But it did and cartoonists and editorialists and people generally were referring to what we now call the baby boomers, at that time, as the Pepsi Generation. And that, of course, is a dream for a product. It made Pepsi part of everything that was going on."

This was soda as a generational statement. If Coke was Americana, Pepsi was America and the cola of cool. The Pepsi Generation wanted to change the world. It was a generation of optimism and postwar wealth that had everything to look forward to. It was also the throwaway generation, as Pepsi made clear in 1966 when it declared that its new nonreturnable bottles were "made to order for the Pepsi Generation." While most people couldn't tell the difference between Pepsi and Coke, they instinctively knew whether they identified with Coca-Cola's traditionalism or Pepsi's youthful future.

Pepsi set out to align itself with the hopes and dreams of the baby boomers. When the Summer of Love turned sour in a cocktail of Vietnam and drugs, Pepsi was there, running reassuring ads that promised "You've got a lot to live, and Pepsi's got a lot to give." For the accompanying 1969 TV commercial, Pepsi gave director Ed Vorkapich free rein—on the condition that there were no jeans, no hippies, and no men with long hair. Vorkapich found inspiration in avant-garde German filmmaker Leni Riefenstahl's use of backlighting in her Nazi propaganda picture *Triumph of the Will*. Flouting filmmaking convention, Vorkapich shot the commercial in the late afternoon to capture the flares of dusky yellow sunlight that are now a staple of TV advertising. On seeing the result one outraged Pepsi executive moaned that Vorkapich had delivered an art film when he was supposed to be making an ad. The commercial ran anyway and pushed exactly the same buttons as the original Pepsi Generation ads, reinforcing Pepsi's image as the baby boomer cola. Coca-Cola's warm and gentle scenes of suburban life and things going better with Coke seemed tame and conservative by comparison.

Pepsi wasn't the only soda maker tuning into the rebellious spirit of the age. While Pepsi drew the line at hippies with hair down to their jeans, Germany's Afri-Cola embraced them with its "sexy-mini-super-flower-pop-op-cola" campaign of 1968, while 7Up embraced the Haight-Ashbury vibe and wrapped itself in psychedelia. 7Up's embrace of hippie culture was fueled by fear. The lemon-lime soda might have been the number-three soft drink in America but as the clash between Pepsi and Coca-Cola intensified, 7Up found itself losing market share even as its sales grew. Worried it was losing out to the colas, 7Up ordered a study to identify the problem. The results made uncomfortable reading. The market researchers reported that people thought of 7Up as an occasional drink and cola as an everyday beverage.

Even worse, 80 percent of people didn't list 7Up among their five favorite sodas. When asked why, they replied that they had forgotten all about 7Up. The message was painfully clear: 7Up was a casual and forgettable drink.

The company responded with a head-on attack on its cola rivals, presenting itself as "the Uncola." To tap into the baby boomer generation, 7Up created ads of trippy fantasy that wouldn't have looked out of place on a Cream album cover or on the streets of San Francisco, the epicenter of hippiedom. By 1969 7Up was commissioning contemporary artists to produce bold billboard posters that smacked of LSD and counterculture. There were primary-colored, *Yellow Submarine*–inspired people playing spraying 7Up bottles like guitars. A spaced-out butterfly with a 7Up bottle for a body and wings decorated with exploding fireworks, a bottle cap sunrise, flowers, and the stars and stripes. Artist Bob Taylor came up with "The Big Un," a bizarre poster that turned an eight-pack of 7Up into the body of a giant bird that was flying over cartoon mountains to its chicks. "No doubt, it's a rather unusual graphic interpretation of an 8-pack," Taylor explained, "but that's what the whole Uncola thing is all about." 7Up's magical mystery tour of psychedelia did the trick. Within a month of launching the Uncola campaign sales were up 20 percent.

With its rivals getting down with the kids, Coca-Cola started to worry about its promotional efforts. While Pepsi and 7Up's eye-catching promotions became conversation topics, no one seemed to register Coke's efforts. "We have become part of the environment," Ira Herbert, Coke's vice president of advertising, wrote in a company memo. "The public is so accustomed to seeing Coke that it literally isn't seeing it." Coca-Cola had become too ubiquitous for its own good. People would walk down streets plastered in Coca-Cola signs and not register a single one. Coke responded with a new logo that encased its Spencerian script trademark in a red box and added a wavy white line called the Dynamic Ribbon that recalled the contours of its famous glass bottle. It also started emphasizing its authenticity, pitching itself as "The Real Thing" before embracing the peace and love vibe of the times with its hit TV ad, "I'd like to buy the world a Coke." But if the big three thought they could carve up the new generation between themselves with their advertising positioning, they hadn't reckoned on Texas.

At the end of the 1960s Dr Pepper was still a regional drink with 60 percent of its sales confined to Texas and the surrounding states. But as the 1970s approached the Dr Pepper Company was ready to take the soda from Waco nationwide. The turning point for the Texan drink came in 1966, when the Food and Drug Administration agreed to accept the company's claim that Dr Pepper was not a cola but something unique—a pepper drink. This might sound like a debate about semantics, but the decision flung open the doors of Coca-Cola, Pepsi, and Royal Crown bottling plants across the United States. The bottlers' deals with the cola companies banned them from producing rival colas but now that Dr Pepper was a pepper and not a cola, they could produce it without breaching their contracts. By the time Woodrow Wilson Clements became Dr Pepper's president in 1970, the company was primed to leap into the national soda wars.

Clements was born in 1914 in Windham Springs, Alabama. His mother named him after the US president in the belief that she had given birth to a future White House resident. His father felt the same, and trained his son to introduce himself as "Woodrow Wilson Clements, future president of the United States." Clements never reached the White House, but he did make it to the top of the Dr Pepper Company, where he used its new network of bottlers to turn the drink into a national, and then a global, brand. Dr Pepper presented itself as "America's Most Misunderstood Soft Drink," making its indefinable fruity flavor a selling point rather than a source of confusion. Sales rocketed. In 1974, Dr Pepper promoted itself as "The Most Original Soft Drink," and the company landed deals with supermarket chains that resulted in a tenfold jump in sales. By the launch of its "Be an Original—Be a Pepper" campaign in 1978 it was no longer a regional soda but a national player that was now being sold in Wendy's hamburger restaurants. The company had even successfully boosted its winter sales by pushing the idea that it was the only soda that could be drunk hot. Hot Dr Pepper, the company advised, should be made by heating the soda in a saucepan until it steams vigorously without boiling, before being served in a carafe with a slice of lemon and, optionally, a stick of cinnamon.

As Dr Pepper became America's number-four soda, 7Up found itself facing the distinct possibility that the Waco soda would soon overtake it

in sales. Feeling that it needed more marketing muscle, 7Up sold itself
to Philip Morris, the marketing giant that had turned Marlboro from an
unpopular ladies' cigarette into an icon of male America and made Miller
the nation's second favorite beer. Coke and Pepsi also responded to the rise
of Dr Pepper. Coke launched a pepper drink of its own called Mr Pibb in a
bid to stop its bottlers from producing Dr Pepper. But for one Pepsi executive it was the entrenched popularity of Dr Pepper in Dallas that was the
problem. Larry Smith was the vice president of Pepsi's bottling plants and
part of a new, more aggressive band of MBA-qualified executives who were
rising up the ranks of PepsiCo, the beverage and snack giant formed when
Pepsi-Cola took over Frito-Lay in 1965. The leading light of this gang of
rising stars was John Sculley, who became the vice president of marketing
at Pepsi-Cola in 1970. "All of us badly wanted to beat Coke," he wrote in his
autobiography. "This wasn't just a marketing war; it was a civil war, and the
South kept winning."

As Sculley took his marketing job the idea that Pepsi could beat Coke
was looking like more than a pipe dream. On the back of its Pepsi Generation campaigns, the company had made solid gains in the supermarkets,
narrowing Coke's lead. Pepsi knew that if it could displace Coca-Cola as
the number-one cola in the supermarkets that would open the doors of the
Coke-dominated fast-food chains. In short, win in the supermarkets, win
everywhere. But the Coca-Cola loyal southern states were a problem. Pepsi
seemed invisible in these Coca-Cola heartlands, so much so that many southerners called all soda Coke and market research suggested that people in the
South gave so little thought to Pepsi that they didn't even have a view about it.

So when Smith went to Dallas to fix the problems at the company's
struggling bottling plant, he found the picture depressing. Texas, he later
reported, was nothing short of a disaster. Not only was Pepsi behind Coke,
but it was also outperformed by Dr Pepper. Coke had 35 percent of the
market, Dr Pepper 25 percent, Pepsi a dismal 6 percent. Eager to boost
sales, Smith visited a major Dallas grocery chain and offered to pay for
ads and in-store displays to promote Pepsi. The grocery chain turned him
down flat, telling him it didn't need Pepsi. The incident convinced Smith
that Pepsi needed a different approach in Texas, one that was more direct

and aggressive than the company's sunny Pepsi Generation promotions. BBDO and Pepsi's ad men in New York resisted, arguing that a special campaign for Texas would undermine the drink's national message and that an aggressive promotion could destroy the drink's upbeat image.

Smith wouldn't take no for an answer and hired Bob Stanford, the creative director for 7-11 in Texas, to devise a campaign for the Lone Star State. Stanford organized a series of blind taste tests to see how people felt about Pepsi compared to Coke. He gave them a choice between two unmarked paper cups filled with cola and asked them to try both before picking the one they preferred. Pepsi won, even with loyal Coca-Cola drinkers. To be sure the findings were right Stanford carried out another two hundred blind taste tests, this time capturing the reactions using a hidden camera, and he found that the result was the same. It was a slim margin—52 percent for Pepsi against 48 percent for Coke—but enough for Pepsi to safely claim that people preferred its cola. Armed with these results the company turned the taste tests into an ad: the Pepsi Challenge.

In May 1975 the first Pepsi Challenge TV commercial aired in the Dallas–Fort Worth area. It showed a loyal Coke drinker testing two unidentified colas, only to be shocked when he opted for the taste of Pepsi. "Pepsi-Cola," he exclaimed. "Well, I'll be darned." More ads followed in Houston, where again Pepsi lagged far behind Coke and Dr Pepper. Again the Coca-Cola drinker picked Pepsi. The ads, with their spontaneous tone, local sights and people, and suggestion that viewers try the challenge for themselves, caused Pepsi sales to rise.

Coca-Cola was outraged at the aggressive campaign and at the claim that people preferred Pepsi over Coke. The company ordered its researchers to carry out its own taste tests, only to find—to its horror and surprise—that Pepsi came out on top. It tried accusing the ads of bias since in the ads the Pepsi cup had the letter M on it, which Coca-Cola claimed people preferred to the Q that adorned the Coca-Cola cups. The next day Pepsi responded by running another Pepsi Challenge ad that featured different letters on the cups but the same "Pepsi tastes better than Coke" message.

In 1977 when Sculley became president of Pepsi-Cola he decided the campaign should go national. The Pepsi Challenge became a sensation. The company turned the arrival of the Pepsi Challenge in each area into a major event, repainting Pepsi trucks to herald the coming of the challenge and inviting TV crews to film the public taste tests as they happened. For Pepsi's bottlers this was nerve-wracking stuff. What if Pepsi lost the challenge in their area? But it didn't. In town after town, city after city, Pepsi came out on top. Soon the Pepsi Challenge went international. In 1977 the campaign turned up at the Canadian National Exhibition in Toronto where it got Coca-Cola devotee Debbie Cowan to take up the challenge. "The commercials on TV are a bunch of hogwash," Cowan stated confidently before taking the taste test and picking out Pepsi. "I can't believe it," she squealed. "OK, I'm not skeptical, not any more." In Australia a blonde-haired surfer took the test on a beach and, inevitably, opted for Pepsi. "I'm going to go with Pepsi for sure," he told the camera after the result was revealed.

Coca-Cola struggled to respond. It tried to intimidate local Pepsi bottlers with threats of price wars and ran an ill-judged TV ad starring a redneck Coke drinker ranting about outsiders coming to Texas and "pulling their wily tricks," but both tactics failed to stop the march of the Pepsi Challenge. Soon the market research reports were indicating that Pepsi had narrowly overtaken Coca-Cola in the supermarket sales. While Pepsi's growth was mainly at the expense of smaller rivals like Royal Crown, the prospect of Pepsi pulling ahead in the supermarkets was frightening for Coke, as it knew that its New York rival would be after its lucrative fast-food contracts next. Coke decided to exploit its dominance of fast-food restaurants, raising prices there to build a war chest before making it clear to Pepsi bottlers that if they brought the Pepsi Challenge to their area, Coca-Cola would hit back hard with a major advertising offensive and unmatchable price cuts. The threat stopped the Pepsi Challenge in its tracks, as Pepsi bottlers chickened out of adopting the campaign. As the 1980s began Pepsi's taste test campaign ground to a halt.

But not before the Coke-beating campaign caught the attention of a Californian businessman named Steve Jobs, the cofounder of Apple Computer. The Pepsi Challenge was already running in Texas when Jobs and his friend Steve Wozniak started their home computer business in a garage in 1976. A year later they launched the Apple II, one of the first mass-produced home computers, and by 1982 their business had grown into a Fortune 500 company. While Apple's success was remarkable, the future looked less certain for the computer firm as it entered 1982. The IBM PC was taking the business world by storm and Commodore's low-priced VIC-20 computer was doing the same in the nation's homes. Jobs wasn't interested in fighting Commodore and other manufacturers of cheap home computers head on. He wanted to present the computer industry as a two-horse race between Apple and IBM that would make the likes of Commodore seem irrelevant—just as the battle between Coke and Pepsi had overshadowed other cola brands.

As it happened, Apple was also on the hunt for a new president. After failing to lure Don Estridge, the IBM man who created the PC, Jobs decided the company needed to look beyond Silicon Valley for its next boss. It didn't take long before he homed in on Sculley, the man under whom Pepsi-Cola had finally broken Coca-Cola's grip on the market. The Pepsi boss was the perfect fit: a marketing wizard capable of winning over Wall Street who had firsthand experience leading an underdog company to victory in a fight against an established rival. In late 1982 Apple sent its headhunter Gerry Roche to approach Sculley about the job. Sculley wasn't interested, but Roche persuaded him that it was worth meeting the exciting young leader of this technology success story anyway. So Sculley went to California to meet Jobs and see what all the fuss was about. He came away buzzing with ideas, and Jobs was equally excited. The pair met again in New York in January 1983 for dinner at the Four Seasons Hotel. As Jobs picked over his vegan meal, Sculley explained the ideas behind the Pepsi Generation and how they were selling a lifestyle rather than a product. Apple, the Pepsi-Cola boss told Jobs, has a chance to create the Apple Generation. Jobs lapped it up. The next morning Roche called Sculley to tell him that Jobs thought their evening together was the most exciting of his entire life.

Jobs was more convinced than ever that it had to be Sculley who became Apple's new president. He needed him to help create the Apple Generation. The two continued their awkward corporate courtship for another two months, eventually ending up spending a day together in New York touring the city's art museums. They talked money—a million-dollar salary and a million dollars just for signing up. But even then Sculley refused to commit. Maybe we should just be friends, Sculley told Jobs. The Apple founder remained silent for a while before looking Sculley in the eye and asking: "Do you want to spend the rest of your life selling sugared water, or do you want a chance to change the world?"

The question haunted Sculley. A few days later he accepted the job offer, and in May 1983 he started work at Apple. What followed was nothing less than the wholesale import of Pepsi's marketing philosophy into the California computer company. Sculley and Jobs devised a new approach to computer marketing to launch the Apple Macintosh computer that would be a far cry from the dry, wordy advertising that Apple and its competitors had been using with their lists of bits, bytes, and processor speeds. Instead Apple would present the Macintosh as a lifestyle choice. It would be the Pepsi of computing, the choice of the young, the free, and the cool. IBM would be the monolithic and outmoded competitor, the Coca-Cola of circuitry representing the status quo, boredom, and control. Commodore and the rest would have to settle for being 7Up, Royal Crown, or Dr Pepper. "We needed a campaign that would focus on a two-horse race to play off of Apple's underdog status," Sculley wrote in his biography *Odyssey: Pepsi to Apple*. "The advertising had to stake out our role as industry innovator in this two-horse race. Perhaps we could even stimulate a public computer war, not unlike the Cola Wars, because of the huge consumer interest in personal computers."

The 1984 launch of the Macintosh did just that. From the iconic Super Bowl commercial showing a young woman rebelling against a dismal world straight out of George Orwell's *1984* to the way Apple turned the arrival of its new computer into a media event, the Pepsi-inspired launch marked the point when the Silicon Valley pioneer stopped being just another tech company and became a business that sold a lifestyle. It was a marketing approach that transformed how computer technology was sold and would still be the basis of Apple's approach twenty years later when the iPod and iTunes turned Jobs's Pepsi-inspired dream of the Apple Generation into a reality. Andrea Cunningham, one of the public relations consultants who worked on the Macintosh launch, said the campaign brought the idea of turning technology launches into media events to the fore. "That was a John Sculley innovation, and I think it was something he had done at Pepsi," she told Stanford University in 2000. "It was more than just getting journalists to cover the product the way we wanted: it was about creating this mystique, this coolness, and this 'I'm on the inside' kind of thing."

While Sculley used the lessons of the Pepsi Generation to reinvent Apple, back in the world of soda the battle for cola dominance was heating up. In March 1981 Coke got a new chief executive: Roberto Goizueta, a Cuban born in November 1931. The son of a successful architect, Goizueta grew up in a wealthy district of Havana and attended the same private school as a sugar plantation owner's son named Fidel Castro. After finishing school, he studied chemical engineering at Yale before returning to Cuba to marry his childhood sweetheart Olguita in 1953. A year later, with his first child on the way, Goizueta spotted a job listing in a newspaper seeking an English-speaking chemist for an unnamed company. He applied and the mystery employer turned out to be Coca-Cola, who hired him as a quality control specialist.

He was still working there when Castro and his men marched into Havana in December 1958 and declared the country a Communist state. In the wake of Castro's revolution, life became tougher for Coca-Cola. Castro's soldiers repeatedly stopped Goizueta in the streets, hoping to find company secrets in his briefcase. In one incident, armed Cuban officials turned up at the Coca-Cola plant and ordered Goizueta to stop coloring the drink with unpatriotic caramel and use burnt sugar instead. They only relented when he cooked up a batch using their preferred coloring and they discovered how vile the result tasted. As relations between the United States and Cuba deteriorated, Coca-Cola worried that its plant would be nationalized by Castro, a concern Goizueta shared. In spring 1960 he and his wife sent their three children to Miami to live with their grandparents; shortly after he and Olguita did the same with nothing but two suitcases to their name. After they left Cuba, Castro seized control of the Coca-Cola plant and banished the drink from the country. Coca-Cola found Goizueta a new job in its Latin American division and within four years he had worked his way into the Atlanta head office. By 1979 he was a vice president and one of just two people in the company who knew the secret formula.

A striking figure, always dressed in sharp tailored suits and chain smoking his Kool menthol cigarettes, Goizueta did not believe in sacred cows. So when Robert Woodruff, who still acted as overseer of the company despite being ninety-one and having suffered two strokes, put Goizueta in charge, the Cuban executive set out to change Coca-Cola's style. He envisaged a feistier Coca-Cola that would be unafraid of change and happy to hit Pepsi where it hurt.

One of Goizueta's first moves was to rid the company of the nonbeverage divisions it had accumulated since the mergers and acquisition mania of the 1960s. Out went the wine business, the water purification division Aqua-Chem, and the Mexican inland shrimp farms. Minute Maid, however, stayed. Coke had bought Minute Maid back in September 1960 for $70 million. Founded in 1945 as the Florida Foods Corporation, the company created the frozen orange juice concentrate market, a revolutionary product that offered shoppers the chance to drink orange juice all year round. The product made Minute Maid a corporate success story, but, under Coca-Cola's guidance, the company would instigate a second revolution in orange juice. The task of overseeing Minute Maid's operations fell to Coca-Cola executive Ben Oehlert, who saw a company—no, an entire industry—in desperate need of Coke's soft drink marketing savvy. "Look at orange juice advertising," he commented. "It tells mothers to see to it that the kiddies take a four-ounce dose of the stuff at breakfast and forget it. It tells old folks to drink it to prevent colds. People don't like medicine; they don't like to do things that are good for them."

Coke decided that this talk of health, colds, and flus simply would not do and transformed how Minute Maid promoted its juice. Instead of presenting it as a source of vitamin C, Minute Maid's orange juice would now be a refreshing drink suitable for all occasions and times of day. The shift in marketing strategy shook up the entire juice business, and the era of orange juice being sold as a medicine was history. As Oehlert put it, "The fundamental change that Coca-Cola has brought to Minute Maid's policies was to go from the business of selling orange juice as a breakfast medicine to the business of selling oranges in any and every form the public will take them."

Having offloaded the company's excess weight, Goizueta turned his attentions to Coca-Cola's core business of selling soda and, as he told Coke employees at a convention in Palm Springs, California, under his leadership the company would take risks. "The days are gone in which an inflexible adherence to a sacred cow will ever give renewed impetus and breathe life into a competitor like it happened when we chose to stick only with the six-and-a-half-ounce bottle for a number of years when our main competitor was going to a larger size," he said.

Those sacred cows included the Coca-Cola formula. Goizueta knew the Coca-Cola recipe, and as a chemist, he knew it was just that: a recipe, not some holy relic with magic ingredients. His job was to increase the value of Coca-Cola shares, not to defend tradition. So he started reducing the amount of sugar in Coke, replacing it with high fructose corn syrup (HFCS), which was cheaper than sugar but tasted pretty much the same. By the end of 1984, Coca-Cola fountain syrup contained no sugar, just HFCS, and sugar accounted for just a quarter of the sweetener used in the bottled and canned versions of the drink. He used the move to signal to Pepsi that Coke was ready to fight back by announcing the recipe change as Pepsi's bottlers gathered for their annual conference. The news that Coke had cut its overheads by dumping sugar stirred up unrest among its rival's bottlers, who now wanted Pepsi to follow suit so they could reap the savings, despite concerns from Roger Enrico, Pepsi-Cola's new man at the top, that HFCS could harm the taste of Pepsi.

Goizueta also dusted off plans for Diet Coke. The concept of launching Diet Coke had been floating around since the early 1960s, when the company was formulating Tab. In 1979 the company revived the idea and developed plans to launch Diet Coke after discovering that just putting Tab in a Diet Coke–branded container would cause a large spike in the proportion of people who said they preferred it to Diet Pepsi. But after the initial work the company's chief executive Paul Austin pulled the plug without explanation. On taking over from Austin, Goizueta relaunched the project, and in August 1982 Diet Coke arrived in a blaze of publicity supported with the slogan "Just for the taste of it, Diet Coke." By the end of 1983 it was the number-one-selling diet soda; a year later it had displaced 7Up as America's number-three carbonated soft drink.

While most of its success was due to the brand, it was also the first diet soda to use the new artificial sweetener aspartame, also known as NutraSweet. Aspartame tasted better than saccharin and, at that time, was free from the cancer scares that so damaged the image of diet soda in the late 1960s and early 1970s. It was also only available to Coke initially, as the company bought all the supplies before Pepsi could react. By the summer of 1984 Diet Coke was sweetened with 100 percent aspartame while Diet Pepsi was stuck with saccharin and its metallic aftertaste for a couple more years.

Diet Coke's launch revived interest in sugar-free soda, and as diet drinks gobbled up market share, it only added to the pressure on 7Up. Diet drinks, Dr Pepper, and Coke's lemon-lime soda Sprite were bad enough, but the Uncola was also finding itself losing ground to a small but fast-growing beverage called Mountain Dew. Mountain Dew started as a joke between two brothers, Ally and Barney Hartman. Back in 1926 the pair opened an Orange Crush bottling plant in Augusta, Georgia, only to watch their business fall apart during the Great Depression. Despite the failure, Orange Crush offered them the rights to bottle the drink in Knoxville, so the pair pulled up stakes and moved to the Tennessee city to start over. To their disappointment they found that Natural Set-Up, the lemon-lime soda that they loved to drink with Old Taylor Kentucky Bourbon, wasn't available in their new hometown. So they concocted an imitation for their personal use and named it Mountain Dew, a slang term for moonshine.

Mountain Dew became an inside joke among the Hartmans and their friends. One day in 1946 the Hartman brothers decided to amuse themselves by pretending to launch it at a soft drinks convention. To prepare for the fake launch they asked John Brichetto, a neighbor who liked drawing cartoons, to create a label they could put on some bottles to take to the convention. Riffing on the Mountain Dew name, Brichetto drew a shoeless hillbilly carrying a rifle and a bottle of moonshine. At the pretend launch in their hotel suite the Hartmans spun a tale of brewing it at their very own moonshine still in the Tennessee mountains. It was a joke, but on the train home they were joined by Charlie Gordon, owner of a Johnson City bottling plant called Tri-City Beverage, which made Hires Root Beer and a grape soda created by the Tip Corporation. As they drank bourbon and chatted, Gordon expressed an interest in bottling their joke soda. In 1951 the Hartmans finally decided to test out Mountain Dew on the market-place, launching it with its hillbilly image intact and the slogan "It'll tickle yore innards." It flopped. Gordon bought the rights to bottle it in Johnson City in 1954, but again it struggled. In 1957 the Hartmans sold off the strug-gling brand to the Tip Corporation.

At the same time over in Johnson City, Tri-City Beverage had a new boss, Bill Bridgforth. Keen to save money, Bridgforth started dropping branded drinks and building a range of Tri-City sodas. One drink he ditched was Sun Drop, a fizzing mix of orange and lemon billed as a "citrus lemon-ade" that had been created by J.F. Manufacturing, the St. Louis business that used to supply Al Capone's soda business with root beer extract. Bridgforth replaced Sun Drop with a citrus lemonade of his own creation, but while people loved the taste the brand failed to connect. So in 1960, feeling that Mountain Dew had a good brand but an unpopular taste, he started sell-ing his citrus lemonade under the Mountain Dew name. By 1962 the Tip Corporation had followed his lead. Two years later the drink had captured enough of the market in the southeastern states for Pepsi to buy the rights to the greenish-yellow beverage.

Pepsi kept the hillbilly image, hoping to tap into the popularity of hill-billies in the wake of the hit TV show *The Beverly Hillbillies.* To help relaunch the drink, the company hired an actor who spent a week in Philadelphia pretending to be a hillbilly from the real-life village of Turkeyscratch, Ten-nessee. The actor spent his time causing traffic jams as he drove around in a bright red 1929 Model A Ford weighed down with jugs of Mountain Dew and petitioning the city authorities to let him open outhouses for making moonshine on Philadelphia's parking lots.

For a while the hillbilly branding worked, but by the start of the 1970s it was clear it wasn't gelling with the nation, so Pepsi dropped it for a less unusual image that was equally unsuccessful. With Mountain Dew making little progress, Pepsi cut back on its advertising of the beverage, but then something strange happened: Mountain Dew started selling. The drink was growing by word of mouth, and so fast that by 1976 its sales had tripled in just two years despite Pepsi's limited promotional efforts.

As Mountain Dew's sales gathered momentum, rivals started launching their own citrus lemonades hoping to cash in. One of the first clones was Rondo from Schweppes, which had finally broken into the United States with its tonic water during the 1950s, thanks to a promotional campaign fronted by its US boss, former British Royal Air Force wing commander Edward Whitehead. With his distinctive ginger hair, long goatee, and English mustache, Whitehead became a well-known figure in America thanks to ads that showed him touring the United States and introducing people to the refined pleasure of the company's mixers and the British cocktail gin and tonic. Thanks to that twenty-year advertising campaign and the company's 1969 merger with the British chocolate giant Cadbury, Schweppes became a sizable force in the US beverage market. Even so, Rondo flopped. Coke did better with its enduring imitation Mello Yello, but it still couldn't match or stop Mountain Dew's rise.

With Mountain Dew coming up fast, 7Up's owners Philip Morris dropped the Uncola campaign and in March 1982 hit back by promoting the lemon-lime drink's lack of caffeine in the hope of attracting health-conscious shoppers. The "Never had it, never will" campaign did little more than spark a rapid counterattack from 7Up's rivals. Before the year was out, people could buy caffeine-free Coke, Pepsi, and Dr Pepper, and 7Up's anticaffeine attack had been defused. Philip Morris never found the magic marketing formula for 7Up. In 1986 it sold 7Up's international operations to Pepsi and two years later offloaded the US business to Dr Pepper.

The defensive rush of Mountain Dew, Dr Pepper, and caffeine-free sodas reflected just how competitive the business had become. The average American was drinking three times as much soda in 1980 as in 1950, guzzling through the equivalent of four hundred twelve-ounce cans a year. As sales soared every sliver of market share became immensely valuable. Even a 0.1 percent slice of the market was worth millions of dollars, and with so much at stake no soda company was willing to give any ground.

So when new flavors proved popular, beverage companies would rush in with their own versions to grab a slice of action or—at the very least—stop their competitors from reaping the rewards. If one company offered a cherry cola then everyone was going to have a cherry cola. This race for market share also inspired a rash of acquisitions and mergers. Coca-Cola snapped up Barq's root beer, Thums Up, and Inca Kola. Pepsi followed up its purchase of 7Up's global business and Mountain Dew by buying Mug root beer. Cadbury Schweppes went on a buying spree, absorbing dozens of famous brands including Hires, A&W, Canada Dry, Dr Pepper, 7Up, Vernors, Royal Crown, and Orangina. By the early 2000s, Coca-Cola, PepsiCo, and Cadbury Schweppes would control more than 90 percent of the soda market.

Advertising became a crucial battleground as the three soda giants fought to outspend and outsell one another. In 1983 Coca-Cola paid big bucks to get the actor and comedian Bill Cosby to star in TV commercials in which he needled Pepsi by holding up a can of Coke and saying: "If you're number two or three or seven, you know what you want to be when you grow up." Pepsi hit back in late 1983 by hiring Michael Jackson, the world's biggest star, to front its revival of the Pepsi Generation concept "Pepsi, The Choice of a New Generation." To get Jackson on board the company handed over an eye-watering $5 million, making the campaign the most expensive ever made at that point in time, even before the cameras rolled. Roger Enrico, Pepsi-Cola's boss, initially balked at the price tag but relented because, as Jackson's promoter Don King told him, "This is Michael Jackson. He is bigger than God."

The deal involved two commercials, sponsorship of the Jacksons' reunion tour, and a personal appearance by Jackson at the press conference where the deal would be announced. Enrico met Jackson for the first time at the New York City press conference. It was, he recalled in his book *The Other Guy Blinked*, an awkward encounter. "What do you say when you meet Michael Jackson? He's so shy he makes you shy. So we stand next to each other and don't say much of anything. After a bit, I make some small talk. And then Michael leans over and whispers in my ear. And what he says is: 'Roger, I'm going to make Coke wish they were Pepsi.'"

But when it came to filming the ads, Enrico probably wished he worked at Coke. After showing the softly spoken pop star the storyboards for the ads, Jackson said it was all fine except he didn't like the music or the commercial. When Pepsi's ad men asked why, the singer responded that his face was on camera too long. "I don't want you to show me for more than a few seconds," he replied. The Pepsi advertising team was stunned; $5 million and he won't let us show his face for more than four seconds? But Jackson insisted. Instead, he told them, they should film his shoes, his gloves, and his silhouette before revealing his face at the very end. There was better news on the music. Why don't you use "Billie Jean" instead, Jackson asked. He didn't have to ask twice. Pepsi dumped their jingle and happily adopted Jackson's mega hit. As anticipation about the Jackson ad spread, the music video channel MTV offered to broadcast it for free if it got an exclusive. Free airtime? OK, said Pepsi.

All was going well. The world's biggest star, free advertising on MTV, "Billie Jean," huge public excitement. Then on January 27, 1984, as the ad was being filmed in Los Angeles, disaster struck. As Jackson danced down a staircase the magnesium flash bombs surrounding him fired early, setting his gelled hair on fire. For a few moments he danced on unaware. "I was dancing down this ramp and turning around, spinning, not knowing I was on fire," Jackson recalled in his biography *Moonwalk*. "Suddenly I felt my hands reflexively going to my head in an attempt to smother the flames." As Jackson was rushed to the hospital with third-degree burns, the Pepsi advertising team looked on in horror. "I remember the medical people putting me on a cot and the guys from Pepsi were so scared they couldn't even bring themselves to check on me," wrote Jackson.

Jackson threatened to sue Pepsi but eventually settled for a payment of $1.5 million, which the star used to fund a burns center at the Los Angeles hospital that treated him. The world's most expensive commercial had just gotten even more expensive, but the advertising deal of the decade was still on. And when the Jackson ad premiered in February 1984, more than eighty-three million people tuned in to watch what was, after all, just a Pepsi commercial.

But while the high-profile commercials captured the imagination of the public and the media, the real fight for soda dominance was an invisible war taking place in the streets, the stores, and restaurants around us. These, says former Pepsi executive Bob McGarrah, were the trenches of the Cola War: "The cola wars were fought in the vending channel, the on-premises channel and the store display stands."

The fast-food chains were one of the biggest of these under-the-radar battlefields. Soda had already played a crucial role in the birth of fast food. Back in 1919, a real estate developer named Roy Allen visited Tucson, Arizona, on business and while he was there, tried a root beer made by a local pharmacist. Impressed, Allen bought the rights to the recipe and later that year opened a roadside restaurant in Lodi, California, that sold hamburgers and his root beer to passing drivers.

It proved so popular that he opened a second, equally successful root beer and burger restaurant in 1920 in Stockton, a few miles south of Lodi. Thrilled with the success and aware of the growing market for roadside service, Allen teamed up with one of his employees, Frank Wright, and formed a partnership called A&W. They opened five outlets around Sacramento. While the food and soda remained the same, these stands focused on serving passing traffic rather than sit-down indoor service. The fast-food drive-in had been born. As the momentum behind the A&W stands grew, Allen bought out Wright and adopted a franchise model that foreshadowed the business models of the fast-food chains that came in its wake. The franchise model worked wonders and A&W Root Beer Drive-Ins spread across America as fast as the roads could be built. By 1941 more than 260 A&Ws had opened across the nation.

The ideas that A&W tapped into with its pioneering fast-food stands evolved rapidly, and by the 1960s a burger joint called McDonald's had become the leader of this culinary revolution. McDonald's started out as a drive-in barbecue joint in San Bernardino, California with carhop service, but in 1948 the McDonald brothers decided to reinvent their popular restaurant. They wanted to serve their customers faster, and their answer was the "Speedee Service System." The carhops were fired, replaced by self-service. Out went the crockery, in came paper cups and plates. To stop wasting time with bills and tips, they got customers to pay up front for their food, which was now churned out in seconds on a cooking assembly line modeled on Henry Ford's car factories.

The new McDonald's with its instant service and standardized meals proved exceedingly popular, but the McDonald brothers barely imagined their drive-in would expand beyond San Bernardino's city limits, let alone spread throughout America and the world. But while the brothers didn't believe they had invented the restaurant of the future, Ray Kroc did. Kroc first got a taste for business while working as a soda jerk at his uncle's fountain in his birthplace of Oak Park, Illinois. "That was where I learned you could influence people with a smile and enthusiasm and sell them a sundae when what they'd come for was a cup of coffee," he recalled in his biography *Grinding it Out*. Kroc first noticed McDonald's after they ordered an unusually large number of the Multimixer milkshake machines he was selling. Curious, he traveled to California to find out why and was so impressed he bought the right to sell McDonald's franchises. Under Kroc's leadership McDonald's grew into the biggest fast-food chain in the world and became the trailblazer of a new generation of restaurant chains that included Burger King, KFC, Pizza Hut, and Taco Bell.

For every fast-food chain, soda was a major source of profit. People almost always wanted a drink with their food, and soda was incredibly cheap to make. A cup of soda would cost mere cents to make but could sell for more than ten times that amount. So great was the markup on soda that fizzy drinks were the most profitable item on fast-food menus. With so much profit to be made from peddling soda, fast-food chains did everything they could to get customers to drink more of it and began increasing serving sizes so that they could make even more from selling beverages. With fast-food chains selling so much fizzy pop, soda companies clamored to win their business. But most fast-food chains wanted the number-one soda, and Coca-Cola won most of these lucrative deals, including the biggest deal of them all: McDonald's.

Coke's advantage in fast food was a constant source of frustration for its rivals. Dr Pepper could infiltrate Coke's stronghold thanks to its classification as a pepper drink, but rival colas faced an uphill struggle in trying to persuade fast-food joints to abandon the market leader. Pepsi tried undercutting Coke without success and eventually resorted to offering generous deals mainly to give the fast-food companies something to use to push down

Coke's prices. In 1976 Royal Crown decided that if it couldn't negotiate its way into fast food, it would buy its way in and snapped up the beef sandwich chain Arby's. PepsiCo followed suit, buying Pizza Hut, Taco Bell, and KFC and converting them to Pepsi sellers. While these acquisitions gave Pepsi a significant presence in fast-food restaurants, it also caused several chains to refuse to buy Pepsi, as they didn't want to fund a rival.

With Coca-Cola dominant in fast food, its rivals looked to the more open battleground of the supermarkets and convenience stores as the prime way to boost sales. In these stores they used a mixture of sweetheart deals, clever display equipment, bigger and better value bottles offering more pop per dollar, and a bit of bullying to make their drinks stand out on the shelves. To grab shoppers' attention soda companies developed equipment that would make their products stand out, which they then handed out to the major retailers. They built reinforced displays that could withstand constant collisions with supermarket carts and constructed increasingly elaborate coolers to keep their soda temptingly cold.

One of the most audacious was a trapezoid Pepsi cooler with three glass-fronted doors that was designed to sit at the end of supermarket checkouts, where it could offer chilled drinks within easy reach regardless of where a customer stood. "It was expensive, but we captured that end-aisle space with it," says McGarrah, who designed the cooler. "Every marketplace wanted it. We said: 'Fine, but if you want that machine, you have to give us that space for two years.' So for two years we owned that end-aisle space and Coke was shut out. That was worth millions of dollars of sales. It was all driven by equipment. You bring it to the store owner and say, 'Look! I have a better mousetrap than the other guy. It will help you sell more product and when you sell more product you make more profit, and we make some more profit too.'"

When not using flashy equipment to gain the in-store edge, soda companies used financial incentives to get their drinks into the best in-store locations and keep the competition at bay. They offered stores discounts on their products or large one-off payments to shops that put their brands on the sought-after eye-level shelves or moved their rivals' beverages to the bottom shelves, which would require shoppers to go to the trouble of bending down to reach them. Alternatively, the deals would require retailers to have more coolers filled with their beverages than their rivals', or to display their drinks in the lucrative impulse-buy zone at the checkout. These deals were also a way for soda companies to get their less popular brands into shops, a tactic that played a crucial role in helping Coca-Cola get its sports drink Powerade into stores back when Quaker Oats' Gatorade had sewn up most of that market.

Usually these deals would merely seek to give a company's drinks greater prominence, but in the early 1990s Pepsi and Coca-Cola started offering deals requiring stores to stop selling rival sodas altogether, carving up the retail landscape into pockets of Coke beverages and Pepsi beverages. In 1994 the Royal Crown Cola bottler in Paris, Texas, found itself on the receiving end of a spate of these deals. As its cola was shut out of stores, its sales collapsed, hurtling down to a quarter of what they had been just a few months earlier. The company sued on antitrust grounds, but while Pepsi made an out-of-court settlement, Coca-Cola refused to give way. Coke initially lost the case but got the decision overturned after appealing to the Texas Supreme Court, which ruled that while such deals had the potential to be anticompetitive there was no evidence suggesting this was the case. Shoppers could go to other stores if they wanted and, the court concluded, Royal Crown seemed more a victim of too much rather than too little competition.

The war of attrition in retail may have been intense, but it looked tame compared to the battle for vending machine dominance. Soda companies found themselves not only fighting each other but also facing down mobsters and armed criminals in their crusade to offer ice-cold refreshment. The first coin-operated soda vending machines had appeared in the late 1930s, and after World War II ended they rapidly spread across America. By 1952 more than six hundred thousand of these silent soda sellers had been installed across the nation, dishing out millions of bottles of pop every year to impulse buyers outside gas stations, in hotels, in shops, in the street, in the workplace, and pretty much everywhere people went. By the end of the 1950s vending machines accounted for 11 percent of Coca-Cola's sales. "Typically vending machines were free to the retailer, but they had to do x cases a week or a month to keep it and they paid for the electricity," says McGarrah. "In return, we were getting these signs—big, beautiful signs. You'd drive past the gas station and there would be vending machines with signs bigger than the gas station's and when the station shut down at night, all you would see were the vending machines all lit up. Even if a place didn't sell much it had a big impact."

Vending machines were also an ideal way to get customers to try new drinks for the first time, says McGarrah: "We called vending 'paid cold sampling'. When Pepsi bought Mug root beer it put it in every vending machine. People would try it out of the vending machine outside the super-market and then buy a six-pack inside. You'd sell them a cold one there and then they would buy warm ones to take home."

Vending machines not only attracted sales, they also attracted trouble. For the delivery drivers who would stock the machines and collect the cash, it was a job fraught with danger. "My wife's brother worked on one of those trucks, and, one time, a guy jumped on his truck and stuck a gun in his face, robbed him of the money," recalls McGarrah. "Another guy I knew carried a gun. This guy jumped on the passenger side of his truck, stuck the gun in and he says: 'OK, OK, I'll get out, I'm going to come round the front of the truck and give you the money box'. He had the box but he also had his gun. So when he got out of sight of the guy he held the box up and pulled out his gun. Got to the front of the truck. Bang! Bang! Shot the guy dead. One year later a guy jumps on his truck—bang!—he shoots him off the truck. It was like the Wild West, fricking crazy."

It wasn't just random criminals who saw opportunity in the hun-dreds, sometimes thousands, of dollars the vending machines swallowed. Coin-operated soda machines were also a handy racket for the Mafia. Mob-sters found the cash-based business of vending machines a handy tool for money laundering. Some would set up vending machine businesses and then shovel the money they made from drugs and other criminal activities into the machines so they could declare it legitimately without any expecta-tion that they could prove where the cash originated. Others would fill their Pepsi and Coca-Cola branded machines with cheap knock-offs for extra profit or simply skim money off the top of what they made while telling the IRS they sold far less soda than they really did. "The vending business historically has been a very lucrative way to make money disappear and a great way to wash money on the other side," says McGarrah. "If you've got drug money coming in and own a vending machine business, it's the most successful vending business you ever saw. For a machine that a normal person would make $400 a week from, you make $4,000 and you've put drug money into a legitimate business."

While Pepsi and Coke tried to catch some of the criminal elements who operated on the fringes of soda vending, it didn't always go according to plan. "The people stealing from the vending machines were organized. They had keys and everything," recalls McGarrah. "We set up one guy in Orlando who we knew was breaking into the machines at this hotel. We set up the camera in a room to watch the vending machine right outside the hotel room. We thought we were so good. So we do this and then all go to off to dinner together. The guy breaks into the room and steals all the video equipment!"

Failed stings aside, by the middle of the 1980s the trench warfare in the supermarkets and streets, the promotional blitz, the barrage of new flavors, ever-growing container sizes, and rush of mergers were going Pepsi's way. Even the fast-food companies were warming to Pepsi, with the company scoring a major victory when it persuaded Burger King to drop Coke and buy Pepsi. As 1984 began Coca-Cola was worried. In the 1950s it had outsold Pepsi two to one, but now its lead was just 4.9 percent, and Pepsi was ahead in retail by a whisker. The Pepsi Challenge had persuaded plenty of people to reassess their cola loyalties too. In 1972 18 percent of soda drinkers only drank Coke; now only 4 percent would drink nothing but Coca-Cola. Coke wondered what was going wrong. It had the ads, twice as many vending machines, the fast-food advantage, a competitive price, and the world's biggest brand. Everything seemed to be in order. As it searched for an explanation it couldn't help but keep coming back to the message of the Pepsi Challenge that maybe people just preferred Pepsi. Maybe tastes had changed and people now wanted a sweeter soda. Could it be, the company's executives wondered, that the secret formula wasn't that good after all?

With its market research studies confirming people's preference for Pepsi, Goizueta decided it was time to slay the ultimate sacred cow and initiated a project to develop and test an alternative Coca-Cola formula. For months the company created and tested new recipes, trying out alternative formulas on thousands of people in blind taste tests that they explained away as an experiment with a new production process. But even as they homed in on a Pepsi-beating formula, whenever the company's market researchers asked people about changing the Coca-Cola formula, the answer was a resounding no. Budweiser sure, Pepsi fine, Coke never. Yet the warning signs went ignored. By September 1984 the company had hit on a new, sweeter formula that significantly outperformed Pepsi in test after test. With a better cola in the bag the company now had to decide what to do with it.

One suggestion was to launch it as a separate cola, but that risked suggesting something was wrong with regular Coca-Cola. That tactic could also split their market and hand the number-one-soda crown to Pepsi. By the end of 1984 Coca-Cola's senior executives had reached their conclusion: they would replace the old formula with the new flavor. They decided to launch the new Coke in 1985 so that it didn't interfere with the celebrations it had planned for its one hundredth anniversary in 1986. In April 1985 Goizueta began hinting that something big was on the way. In an interview with *Financial News* magazine Goizueta gave a tantalizing response when asked about the news that Coke had lost another percent of market share while Pepsi had gained another 1.5 percent: "We will soon be unfolding what is probably the strongest marketing program in the history of the company behind our brand Coca-Cola."

On Friday April 19, 1985, Pepsi-Cola boss Roger Enrico got a call from a man he nicknamed "Deep Palate," a Coke insider who regularly tipped him off about what his archrival was up to. Deep Palate told him that Coca-Cola had summoned its bottlers to Atlanta for an unknown reason. A few moments later, Enrico got word that Coke was holding a big press conference in New York the following Tuesday. After a bit more digging he discovered the big secret: Coke had a new amazing formula. Pepsi was shocked. This it didn't expect, and if the new formula Coke had was so good that they were willing to tear up the secret formula, it had to be a serious threat. Pepsi's bosses spent the day in the doldrums worrying about how to respond. Then, while driving home on Manhattan's Franklin D. Roosevelt East River Drive, Pepsi vice president Joe McCann had a revelation that almost caused him to crash his car. This wasn't an offensive move by Coke but an admission of defeat. He called Enrico. We've been looking at this the wrong way, he told him. They are admitting Pepsi is better by doing this; they've lost and we've won the Cola War.

Instantly a strategy to undermine Coke's relaunch came together.

To announce its victory, Pepsi bought full-page ads in the country's leading newspapers, to run on the day of Coca-Cola's announcement. It then prepared a $6 million promotional assault that included dishing out coupons for free Pepsi so that Coke drinkers could get a taste of the winner of the Cola War, and also started booking airtime for a TV commercial it had in the bag called "Archaeology." Set in a Pepsi-drinking future, the ad showed an archeologist leading a group of students around a twentieth-century ruin. One student picks up an object covered in mud. "Professor, what is it?" she asks. The professor cleans off the mud to reveal a dusty Coke bottle. He looks at it with a quizzical expression and replies: "I have no idea."

As Pepsi's ads hit the newsstands on April 23, Coca-Cola prepared to reveal its new formula to more than two hundred reporters, TV crews, and photographers at the Vivian Beaumont Theatre in New York City. The new formula, Goizueta told them, was the result of nearly two hundred thousand consumer taste tests. The best, he declared, just got better. But thanks to Pepsi's publicity team, the reporters were already primed with critical questions. As the question-and-answer session dragged on, it was becoming clear that Coca-Cola's relaunch was going badly wrong. One reporter asked Goizueta to describe the new taste. He stumbled around muttering about "a more harmonious flavor" as reporters smirked. "Assuming it's a success, are you planning on reformulating Diet Coke?" asked another. Goizueta irritably replied: "No. And I don't assume that it is a success. It is a success."

If the sixty-minute barrage of questions left the Coca-Cola boss feeling bruised, it was nothing compared to what the team answering the calls to its consumer hotline were feeling. Within hours of the announcement more than a thousand people had called to express their shock and dismay. The next day even more people called in to express their disgust. The next day, even more. Once people started to try the new Coca-Cola, even more again. One caller declared: "There are two things I don't ever want to change. My Coke and my man, in that order." Another said: "The sorrow is knowing not only won't I ever enjoy the real Coke again, but my children and grandchildren won't either."

Across the country loyal Coca-Cola drinkers rushed to stores to stockpile the last cans and bottles of their treasured soda before it vanished for good. One eleven-year-old wrote a letter to tell Coca-Cola she was angry because her little sister hadn't stopped crying since they announced the change and she was sick of her whimpering. Another Coke fan wrote to Robert Woodruff, who had died in March, to express her anguish, telling the deceased Coca-Cola boss that "you boys made a BIG mistake."

Customers talked of betrayal, of the news of the reformulation being like hearing that a loved one had died, of the destruction of an American icon. Coca-Cola staff found anger wherever they went. In Marietta, Georgia, a Coca-Cola deliveryman dropping off the drink at a supermarket was attacked by a woman brandishing an umbrella who screamed: "You bastard! You ruined it! It tastes like shit!" A Pepsi delivery driver who witnessed the scene burst out laughing, only for the furious Coke drinker to turn on him: "You stay out of it. This is family business. Yours is worse than shit." Coke's West German operation, which was next in line after the United States to introduce the new formula, claimed it was too busy launching Cherry Coke to handle another launch, in order to receive a stay of execution. Sales of Coca-Cola plunged, falling 10 percent in some states. Nielsen market researchers reported that Coca-Cola had lost a 2.5 percent chunk of market share as a result of the new Coke, a slice worth $625 million.

With no letup in the backlash in sight, Coca-Cola decided to eat humble pie. On July 10 the company announced it had listened to its customers and was bringing the original formula back as Coca-Cola Classic, which would be sold alongside the new Coke. The reversal not only quelled the storm but made customers fall in love with the company all over again. The deluge of angry calls was replaced by an outpouring of love. "You have given us back our dream," one grateful Coke fan wrote. Another told the company, "I feel like a lost friend is returning home."

New Coke remained on sale, but it would die a long, slow death. As soon as Coca-Cola Classic returned, McDonald's dumped new Coke and within a year the revived original was outselling its sweeter offspring ten to one. By 2000 new Coke had been, in the company's own words, "phased out and totally eliminated." New Coke proved to be one of the biggest blunders in marketing history.

Yet what seemed like a disaster for Coca-Cola turned out not to be the moment that Pepsi won the Cola War but the moment that Coca-Cola reconnected with its consumers. The outburst of passion among loyal Coca-Cola fans caused many Americans to remember why they liked the drink. Somehow it took the threat of losing the soda that had become part of the furniture to reignite the love for brand. Soon Coca-Cola sales were heading toward new heights. So strong was the rebirth after the new Coke fiasco that some accused the company of engineering the whole shambles in some kind of soda conspiracy. But that wasn't the case. As Coca-Cola president Don Keough put it, "We are not that dumb and we are not that smart."

By the end of the 1980s Pepsi's advances in the Cola War had ground to a halt. The battle continued, of course, as the soda giants flung Molotov cocktails of celebrity endorsements, vending machine innovations, retailer contracts, and new flavors at each other. But for all the heat generated, there would—in America, at least—be no big breakthroughs beyond the steady growth of Pepsi's dark horse Mountain Dew, which had risen to become the country's fourth most popular soda by the year 2000.

It was a high-profile, sales-driving stalemate, though, and in 1998 soda sales in America hit an all-time high. The average American now drank the equivalent of 576 twelve-ounce cans of soda every year. The Cola War with its big promotions and clashes over retail appeal had lifted American soda consumption to incredible heights. It had, almost unseen, changed the very environments we shopped in, smashed advertising records, delivered one of the biggest marketing misjudgments of all time, armed Apple with the marketing tools it would use to grow into the biggest company by stock market value in American history, and helped fast-food chains rake in the profits. But as carbonated soft drinks entered their fourth century, the tide of almost uninterrupted upward growth was about to come to a screeching halt.

10

Beverage Backlash

The perennial topic of conversation at the Rapp family home was soda. It was, after all, the family business, and their bottling plants pumped out most of the 7Up, Canada Dry, and Dr Pepper in upstate New York. "Beverages for me are a way of life," says C. J. Rapp, whose father Joseph built their bottling empire. "I worked in my father's factory in the summers from the age of twelve onwards." So when the Rapps got together over meals at their home in Rochester, New York, their discussions usually came around to the state of the soft drink industry. In 1983, these conversations had taken a downbeat tone.

It wasn't because soda wasn't selling; in fact, it had never been bigger. What upset the Rapps was that soda seemed to be losing its magic, and the new diet and caffeine-free sodas landing on the nation's shelves were to blame. "Americans at that time were going through their first-ever wave of health-conscious products and starting to understand, arguably for the first time, the concept of moderation," Rapp recalls. "We felt that the soft drink giants were abandoning their roots. When you look back at history, soft drinks were intended to be an indulgence, consumed for no other reason than pleasure. They were never intended to be health foods, and the large companies had begun running campaigns that were, for want of a better term, apologetic."

It was a conversation topic that refused to go away. Time and time again they talked about how Big Soda was abandoning everything that made fizz special as they tried to capture the health-aware drinker. The Rapps were still talking about it two years later when they hit on the idea of launching a new soda, a soda that would take the industry back to its roots and be proud, rather than ashamed, of being full of fun, sugary sweetness and the tingling buzz of caffeine. "We saw an opportunity to pull in the complete opposite direction," says Rapp. "So instead of less sugar or no sugar and less or no caffeine, we did the opposite and came up with Jolt Cola."

Launched in March 1985, Jolt swam against the health tide. It offered its drinkers more sugar—and real cane sugar at that too, not the high fructose corn syrup stuff to which the big soda makers had switched to extract a few more cents out of every drink they sold. It also came with as much added caffeine as the law would allow. "The caffeine level of Jolt was literally twice that of Coke and Pepsi, which brought us to the Food and Drug Administration maximum," says Rapp. "At the time Coke and Pepsi were thirty-six to thirty-eight milligrams per twelve ounces. Jolt was seventy-two milligrams."

This amount was still significantly less than the one hundred milligrams or more of caffeine that could be found in a twelve-ounce cup of coffee, but compared to the average cola, Jolt certainly lived up to its name. "There wasn't anything, at least in the United States, along the lines of cold coffee then," recalls Rapp. "If you wanted caffeine most Americans found it in a hot cup of coffee. Jolt became the espresso cola, something that refreshed and stimulated."

Making a caffeine-packed cola was straightforward enough, but getting into shops was a trickier task. Almost every soft drink bottling plant in America already had a contract to produce a brand name cola that also banned them from producing any other cola. Jolt found itself all dressed up and with nowhere to go. So the twenty-three-year-old Rapp looked beyond the soda industry and found a back door into the shops: beer.

The beer industry had distribution networks just as far reaching as those of the soda business; the only difference was, they carried alcoholic drinks. Everything else was much the same. Rapp decided to see if he could get one of Rochester's beer distributors to put Jolt into the stores. "We convinced one to adopt it and it worked out well. That gave us a business model we could emulate swiftly and easily. So, as we entered each new market, we approached two or three beer distributors and would usually persuade one to take Jolt. In six or seven months we achieved national distribution through 700 beer wholesalers and, in doing so, created an alternative national route to market."

Jolt became a sensation. Its extra caffeine and sugar stance won over people who were keen for a cola with a kick, and it horrified those who wanted America to eat and drink more healthily. "The reaction was strong on both sides," says Rapp. "There were people who were outraged and people who were excited. It was a very polarizing product. It had a shock value in being so brazen as to put 'twice the caffeine' on the label. Some thought we were irresponsible, others liked the irreverence and the return to soft drinks' origins."

More than anything else, it was caffeine that drew people to Jolt. They wanted a cola capable of zapping them with its caffeine content. "What resonated with the core audience was the caffeine, not so much the sugar or the taste," says Rapp. "It was the whole idea of a cold, thirst-quenching, and refreshing alternative to coffee."

By 1988 Jolt was a fast-growing cult favorite. Bon Jovi insisted on having cases of Jolt on hand as they toured America promoting their hit album *New Jersey*. Stephen King turned the heroes of his 1996 horror novel *Desperation* into a group of obsessive Jolt guzzlers. It also became the cola of choice for programmers and hackers as they hammered at their computer keyboards building the World Wide Web. "Jolt stood for more than a soft drink—it stood for a way of life," says Rapp. "The programming industry in particular took to it. The techno-geeks were noted for being lovers of junk food— pizzas, Twinkies and so on. They loved their sugar and junk food and Jolt. That's how it ended up in *Jurassic Park*. They had a lot of programmers and animators working on the movie who were Jolt drinkers. We were told that they just grabbed a couple of cans from the programmers' own desks when shooting the movie and threw them into the set. We didn't even pay for it."

As Jolt weaved its way into pop culture, it revealed that just as there were people who wanted their fizz free from caffeine, there were plenty who craved a bigger buzz from their beverage. And while Jolt led the way, it would be an Austrian toothpaste promoter who would take what Rapp had stumbled upon to its logical conclusion.

Dietrich Mateschitz was born in 1944 in Sankt Marein im Mürztal, an Austrian town about eighty miles southwest of Vienna. After studying marketing in college, he joined Unilever, where he marketed detergents before moving to Procter & Gamble to head up the international marketing of the toothpaste Blendax. His dentifrice-marketing role took him all over the world. One day in 1982 his globetrotting business trips took him to Thailand, where the badly jet-lagged businessman tried Krating Daeng for the first time. Launched in 1976 by the Thai pharmaceutical entrepreneur Chaleo Yoovidhya, Krating Daeng was a sweet, still beverage promoted as a means of replenishing energy. The drink had a label that showed two gaur, a bison-like bovine native to southern Asia, charging at each other. "One glass and the jet lag was gone," Mateschitz later told the *Economist*.

Mateschitz became obsessed, ordering the taxis ferrying him around Bangkok to stop at stores so he could grab a bottle whenever he felt tired. Then in 1984, while he sat at the bar of the Mandarin Hotel in Hong Kong on another business trip, he read a story about how Japan's biggest taxpayer was a pharmaceutical company that sold tonics similar to Krating Daeng. Then and there, Mateschitz decided he should bring the Thai pick-me-up to Europe. After striking a deal with Yoovidhya, the Austrian marketing expert began thinking about how to best promote the drink. He knew he needed to do more than just import the beverage and, calling on the marketing skills he learned at Unilever and Procter & Gamble, set to work reinventing the Thai energy drink. "The only things we took back to Europe were the active ingredients from the original formula," he told the drinks industry website *BevNet* in 2007. "Everything else, including package design, advertising and promotion, positioning, distribution, and price strategy, was developed individually for the European markets."

The result was Red Bull. The renamed drink carried a similar logo to Krating Daeng, but now the charging bovines were bulls rather than the gaur that few Europeans or Americans would have recognized. He opted for thin, tall eight-ounce cans that made the drink stand out on the shelves and, to underline Red Bull's status as something more powerful than the average beverage, he gave it a premium price. To give it an extra zing he made his sole addition to the drink's formula by carbonating it. Finally, Mateschitz devised a marketing strategy that promoted Red Bull as a new type of beverage, an energy drink, and he developed campaigns designed to link its consumption with extreme sports and other energetic activities.

There had been energy drinks before. In 1927 a British pharmacist named William Owen developed Glucozade, a sugary carbonated drink with a vague taste of oranges that was sold as a beverage that could reenergize the ill. Two years later it was renamed Lucozade. Lucozade continued to be pushed as a drink for the unwell for decades until, in 1985, the pharmaceutical company Beecham relaunched it with TV ads showing Daley Thompson, the British Olympic decathlon gold medalist, racing around an athletic track to the feisty heavy metal of Iron Maiden's "Phantom of the Opera." The result positioned Lucozade somewhere between a sports drink and an energy drink, but while the high-glucose and high-caffeine drink was popular in the United Kingdom, little effort was made to spread it beyond British shores. Even in 2009, by which time it was owned by the global pharmaceutical giant GlaxoSmithKline, the eighty-year-old energy drink had yet to reach Germany, let alone the United States.

Like Lucozade and Jolt, Red Bull was high in caffeine, boasting 9.5 mg of the stimulant per fluid ounce, well above Coca-Cola's 2.8 mg and even Jolt's 6mg although still less than the 18.1 mg in filter coffee and 51.3 mg in a shot of espresso. But Red Bull featured more than just caffeine and sugar. Another part of its energy blend was a dose of synthetic taurine, an amino acid that occurs naturally in the body and is present in meat and fish. Some studies suggest that taurine enhances endurance and reduces the build up of lactic acid after exercise, but its full role in bodily functions is not fully understood. Red Bull also contained B-group vitamins, which can also be found in a wide variety of foods and play important roles in cellular processes. While these vitamins are vital, evidence suggests that excess B-group vitamins provide no additional benefits and are simply excreted in urine. Finally there was glucuronolactone, a stimulant believed to increase alertness. These ingredients would, in similar quantities, become features of almost all energy drinks, although many also contain guarana, a small berry-like fruit found in the Amazon basin that bears caffeine-rich seeds and is the basis of several popular Brazilian sodas, the most successful of which, Guaraná Antarctica, launched in 1921 and is the South American nation's second-best selling soda after Coca-Cola.

In 1987, with his planning finished, Mateschitz launched Red Bull in Austria. From the start the beverage associated itself with the fast lane and daredevil challenges, sponsoring Austrian Formula 1 racing driver Gerhard Berger and the Dolomitenmann, an exhausting marathon of kayaking, paragliding, and running through the Dolomites, a mountain range in Austria. By the start of 1994 the company had its whimsical TV cartoon ads with the "Red Bull gives you wiiings" slogan in place, and Europeans were embracing its promise of liquid zing, sometimes with too much fervor. "When we launched in Germany in 1994, we dramatically underestimated the demand our product would have," Mateschitz told *BevNet*. "We were selling an average of a million cans a day and ran out of stock after a few months. We were not able to buy additional cans anywhere in the world to keep up production. As a consequence, we. . . had to re-launch Red Bull six months later."

Red Bull finally charged into America in 1997, bringing its cartoons, sprightly promotions, and energy drink positioning with it to nearly instantaneous success. Red Bull's spread proved unstoppable. By the end of 2006 Red Bull could be found in 141 countries, Mateschitz was a billionaire, and the company even had its own NASCAR and Formula 1 teams.

Red Bull thrived on its groundbreaking marketing approach, which focused on creating and owning—as opposed to sponsoring—attention-grabbing promotions that would engage its target audience and keep its brand in everyone's mind, whether that was having its own motor racing teams, producing *The Art of Flight*, an acclaimed film about snowboarding, or publishing the global monthly magazine the *Red Bulletin*.

Its most spectacular and daring marketing move, however, was the decision to spend tens of millions of dollars bankrolling the Red Bull Stratos project, a record-breaking high-altitude skydive from the edge of space by the Austrian daredevil Felix Baumgartner. Seven years in the making, Red Bull Stratos involved the development of a special pressure suit for

Baumgartner, a high-tech hot air balloon capsule to take the skydiver into the stratosphere, and custom-made equipment to monitor his descent. When Baumgartner finally made his jump on October 14, 2012, more than eight million people around the world were watching as he dropped twenty-four miles down to earth and achieved a top speed of 833.9 miles an hour before gently landing by parachute in a New Mexico desert. The dive smashed world records. It was the highest-ever skydive with the longest-ever freefall, and Baumgartner was also the first person to break the sound barrier. Baumgartner's Red Bull–funded feat was a stunt of epic proportions, one that some declared "the greatest marketing stunt of all time." Red Bull might not have taken its beverage into space, but the daring dive certainly outstripped the excitement generated by Pepsi and Coca-Cola's own space travels.

Red Bull's more direct and masterful marketing made Jolt yesterday's news. "The way Mateschitz positioned Red Bull was much more about providing energy to fuel an active lifestyle than Jolt, not necessarily physically active, but staying up all hours and living life to the fullest," says Rapp. "We played a role in the development of the energy drink category but the credit goes to Red Bull and Monster for being better marketers than we were."

Launched in 2002 by the California soft drinks firm Hansen's Natural, Monster Energy was the American answer to Red Bull. It evolved out of Hansen's Energy, an unsuccessful energy drink that found itself outgunned by the Austrian market leader. "We realized that if we were going to survive in the category, we really needed a product with a different positioning," Mark Hall, the president of Monster Energy told *Beverage World* in 2009. "We've always looked at Red Bull as the sleek, sophisticated European brand and Monster is a rough-and-tumble American product."

And America, as far as Monster was concerned, meant bigger, so instead of Red Bull's petite silver and blue containers, Monster came in sixteen-ounce jet-black cans. Like Red Bull, it also associated itself with a daredevil lifestyle. "Monster is about action sports, punk rock music, partying, girls and living life on the edge," Hall said. When Red Bull eventually upped its can size too, it only underlined how Monster's bigger size had helped it become the Austrian energy drink's main challenger.

By 2011 Americans were guzzling down more than 1.8 billion liters of energy drinks every year. But compared to soda this was small potatoes. Even Red Bull, the biggest energy drink of them all, falls well short of making it into the list of America's top-ten-selling sodas.

But there was little doubt that energy drinks were chipping away at soda's sales, and they became popular enough to inspire a Jolt-style backlash of their own in: Slow Cow, a French Canadian "relaxation" drink. Eric Marcoux, vice president of the Quebec-based Boisson Slow Cow, says the idea for a relaxation drink began in a store filled with displays of energy drinks. "One of my friends, who hated those energy drinks, was in this store and he said to me: 'Why don't we do the other side? If they have energy drinks, we'll do one just to relax with,'" he says. "These energy drinks were everything that we hate. You see children eight years old and they have a Red Bull or Monster in their hands. The kids, they drink one in the morning before they go to school, they drink another before they play hockey or soccer and by the end of the day they will have had between two and ten. I believe that is bad. The kids think it will help them concentrate, but instead they become excited and can't concentrate. So we made a drink you can drink once or ten times a day that is going to help you focus and concentrate."

Marcoux's answer, Slow Cow, launched in 2009 with a logo that replicated the charging bovines of Red Bull, but replaced them with snoozing cattle. Red Bull's lawyers were onto it like a shot. "I wanted to do it to make people talk about the drink and we knew somebody would call us," says Marcoux. "But you don't want to fight with Red Bull, so we made an agreement and now it's a single cow." Not that Slow Cow's relationship with the Austrian energy drink powerhouse improved as Slow Cow steadily expanded across Canada and into the United States. "I'm not the best friend of theirs," Marcoux laughs. "What they do in Canada is they go someplace and say: 'We will give you this if you remove them.' They don't like us. They try to stop us getting into shops."

But Slow Cow and the energy drink boom that inspired it were not the only ones to follow in the wake of Jolt's kick against diet and caffeine-free soda, as the beer distribution network that Rapp used to launch Jolt opened the doors for an explosion of new still and fizzing drinks—drinks that the industry took to calling "new age beverages." "That's probably Jolt's largest legacy," says Rapp, who has since launched the vitamin water Karma Wellness Water. "Jolt's route to market system in the United States created another way into the market that brands like Clearly Canadian and others emulated. In two to three years of us doing that with Jolt, there were enough brands collectively to create what became known as the new age beverage category. The common denominator was that these were products sold at a premium price and since the large companies are risk adverse that system became the hotspot of innovation because the risk factor was minimal. The commercial success of the innovative drinks that came through the new age beverage system had a profound impact on Coke and Pepsi."

Individually none of these drinks were a serious threat to Coca-Cola or Pepsi, but collectively these new beverage brands began to win over sizeable numbers of people who might otherwise have opted for one of their sodas. Brands such as Jones Soda, founded in 1996 by former ski instructor Peter van Stolk, who started selling his pop in snowboarding shops and tattoo parlors. Van Stolk had a hunch that his Generation Y customers were cynical about big business and would buy into a brand that they could feel a connection with. So he encouraged people to send in photographs so he could put them on his ever-changing labels. By 2006 more than a million photos had been submitted by fans who hoped to one day see their images lurking on the shop shelves.

"We allowed the labels to be discovered and that gave consumers a sense of ownership," van Stolk told *Bloomberg Businessweek* in 2005. Jones Soda also made itself stand out by offering novelty flavors that ranged from the odd to the downright disgusting, such as smoked salmon pate, mashed potato, and their Thanksgiving special of turkey and gravy. They might not have tasted great, but Jones Soda fans loved trying the off-the-wall choices just to see what the result tasted like. This was soda, but not as Coca-Cola or PepsiCo knew it.

But as the twenty-first century dawned, the new age beverage makers offering green bean casserole–flavored fizz were the least of the soda giants' worries. They had a bigger problem. A much bigger problem, and one shared by millions of Americans: obesity. American waistlines had been expanding for years, and by the year 2000 the idea that something needed to be done was taking root. In the early 1960s 13.3 percent of American adults were classified as obese by the Centers for Disease Control and Prevention, but at the start of the new century the figure had grown to 31.1 percent, almost one in three people. Children were getting fatter too. In 1980, 6 percent of American children and young people were considered obese; by 2012 the proportion had tripled. And with obesity linked to strokes, heart disease, cancer, and type 2 diabetes, estimates put the cost to the nation of all this excess weight and associated diseases at $150 billion a year. This was not just an American problem; a similar upward trend could be seen in Australia, Britain, Chile, and Mexico. But America led the pack among Organisation for Economic Co-operation and Development (OECD) member nations with 33.8 percent of American adults classified as obese in 2009. In contrast the average OECD nation had an adult obesity rate of 16.9 percent, and Mexico, the next most obese country, had an obesity rate of 30 percent.

Without question the rising levels of obesity were the result of a great many interlinked contributory factors. The shift toward office-based work. The trend for eating out and fast food. Increased portion sizes. A lack of physical activity. The shift to home entertainment. Urban planning that prioritized cars over other forms of transportation. Our own food and drink preferences. Where soda fit into this complex cocktail was an obvious question. The ancient belief in the healing power of fizz had turned out to be nothing more than a myth; all carbonation did was make water look prettier, tickle the tongue, and encourage more burping. But the caloric content of sodas did have the potential to make us fat, a potential that more and more studies were concluding was being realized as sales of fizzy drinks soared.

The idea that the sugar in soda might cause weight gain had dated back years, but there was little evidence to support the link. Even in the early 1970s, when Michael Jacobson cofounded the consumer advocacy group Center for Science in the Public Interest, there were few studies to support the notion that soda could make you fat. "It made sense, but there were no scientific studies to show that soda promoted obesity and obesity was a much smaller problem back then, so the focus was on tooth decay," he recalls.

Studies linking the sugar and acidity of soda to tooth decay and the erosion of tooth enamel first gained public attention in the late 1940s, as dentists began warning their patients about the damage that sugary pop and candy could have on oral health, and advising them to cut down soda consumption. By the summer of 1951 Coca-Cola estimated that the talk of soda damaging teeth had cost the company a million gallons in syrup sales, and internal memos discussed how to stage a "counter-offensive against attacks on Coca-Cola on the dental and nutritional fronts." The resulting plan sought to emphasize the complexity of the issue by highlighting how regular brushing, fluoridation of water, and the amount of time food spent in the mouth also played a role in tooth decay and erosion. As one company memo put it: "We want to dislodge the cocksure attitude in the minds of dentists, which incites them to tell their patients they should avoid candy and soft drinks."

The counteroffensive made little difference. Dentists continued to advise the public that sugary soda could harm teeth but, says Jacobson, the issue of rotting teeth simply wasn't compelling enough to persuade many people to change their drinking habits. "People didn't care all that much about tooth decay, so we didn't get much traction back in the 1970s," he says. "But we certainly called soda a junk food and bad mouthed it when we could. It was just junk. Total junk. It stood apart from just about every other food in that it was consumed in fairly large volumes and had no vitamins, minerals, protein, fiber—nothing. Just sugar. So we told the public and people didn't care that much."

The Cola War deepened. Soda serving sizes grew. More people took to drinking soda. Those who already drank soda drank even more. Soda shifted from a treat to a several times a day drink suitable for every occasion. "I grew up in the '50s," recalls Jacobson. "My family would have a soda on a Sunday with dinner or maybe if we went on a picnic. It just wasn't the kind of thing you get anywhere. Sometimes I worked in my father's store and one of the guys working there would go out and get a few sodas for us. We saw that as a treat and not a big deal, but it's become a big problem. One reason is larger serving size. You have to remember that when family sized Coca-Cola was introduced in the '50s that was marketed as something the whole family could consume. It was twenty-six ounces, four six-and-a-half-ounce servings—today that's a single serving for some people. Then the proliferation of fast-food restaurants helped to standardize soda as the beverage you would drink with your meal."

There was no doubt that by the end of the 1990s Americans were drinking soda in quantities that would have been unthinkable in the 1950s, and with much of the growth in sales coinciding with the nation's weight gain, soda became a prime suspect in the hunt for who made the nation fat. Research intensified and soon more and more studies were concluding that nondiet sodas were the source of some, possibly many, of the extra calories that were making America fat. These findings were followed by the Centers for Disease Control and Prevention publishing maps that vividly illustrated the extent of obesity state by state. Soon the issue of weight had become the foremost health issue in America.

As soda sales peaked in 1998, Jacobson published *Liquid Candy*, a report that picked out some of the most damning evidence about soda's role in obesity and pointed an accusatory finger at Big Soda for fattening up the kids. In the wake of its publication, orchestrated stories about the Cola War from their own publicity departments gave way to newspaper and TV reports citing the research that painted soda as the enemy of good health.

Then in 1999, as the debate about soda and health gathered speed, a revolution began in Venice, California. Beverage companies had long sought access to schools. Not so much for the sales, but for the chance to get their products in front of the next generation in the hope of turning them into loyal fans of their brands. In the 1950s every successful push into a school was a cause for celebration among soda makers. "Orange Crush is served to the children and they love it," the orange soda's internal newsletter *O.C. News* proudly reported about one such deal in May 1951. The children, it continued, even spontaneously burst into song to express their love of Orange Crush and "mothers have been writing in to state that consumption of milk has been on the decline since the advent of the program." Whether the mothers' letters were thanking Orange Crush for weaning their children off milk remained unrecorded. This push into education evolved into long-term deals where soft drink companies got the exclusive right to provide beverages to a school and, in return, cash-strapped schools got money. As the 1990s ended, these deals, which could last as long as ten years, existed in 92 percent of high schools, 74 percent of middle schools, and 43 percent of elementary schools.

Jacqueline Domac, a teacher at Venice High School, knew nothing about these deals. So when in 1999 one of the students in her health classes asked her why there was no pure fruit juice on sale in any of the school's twenty-two vending machines, she was surprised at the absence. Simple enough to fix, she reckoned, and she sent a request to the school's finance manager asking for fruit juice to be added. The next day she got a reply in her mailbox: "Sorry, selling this juice would conflict with our soda contract."

Venice High School had an exclusive deal with Coca-Cola worth $3,000 a year plus several hundred cases of free beverages. As far as soda-school deals go it was a poor one, given that similar schools were getting $50,000-plus a year, but what angered Domac was that this contract was stopping students from accessing healthier drinks. In response, she and her students launched a campaign pushing for the Coke deal to be canceled and for healthier options to be introduced. As part of the campaign Domac obtained a copy of the school's beverage contract and sent it to the *Los Angeles Times*, a move that earned her a stiff telling-off at work but also shoved the nature of these school contracts into the public eye.

Domac wasn't alone. As concerns about obesity deepened, grassroots campaigns against the sale of soda on school premises were bubbling up all across the country. By 2002 Domac and her fellow campaigners scored their first major victory when Los Angeles Unified School District, one of the largest in the United States with more than 750,000 students, voted in favor of a ban on soda in its schools, despite the objections of several schools that said they would be thousands of dollars worse off as a result. Many kids weren't too pleased either, as one Pepsi-loving eighth-grader told the *Los Angeles Times*: "It's unfair because when we get thirsty we need something to drink, and we don't want water. We want something that has sugar."

But the tide had turned. In district after district, state after state, the soda was kicked out and the industry's contracts ripped up. Similar bans followed in Europe, including the United Kingdom and France. The beverage industry fought back for a while, arguing with little success that pulling soda out of schools would take money away from children's education. But the momentum was unstoppable. In May 2006 the soda industry struck an agreement with the Alliance for a Healthier Generation, the childhood obesity campaign group founded by Bill Clinton and the American Heart Association. As part of the deal the big three soda giants pledged to phase out nondiet soda in the nation's schools by 2010. By the fall of 2009 shipments of regular fizzy drinks to schools were down 95 percent compared to 2004–05, and water had become the most common drink on sale in schools.

By the time the industry agreed to start removing fizzy drinks from schools, soda was clearly in trouble. Studies linking it to obesity had continued to pile up, and sales were dropping as weight-watching consumers turned their back on full-calorie soda and opted for bottled water instead. Bottled water had come a long way since the days when Perrier's mineral water became the fizz of choice for the go-getting yuppies of the 1980s. In 1986 Americans bought 1.4 billion gallons of bottled water, but in 2006 bottled water sales had reached 8.3 billion. Soda still topped the beverage industry, of course, with more than 15 billion gallons sold every year, but it was losing ground fast as water, new age beverages, and energy drinks peeled away its consumers and concerns about obesity damaged its image.

As it happened, the soda giants had been looking beyond the world of fizz for several years. Coca-Cola was accelerating its efforts to turn itself into an all-around beverage company that produced water, juice, energy drinks, and sports drinks, as well as the soda that made the company famous. Cadbury Schweppes tried unsuccessfully to reinvent soda's image with 7Up Plus, a diet version of the lemon-lime drink that featured added vitamin C and calcium. PepsiCo went furthest of all. In the late 1990s it started hunting for healthy brands to add to its portfolio of soda and snacks. It sold off its fast-food chains, bought Tropicana, and then swallowed Quaker Oats. By the time Indra Nooyi became its chief executive in 2006, PepsiCo had become bigger than Coca-Cola in market value by reaching far beyond the world of soda in its hunt for a less sugary future.

While Pepsi and Mountain Dew would remain top sellers for the company, PepsiCo now saw its future as a maker of "fun for you" products like Pepsi, "better for you" products like the zero-calorie Pepsi Max and, increasingly, "good for you" lines such as Quaker Oats. For Nooyi the Cola War battles for slivers of market share were history. "We, Pepsi, would push like hell . . . and get a tenth of a point of market share," she told the *Wall Street Journal* in June 2011. "The next period, Coke would come along, push like hell, and gain a tenth. This was a zero-sum game. The cola category was profitable, but didn't grow profits."

But even as the soda companies reinvented themselves and their products, the number of obesity studies connecting soda to the problem of fat continued to grow. An examination of the obesity studies published in the journal *Public Health Nutrition* concluded that the consumption of sweetened beverages might account for as much as a fifth of the weight gained in America between 1977 and 2001. Another review of the studies, this time in the *American Journal of Public Health*, reported that there were "clear associations of soft drink intake with increased energy intake and body weight," and that studies funded by the food industry tended to conclude that soft drinks had less of an effect than studies funded by other organizations.

Some researchers claimed that high fructose corn syrup, the money-saving sugar substitute that the industry adopted in the late 1970s and early 1980s, caused even more weight gain than sugar. The finding prompted a spate of sodas such as Mountain Dew Throwback that made a virtue out of containing cane sugar instead of corn syrup. But the evidence that high fructose corn syrup was worse than sugar was weak. Obesity was rising just as fast in Europe, where the industry had stuck with sugar, and even the ardent soda critics at the Center for Science in the Public Interest felt corn syrup made little if any difference compared to sugar. But even without the unconvincing claims about high fructose corn syrup, by the start of the 2010s soda was being compared to cigarettes with the *New York Times* posing the question: "Is soda the new tobacco?"

Comparing soda to tobacco was a real stretch, but that such a comparison was even being made only underlined how the concern about obesity had turned fizz into public health enemy number one. The American Beverage Association, the trade body representing the beverage industry, argued that the research wasn't conclusive or thorough enough and that it was unfair to blame soda alone for something as complex as obesity, but just as with the fight over soda in school, the momentum was with the health campaigners. "It's clear that soda is losing," says Michael Jacobson. "It's been kicked out of schools and some city government properties. They are really feeling the pressure from a bunch of different directions. Sales of the sugary drinks have been going down year after year."

Soon cities and states across America were floating proposals designed to curb soda drinking. Most looked to taxes as a way of not only encouraging people to drink fewer fizzy drinks but also raising revenue. Attempts to impose such a tax in the small California cities of Richmond and El Monte were firmly rejected by voters in November 2012 after heavy campaigning by the beverage industry. But while soda taxes remain more idea than reality, Jacobson is convinced that the soda industry will ultimately fail to stop the introduction of such levies: "The industry wants to crush every tax initiative. They got a tax repealed in the state of Maine and a temporary tax in Seattle repealed. They spent millions of dollars to fight off taxes in Philadelphia and New York State. They are willing to put any amount of money into killing these proposals. But as the health evidence continues to build up and as cities and states need money, I think our governments will continue to look at soda taxes as a way to reduce sales and generate revenue."

Price, however, is just one battlefront in the new obesity-inspired war on soda. Another is portion size, where New York City mayor Michael Bloomberg's bid to limit soda serving sizes in the city's food establishments to sixteen ounces is leading the charge. A clash between Bloomberg and the soda industry had been brewing for some time. The New York mayor had already required the city's restaurants to display calorie counts on their menus and tried—unsuccessfully—to get the federal government to ban people from buying soda with food stamps. Then there was "Don't drink yourself fat," an off-putting TV ad in which a man pours a vile gloop of liquid and solid fat into a glass from a cola can before messily guzzling away. "All over the United States, public health officials are wringing their hands saying, 'Oh, this is terrible,'" Bloomberg told the *New York Times*. "New York City is not about wringing your hands; it's about doing something."

The serving-size ban became yet another big-budget fight between public health officials and the soda industry, which ran ads showing Bloomberg dressed up as an old woman, with the slogan "New Yorkers need a mayor, not a nanny." But this time the only votes that counted were those of the city's Board of Health, and its members were all appointed by Bloomberg. On September 13, 2012, the measure got approval, limiting the Big Apple's restaurants, food trucks, concert halls, delis, stadiums, and movie theaters to serving sizes of sixteen ounces or less for nondiet soda. "This is the biggest step a city has taken to curb obesity," said Bloomberg as he announced the decision. "Simply by proposing limits on sugary drinks, New York City pushed the issue of obesity—and the impact of sugary beverages—onto the national stage. The Board of Health's passing of this proposal means that New Yorkers will soon consume fewer junk calories and eventually begin turning the tide of the obesity epidemic that is destroying the health of far too many of our citizens."

The following month a group of business groups, including the American Beverage Association, launched a joint lawsuit against the measure on the grounds that the New York City health authorities had overstepped the limits of their power by introducing such a ban. The lawsuit worked. On Monday June 11, 2013—the day before the ban was due to start—the Supreme Court of the State of New York ruled against Bloomberg, who immediately announced plans to appeal. Yet even as Bloomberg slugged it out with Big Soda in the New York courts, just a short stroll away from his Manhattan office over the East River, a new breed of soda could be found amid the food stalls of the Brooklyn Flea's Smorgasburg food market.

Brooklyn Soda Works started out in 2010 as a search for the perfect cocktail mixer by installation artist Caroline Mak and chemist Antonio Ramos. "We both love making things and always liked to do projects together," recalls Ramos. "In the beginning of 2010, we started with a project to make the perfect mixer, starting with a classic Dark 'n' Stormy ginger beer. We tried carbonating it with yeast to make an alcoholic ginger beer and had a lot of fun with it."

The ginger beer experiments got the couple interested in taking their carbonation adventures further. "Around the same time a lot of the DIY soda siphons came out in the home ware supply stores," says Mak. "They all said only use these to carbonate water, nothing else, but the two of us went: 'Screw that, let's try and carbonate whatever we can.'"

And that they did, zapping any liquid they could with bubbles of carbon dioxide. "We just threw everything we could think of in there to see what happened," says Ramos. "We tried carbonating milk. It was gross. We tried bourbon. That was wrong. It gets you really drunk, really quick. It's almost like champagne, the bubbles make it go to your head. It was a little too intense with all the alcohol burn and the carbonation burn. It was an assault on the senses, but it was fun."

They also tried carbonating juices, starting with orange and apple before progressing to more exotic combinations. Soon they found themselves with soda recipes that, unlike the fizzy milk and bourbon, tasted great while still offering something far removed from the likes of Fanta. Drinks like apple and ginger ("our signature flavor," says Mak); or grapefruit, jalapeño, and honey; or cucumber, lime, and sea salt (a mix of freshly squeezed cucumber and lime juice plus a pinch of salt and a dash of cane sugar). The pair wondered if other people would enjoy their unusual soda combos as much as they and their friends did, so they decided to test it out by getting a stall on the Brooklyn Flea food markets, where they charged around four dollars a cup. "We hooked up a few kegs onto our draw system—we don't bottle, everything is in kegs. We sold out in four hours and realized we that we had a potential mini-business we could develop," says Mak.

Brooklyn Soda Works was born, and in the two years since its public debut in 2010, the hobby-turned-business has grown into a six days a week operation with three employees and an eighteen-hundred-square-foot production space. Not to mention deals to supply several upscale restaurants, including Blue Hill, the swanky Greenwich Village eatery where the Obamas dined when they visited New York in 2009. "Most of our customers, I would say, are people who had given up on soda for health reasons or because they didn't like the idea of the preservatives or the sugar and drank juice most regularly, but can now go: 'Wait, I can have something carbonated without all the sugar and additives,'" says Ramos. "There's no shortage of products at the lower-end price scale of soda, but what's missing is a premium, artisanal product. There was a big desire for that, but not much going on in nonalcoholic beverages so people were very excited by it."

Brooklyn Soda Works' small-scale soda production offers its customers something very different from Coca-Cola and Pepsi: a chance to feel a personal connection with their drink. It is an appeal not far removed from that of the craft beer makers, which have exploded in number so much that they make up almost 98 percent of the breweries operating in the United States today. And nor was Brooklyn Soda Works a one-off. Although still tiny in number, all across the United States small artisan soda companies are popping up. From Oregon to Maine tiny soda outfits are putting the passion back into fizz and winning over lapsed soda drinkers. Outfits such as Humdinger Craft Soda, making its soda in the basement of St. Patrick's Church in Richmond, Virginia, or Maria's Packaged Goods & Community Bar in Chicago, which came up with a custom ginger ale to use in its cocktails.

The craft soda movement might yet prove to be a false dawn, but if the trend for craft beer is anything to go by, a new alternative soda boom may be in the works. None of that, of course, helps the giants of the soda world, who increasing resemble Gulliver, tied down by the miniature people of Lilliput, as changing consumer tastes, craft sodas, energy drinks, health campaigners, lawmakers, research studies, bottled water, falling sales, and new age beverages assail them.

Soda has come a long way since Joseph Priestley first began experimenting with water over the fermenting beer vats in the English city of Leeds back in 1767. The sticky sugary fingerprints of the Age of Soda can be found all over the world. Soda spawned laws of physics, occupied the attentions of some of humanity's greatest figures, and provided the tools for some of the first anesthetists. Their fizzy pleasures introduced us to new flavors, encouraged us to drink ice-cold beverages, made us smile, and even became part of our national identity. The soda business gave us the world's most famous brand, the concept of coupons, the drive-in restaurant, and new approaches to advertising. It reshaped our shops and our streets, encouraged prohibition, covered up the moonshine, helped us become a throwaway society, and set Michael Jackson's hair on fire. Soda even influenced geopolitics, priming US presidents, puncturing holes in the iron and bamboo curtains, and pumping money into underdeveloped nations when no one else would. And it also helped to make us fat.

But even as the sales slide and the health criticism mounts, soda is far from dead. Soda is still—by a substantial margin—the most popular type of beverage in America. The soda giants have barely started tapping into the potentially enormous markets of India and China, where people still drink far less soda than the worldwide average. And then there's the holy grail: a no-calorie, natural sweetener with no aftertaste. Sounds too good to be true? Maybe, but those in the soda business who are searching for this miracle sweetener are confident. The Dr Pepper Snapple Group, the US beverage company formed in 2008 after Cadbury Schweppes split its beverage and confectionery businesses, expects a breakthrough in the next few years. Al Carey, head of the beverage unit for the Americas at PepsiCo, told the *Huffington Post*: "I can't say when it will be here, but it's in the reasonable future."

What form this ultimate sweetener will take is unknown. It could be a single sweetener or a mix of several different sweeteners. It could also be a fusion of natural calorie-free sweeteners, natural sweetness enhancers such as the miracle fruit plant that makes sour taste sweet, and a small amount of sugar. "I think that's the way the industry is going to go and I don't think it is pie-in-the-sky at all," says Jacobson. "A combination of a high potency sweetener and a sweetness enhancer, maybe with a little sugar, will—I think—yield good-tasting products with very few problems. If they do achieve this then the problems with soda would be greatly diminished."

Whatever the exact combination, there's no doubt that the ultimate sweetener would be a game changer, shooting down both the cancer fears that still plague artificial sweeteners and the accusations that soda is fattening the nation. Soda might be on the ropes, but it's far from dead, and its world-changing story may have only just begun. The Age of Soda might not be over yet.

Acknowledgments

As with any book there are many people whose help has been invaluable. First and foremost my partner Jay Priest for, well, just about everything. Not least acting as a human photocopier in various archives, driving ludicrous distances across America, and being willing to put up with me and a fridge filled with random sodas while I researched and wrote this book.

Another big thanks goes to my tireless, go-getting agent Isabel Atherton of Creative Authors, without whom you wouldn't be reading this now, and to Chicago Review Press for taking on the book and my editor Yuval Taylor and project editor Devon Freeny for their insights, suggestions, and patience.

The research for this book would have been a lot harder without the staff at the various museums, libraries, and archives I found myself in while researching *Fizz*. A special thank-you goes to the staff at the Dr Pepper Museum in Waco, in particular Joy Summar-Smith, Mary Beth Tait, and Charlie Stanford (who deserves extra credit for his sterling work in tracking down much of the information I was looking for before I even got to Waco).

Equally deserving of thanks are the staff at the Manuscript, Archives, and Rare Book Library at Emory University for their help with my epic trawl through their Coca-Cola collections. I'm also much obliged to the staff at Lewes Library in East Sussex, the Mass Observation Archive team at the University of Sussex, and Marie Force of the Delta Air Transport Heritage Museum.

Thanks also to: Bob and Ann McGarrah for their generous hospitality, recollections, and the Pepsi space cans; Colin Emmins for his pointers on British soda history; Amanda Rosseter and the archivists of the Coca-Cola Company; Caroline Mak and Antonio Ramos of Brooklyn Soda Works; John Risse for his insights on Robert Woodruff's time at Coca-Cola; and Keith Blount for inventing Scrivener, which made the process of writing this book so much easier than my last. Further thank-yous go to Michael Jacobson, Eric Marcoux, C. J. Rapp, Neil Verlander, and Douglas Woodward for taking the time to be interviewed for this book.

I'd also like to say thanks to Mark Pendergrast, author of *For God, Country & Coca-Cola*; Frederick Allen, author of *Secret Formula*; and Douglas Simmons, author of *Schweppes: The First 200 Years*. All three books were valuable sources of information, and Mark deserves an extra thank-you for helping to weed out Coke-related errors and myths.

Finally, thanks to the A&W server who provided me and Jay with endless amusement on long, energy drink–fueled drives by greeting us with an enormous burp and, without skipping a beat, the words "What you having?"

References

Introduction: To the Stars

"As more people explore outer space . . ." Barbara Reynolds, "Sodas, Food, Movies—It's All Refreshment," *USA Today*, August 7, 1984.

"PepsiCo is strongly identified . . ." "It's Pop Politics: Pepsi, Coke Battle Spills Over into NASA," *Ludington Daily News*, July 13, 1985.

"We're not up there to run a taste test . . ." Roger Enrico and Jesse Kornbluth, *The Other Guy Blinked: How Pepsi Won the Cola Wars* (London: Bantam, 1986), 245.

"On Earth, that's not such a big deal . . ." Vickie Kloeris, "Eating on the ISS," *NASA Quest*, May 1, 2001, http://quest.arc.nasa.gov/people/journals/space/kloeris/05-01-01.html.

"have generally remained grossly ignorant" . . . Friedrich Hoffmann, *New Experiments and Observations upon Mineral Waters* (London: J. Osborn & T. Longman, 1731), 43.

"We must here note and reject . . ." Ibid., 44.

"No less preposterous . . ." Ibid., 12.

Instead, he argued, physicians needed . . . Ibid., 84–88

Priestley presented his findings . . . Joseph Priestley, *Directions for Impregnating Water with Fixed Air* (London: J. Johnson, 1772).

1. The Beverage of Kings

"Guts and all the nastiness . . ." Charles P. Moritz, *Travels, Chiefly on Foot, Through Several Parts of England in 1782* (London: G.G. and J. Robinson, 1797), 138.

Dr. John Watson . . . Arthur Conan Doyle, *The Adventures of Sherlock Holmes* (Lewes, UK: Vigo Essential Classics, 2011), iBooks ed.

"aerated lemonade" . . . Sutcliffe & Co., print advertisement, *York Herald and County Advertiser*, March 14, 1807.

2. Meet Me at the Soda Fountain

"laying gunpowder, grain by grain . . ." Joseph Priestley, *The Importance and Extent of Free Inquiry in Matters of Religion* (London: J. Johnson, 1785), 40.

"every enemy to civil and religious despotism" . . . Quoted in Joseph Priestley, *An Appeal to the Public on the Subject of the Riots in Birmingham* (London: J. Thompson, 1791), 129.

"I cannot but feel better pleased . . ." Quoted in F. W. Gibbs, *Joseph Priestley: Adventurer in Science and Champion of Truth* (London: Thomas Nelson and Sons, 1965), 204.

"has a slight fetid smell . . ." Benjamin Rush, *Experiments and Observations on the Mineral Waters of Philadelphia, Abington, and Bristol, in the Province of Pennsylvania* (Philadelphia: James Humphreys Jr., 1773), 6.

"The water . . . cannot be confined . . ." Quoted in John J. Riley, *A History of the American Soft Drink Industry: Bottled Carbonated Beverages, 1807–1957* (New York: Arno Press, 1958), 38–39.

"brisk with carbonic acid gas" . . . Quoted in George P. Fisher, *Life of Benjamin Silliman, M.D., LL.D.* (New York: Charles Scribner and Company, 1866), 308.

"made noonday in the streets" . . . Quoted in Fisher, *Benjamin Silliman*, 146.

"quite impossible with my present means . . ." Quoted in Riley, *American Soft Drink Industry*, 48–49.

"combine amusement with utility . . ." Quoted in Riley, *American Soft Drink Industry*, 50.

"During the hot season . . ." Adlard Welby, *A Visit to North America and the English Settlements in Illinois, with a Winter Residence at Philadelphia* (London: J. Drury, 1821), 172.

3. The Medicine Men

"The whole of her practice . . ." Quoted in John Uri Lloyd, *Life and Medical Discoveries of Samuel Thomson and a History of the Thomsonian Materia Medica* (Cincinnati: The Lloyd Library of Botany, Pharmacy and Materia Medica, 1909), 12.

"Java's deadly trees". . . Quoted in James Harvey Young, *The Toadstool Millionaires: A Social History of Patent Medicines in America Before Federal Regulation* (Princeton: Princeton University Press, 1961), 47.

"the fishermen of Newfoundland, Labrador . . ." "National Drinks: Queer Beverages Peculiar to Some Countries," *Canaseraga Times*, November 11, 1887.

all that remains of their efforts is a patent . . . Henry Smith and Hiram F. Snow, improved beverage, US Patent 56,458, filed May 31, 1866, and issued July 17, 1866.

"For Heaven's sake don't call it herb tea" . . . Unattributed and undated history of Hires Root Beer, Dr Pepper Museum Collection, Dr Pepper Museum, Waco, TX.

"I have had a taste of your root beer . . ." "The Story of My First Job: Charles E. Hires' Experience," *Printers' Ink Monthly*, undated news clipping, Dr Pepper Museum Collection.

"Sales increased slowly at first . . ." Quoted in John S. Grey, "The Advertising of Hires' Rootbeer," *Printers' Ink* 24, no. 12 (September 21, 1898), Dr Pepper Museum Collection.

"Business success is built upon two foundation rocks . . ." "Industrial Philadelphia: The Charles E. Hires Company," unattributed and undated news clipping, Dr Pepper Museum Collection.

"recover brain and nervous exhaustion . . ." Quoted in Frank N. Potter, *The Moxie Mystique* (Virginia Beach: Donning Company / Publishers, 1981), 1.

"Behind us lay Atlanta . . ." William Tecumseh Sherman, *Memoirs of General W. T. Sherman* (New York: Library of America, 1990; orig. publ. 1886), 655.

"There was a South of slavery . . ." Quoted in Norman Shavin and Bruce Galphin, *Atlanta: Triumph of a People* (Atlanta: Capricorn Corporation, 1982), 132.

"I would rather have a life span of 10 years . . ." Quoted in Jerome J. Platt, *Cocaine Addiction: Theory, Research and Treatment* (Cambridge, MA: Harvard University Press, 2000), 3.

"the many worthless, so-called coca preparations" . . . Angelo Mariani, *Coca and its Therapeutic Application*, 3rd ed. (New York: J. N. Jaros, 1896), 52.

"a feeling as though the body . . ." Quoted in Frederick Allen, *Secret Formula: How Brilliant Marketing and Relentless Salesmanship Made Coca-Cola the Best-Known Product in the World* (New York: HarperCollins, 1994), 22.

"nerve trouble, dyspepsia . . ." Quoted in Mark Pendergrast, *For God, Country & Coca-Cola: The Definitive History of the Great American Soft Drink and the Company That Makes It*, 3rd ed. (New York: Basic Books, 2013), Kindle ed.

"the black population would scarcely . . ." Quoted in *Cambridge World History of Food*, s.v. "The Kola Trade," 2000, www.credoreference.com/entry/cupfood/the_kola_trade.

"to avert, as far as practicable . . ." Quoted in *World History of Food*, s.v. "The Kola Trade."

"especially good for keeping . . ." Pure Water Co. Ltd., print advertisement, *Illustrated London News*, April 14, 1894.

hot chocolate maker Cadbury . . . Cadbury advertisement, *Illustrated London News*, October 22, 1898.

"The general condition has materially improved . . ." Quoted in *Cambridge World History of Food*, s.v. "Uses of Kola," 2000, www.credoreference.com/entry/cupfood/uses_of_kola.

The kola nut buzz . . . Details of the Coca-Cola formula from Pendergrast, *For God, Country & Coca-Cola*.

"Coca-Cola. Delicious! Refreshing! . . ." Quoted in Allen, *Secret Formula*, 28.

"You know how I suffer with headaches . . ." Asa Candler, letter to Warren Candler, April 10, 1888, Asa Griggs Candler Papers, Manuscript, Archives, and Rare Book Library, Emory University, Atlanta, GA.

"a shot in the arm" . . . Quoted in Pendergrast, *For God, Country & Coca-Cola*.

"a man would explode" . . . Quoted in Allen, *Secret Formula*, 45.

"breakdown was not so much due to . . ." "Greenway Found a Deranged Man," *Richmond Times*, July 25, 1902.

"I am satisfied that many of the horrible crimes . . ." "Cocaine Sniffers: Use of the Drug Increasing Among Negroes of the South," *New-York Daily Tribune*, June 21, 1903.

4. A Snail in a Bottle

"If ever you should visit the Smithsonian . . ." Quoted in Richard Swiderski, *Poison Eaters: Snakes, Opium, Arsenic, and the Lethal Show* (Boca Raton: Universal-Publishers, 2010), 234.

"I recommend that a law . . ." Quoted in Young, *The Toadstool Millionaires*, 236.

"be contented with water . . ." Quoted in E. J. Kahn Jr., *The Big Drink: An Unofficial History of Coca-Cola* (London: Max Reinhardt, 1960), 109.

"In England, I have seen women . . ." Quoted in Clayton A. Coppin and Jack C. High, *The Politics of Purity: Harvey Washington Wiley and the Origins of Federal Food Policy* (Ann Arbor: University of Michigan Press, 1999), 148.

"Anybody who says saccharin is injurious . . ." Harvey Wiley, *The History of a Crime Against the Food Law* (New York: Arno Press, 1976; orig. publ. 1929), 163.

"It is remarkable what the fear . . ." Quoted in Allen, *Secret Formula*, 57.

"Dr Pepper stands alone on the bridge . . ." Quoted in Harry E. Ellis, *Dr Pepper: King of Beverages* (Dallas: Dr Pepper Company, 1979), 144.

"It's a bully drink . . ." Quoted in Bob Stoddard, *Pepsi-Cola: 100 Years* (Los Angeles: General Publishing Group, 1997), 28.

"a poisonous ingredient" . . . United States v. Forty Barrels and Twenty Kegs of Coca-Cola, US District Court, Eastern District of Tennessee, Southern Division, Chattanooga, court transcripts, March 13, 1911, US National Archives Online Public Access, http://research .archives.gov/search?expression=parent-id-lnk:279312.

"a dirty undershirt" . . . Ibid.

"not one indivisible atom . . ." Quoted in Allen, *Secret Formula*, 193.

"I did not say anything to Mr Candler . . ." Quoted in Wilbur G. Kurtz Jr., "Joseph A. Biedenharn," *Coca-Cola Bottler*, August 1944, Robert Winship Woodruff Papers, Manuscript, Archives, and Rare Book Library, Emory University, Atlanta, GA.

"Those first salesmen . . ." "Fifty Fabulous Years of Overseas Growth for Coca-Cola, 1926–1976," *Refresher USA* 8, no. 3 (1976), Coca-Cola Collection, Manuscript, Archives, and Rare Book Library, Emory University, Atlanta, GA.

"the most perfectly designed package . . ." Quoted in "The Story Behind . . . Coca-Cola," *Changing Times: The Kiplinger Magazine*, November 1959.

5. The Bar Is Dead, Soda Is King!

"The slums soon will be only . . ." Quoted in Anne Cooper Funderburg, *Sundae Best: A History of Soda Fountains* (Bowling Green, OH: Bowling Green State University Popular Press, 2002), 123.

"liquor stampedes". . . Quoted in Michael A. Lerner, *Dry Manhattan: Prohibition in New York City* (Cambridge, MA: Harvard University Press, 2008), 43.

"might have been dreamed up . . ." Quoted in Max Rudin, "Beer and America," *American Heritage*, June–July 2002.

"Since the country's turned prohibitin' . . ." Quoted in Leah A. Zeldes, "Two Rivers: Drinking Green in Chicago This St. Patrick's Day," *Dining Chicago*, March 9, 2010.

"In my neighborhood, if you went . . ." Quoted in Hank Bordowitz, *Bad Moon Rising: The Unauthorized History of Creedence Clearwater Revival* (Chicago: Chicago Review Press, 2007), 71.

"the new American bar" . . . Quoted in Funderburg, *Sundae Best*, 103.

"The bar is dead . . ." Ibid.

"getting hilarious" . . . "Jake and Coca Cola Caused Several Arrests," *Cincinnati Press*, March 8, 1929.

"But Mr. Woodruff . . ." Quoted in Pendergrast, *For God, Country & Coca-Cola.*

"I feel that to work . . ." Quoted in Allen, *Secret Formula*, 165.

"The offering of a product . . ." Archie Lee, letter to Robert Woodruff, November 21, 1945, Robert Winship Woodruff Papers.

Its impact was still . . . "Ad Age Advertising Century: Top 10 Slogans," *Advertising Age*, March 29, 1999, http://adage.com/article/special-report-the-advertising-century/ad-age-advertising -century-top-10-slogans/140156.

"hydra-headed menace . . ." Quoted in Constance L. Hays, *Pop: Truth and Power at The Coca-Cola Company* (London: Hutchinson, 2004), Kindle ed.

"There has been a tremendous loss . . ." Harrison Jones, memo to Robert Woodruff, August 22, 1932, Robert Winship Woodruff Papers.

"In the last four years . . ." Harrison Jones, memo to Robert Woodruff, undated, Robert Winship Woodruff Papers.

"He embodied all the features . . ." Quoted in Coca-Cola Company, "Haddon Sundblom," undated biography, Coca-Cola Collection.

"If you think you can do better . . ." Daniel J. Forrestall, "The History of the Seven-Up Company," unpublished manuscript, 1989, Dr Pepper Museum Collection.

"simply in order to line up . . ." Ibid.

"There may be war" . . . Quoted in Pendergrast, *For God, Country & Coca-Cola.*

"We'd bring him a sample . . ." Quoted in Robert Lockwood Mills with Harry Maurer, *Thomas Elmezzi: The Man Who Kept the Secret* (Great Neck, NY: JET Foundation Press, 2004), 28.

"under no circumstances . . ." Pepsi-Cola Company v. The Coca-Cola Company, Supreme Court of the State of New York, County of Queens, motion for the defense, September 17, 1940, Robert Winship Woodruff Papers.

"A lot of people thought I was . . ." Walter Mack, speech to the Pepsi-Cola Bottling Association Annual Meeting, November 21, 1975.

"It was like a two-headed monster . . ." Walter Mack with Peter Buckley, *No Time Lost: The Autobiography of Walter Mack* (New York: Atheneum, 1982), 120.

"For whatever reasons, our several radio experiments . . ." Ralph Hayes, letter, September 8, 1938, Robert Winship Woodruff Papers.

"When I listen to some of the jingles . . ." Mack, *No Time Lost,* 136.

6. Was Ist Coca-Cola?

In 1919 the company granted . . . Pendergrast, *For God, Country & Coca-Cola.*

"If Hitler comes to power . . ." Ray Powers, letter to Robert Woodruff, October 7, 1930, Robert Winship Woodruff Papers.

"We had millions and millions . . ." Max Keith, interview, June 29–30, 1966, Robert Winship Woodruff Papers.

"loud and arrogant manner" . . . "Coca-Cola?—What Is It and Where Does It Come From?," German leaflet, trans. September 4, 1936, Robert Winship Woodruff Papers.

"They claimed we were an American-Jewish company . . ." Keith, interview.

As the German assault smashed through . . . Allen, *Secret Formula,* 245–46.

"not sufficiently important . . ." Ministry of Food, "History of the Soft Drinks Industry (War-Time) Association Ltd.," report, 1946, National Archives of the United Kingdom, London, UK.

"the time will come . . ." Pepsi-Cola, print advertisement, *Bath Chronicle and Weekly Gazette,* July 15, 1944.

"We, members of the Associated Press . . ." Quoted in Allen, *Secret Formula,* 250.

"not merely with guns . . ." James A. Farley, speech to the 23rd Annual Convention of American Bottlers of Carbonated Beverages, November 13, 1941, Robert Winship Woodruff Papers.

"I have the honor to inform you . . ." US Office of the Military Attaché, Pretoria, Transvaal, letter to R. Stuttaford, September 18, 1942, Coca-Cola Company Archives, Coca-Cola Company, Atlanta, GA.

"Yesterday was a red letter day . . ." Lt. W. J. Forbes, letter to Mrs. Williams, August 15, 1949, Coca-Cola Company Archives.

"After eyeing it till . . ." Lt. W. P. Gaddis Jr., letter to his mother in Berkeley, California, undated, Coca-Cola Company Archives.

"If anyone asked us . . ." Walt Bielski et al., letter to Robert Woodruff, September 8, 1943, Coca-Cola Company Archives.

"I don't know exactly . . ." Robert L. Scott, *God Is My Co-Pilot* (Broomfield, CO: Summa Iru Speciality Publishing, 2011). Kindle ed.

"Memories started coming back to me . . ." Quoted in Kahn, *The Big Drink*, 13.

"I could have hit that . . ." Mack, *No Time Lost*, 147.

"This to my mind is . . ." F. J. H. Corbyn, letter to D. R. Lamb, May 8, 1944, National Archives of the United Kingdom.

"It would be a gross waste of transport . . ." F. J. H. Corbyn, letter to E. M. Hugh-Jones, May 9, 1944, National Archives of the United Kingdom.

"America never contributed anything . . ." Quoted in Pendergrast, *For God, Country & Coca-Cola.*

"the leftovers of the leftovers" . . . Keith, interview.

"One of Carl West's employees . . ." Keith, interview.

7. Cola-Colonization

"It was a product saying . . ." Bill Backer, "Bill Backer Interviewed About 'I'd Like to Buy the World a Coke,'" interview by the Coca-Cola Archives, 2007, YouTube video posted by CokeConversations, October 7, 2011, www.youtube.com/watch?v=tSNU1TvF4pc.

"It was so drab . . ." Quoted in David Ellwood, "The American Challenge in Uniform: The Arrival of America's Armies in World War II and European Women," *European Journal of American Studies*, special issue 2012, document 8 (March 29, 2012): http://ejas.revues .org/9577.

"American social invasion" . . . Fred Moten, "The New International of Rhythmic Feeling(s)," in *Sonic Interventions*, edited by Sylvia Mieszkowski, Joy Smith, and Marijke de Valck (Amsterdam: Rodopi, 2007), 42.

"fresh out of Japans" . . . J. Paul Austin, letter to Robert Woodruff, May 4, 1973, Robert Winship Woodruff Papers.

"empty Coca-Cola bottles . . ." Yukio Mishima, *The Decay of the Angel* (London: Vintage Books, 2001; orig. publ. 1971), 7.

"the foreboding noises . . ." "The Greatest Commercial Mystery of the Century," *Paris Match*, undated translation, Robert Winship Woodruff Papers.

"Are we being Coca-Colonized?". . . Richard F. Kuisel, *Seducing the French: The Dilemma of Americanization*, (Berkeley: University of California Press, 1993), http://publishing.cdlib .org/ucpressebooks/view?docId=ft4w10060w.

"personal grudge against us" . . . Ibid.

"Coca-Cola was not injurious . . ." Quoted Pendergrast, *For God, Country & Coca-Cola.*

"the generous supply of home-grown sorghum" . . . Richard Nixon, letter to Robert Woodruff, December 15, 1959, Robert Winship Woodruff Papers.

"That is home-grown Georgia cane syrup . . ." Robert Woodruff, letter to Richard Nixon, December 21, 1959, Robert Winship Woodruff Papers.

"You will never get any real trade . . ." Quoted in Stephen Aris, "Things Went Better for Pepsi than for Coke in Moscow," *Age*, December 5, 1972.

"Georgia has a particular advantage . . ." Quoted in Joe Albright, "Lawyers Study Question of Duncan's Coke Stock," *Atlanta Constitution*, undated news clipping, Robert Winship Woodruff Papers.

"degenerate capitalism" . . . Quoted in Pendergrast, *For God, Country & Coca-Cola*.

"This agreement is more than just a sales contract . . ." Ian Wilson, "Remarks for China Agreement News Conference," undated, Coca-Cola Collection.

"We're here to cure people . . ." "Mount Sinai Ends Coca-Cola Boycott," *New York Post*, April 12, 1966, Robert Winship Woodruff Papers.

"evidence of the company's independence . . ." Morris B. Abram, statement, April 15, 1966, Robert Winship Woodruff Papers.

"bad faith" . . . B. H. Oehlert Jr., letter to John R. Talley, April 25, 1966, Robert Winship Woodruff Papers.

"the American ambassador is particularly . . ." Alexander Makinsky, letter to John R. Talley, July 11, 1966, Robert Winship Woodruff Papers.

"Coca-Cola is non-essential to Egypt . . ." Ibid.

"I feel sure that the administration . . ." B. H. Oehlert, letter to James H. Bahti, August 11, 1966, Robert Winship Woodruff Papers.

Rashad Mourad . . . V. G. Hoppers, letter to John R. Talley, July 27, 1966, Robert Winship Woodruff Papers.

"Cola is like beer . . ." Samanth Subramanian, "The Real Thing," *PORT Magazine*, winter 2011.

"I tell [my daughter] . . ." Calvin Sims, "Lima Journal; Peru's Pride That Refreshes," *New York Times*, December 26, 1995, www.nytimes.com/1995/12/26/world/lima-journal-peru-s -pride-that-refreshes-kola-of-a-local-color.html.

"a grand pick-me-up . . ." Robin Barr and Mark Jephcott, *Robert Barr, 1875–2001.* (Glasgow: A. G. Barr plc, 2001), 12.

"a foreign policy whose principal accomplishment . . ." Quoted in "Guided Readings: American Foreign Policy in the 1970s," Gilder Lehrman Institute of American History, accessed February 25, 2013, www.gilderlehrman.org/history-by-era/seventies/resources/guided -readings-american-foreign-policy-1970s.

One witness . . . Graham Davies, "The Week the Wall Came Down," December 1, 1989, www.camsoftpartners.co.uk/berlin.htm.

"There were thousands of cars . . ." Quoted in Neville Isdell with David Beasley, *Inside Coca-Cola* (New York: St Martin's Press, 2011), 121.

8. Racists, Eco-Freaks and Cancer Rats

"an unrepentant capitalist . . ." Mack, *No Time Lost*, viii.

"a forward step by business . . ." Quoted in Stephanie Capparell, *The Real Pepsi Challenge: How One Pioneering Company Broke Color Barriers in 1940s American Business* (New York: Wall Street Journal Books, 2007), 20.

"No one knew anything . . ." Allen McKellar Jr., "Pepsi's Real Challenge: Integrating Corporate America," Walker Speaker Series, Webster University, accessed February 23, 2013, http://blogs.webster.edu/webstertoday/2012/02/17/walker-speaker-series-integrating -corporate-america-at-pepsi.

"She couldn't understand . . ." Quoted in Capparell, *The Real Pepsi Challenge*, 22.

"Yassuh . . . it's genu-wine Hires". . . Hires, print advertisement, *Life*, September 6, 1937.

"the second-greatest governor . . ." Quoted in Capparell, *The Real Pepsi Challenge*, 179.

"Below, Picture of Negro vice president of Pepsi-Cola . . ." Quoted in Capparell, *The Real Pepsi Challenge*, 269–70.

Cans, the company's ads . . . Cantrell & Cochrane, "Now! Your Favorite Soft Drinks in Cans!," print advertisement for Super Beverages, *Daily Mirror*, June 10, 1953, Robert Winship Woodruff Papers.

"The time has come for you . . ." Quoted in Allen, *Secret Formula*, 276.

Back then its vision of the legendary symbol . . . "History of Psyche," White Rocking, accessed February 19, 2013, www.whiterocking.org/pwc.html.

"The modern woman owes a lot . . ." Pepsi-Cola, "Pepsi, the Light Refreshment," print advertisement, *American Weekly*, January 25, 1953, Robert Winship Woodruff Papers.

pretending to be a fat man . . . W. T. Johnson, memo to Hunter Bell, March 3, 1953, Robert Winship Woodruff Papers.

"A dollar's worth of sugar . . ." Douglas W. Cray, "Battle over Sweeteners Turns Bitter," *New York Times*, June 1, 1969.

"to induce cancer in man . . ." "The Delaney Paradox and Negligible Risk," Pesticide Safety Education Program, accessed January 7, 2013, http://psep.cce.cornell.edu/issues/delaney -negrisk.aspx.

"Action affecting the use of saccharin . . ." J. Paul Austin, letter to Robert H. Finch, April 14, 1970, Robert Winship Woodruff Papers.

"Use of this product . . ." W. F. "Bill" Massmann, "Government Intervention," *Clock Dial*, July– August 1978, Dr Pepper Museum Collection.

"ecology freaks . . ." "Earth Week April 17-26: It's the Real Thing," *Great Speckled Bird*, April 20, 1970.

"We had about a week . . ." Quoted in Robert Lamb, *Promising the Earth* (Abingdon, UK: Routledge, 1996), 40.

"There is a definite feeling . . ." Eugene C. Smith, memo, June 30, 1967, Robert Winship Woodruff Papers.

"Even though it's far more economical . . ." J. Paul Austin, "Environmental Renewal or Oblivion . . . Quo Vadis?," speech to the Georgia Bankers Association, April 16, 1970, Robert Winship Woodruff Papers.

9. A Better Mousetrap

"After the Second World War . . ." "Giants of Advertising: Alan Pottasch," Advertising Educational Foundation, accessed February 26, 2013, www.aef.com/industry/industry_leaders/giants _of_advertising.

"made to order for the Pepsi Generation". . . Pepsi-Cola, "Pepsi One Way," print advertisement, *Victoria Advocate*, June 3, 1966.

"No doubt, it's a rather unusual . . ." Seven-Up Company, *The Uncola: American Contemporary Graphics Exhibit*, undated booklet, Dr Pepper Museum Collection.

"We have become part of the environment" . . . Quoted in "Coke's Formula: Keep the Image Fresh," *Business Week*, April 25, 1970.

"Woodrow Wilson Clements . . ." Quoted in Jeffrey L. Rodengen, *The Legend of Dr Pepper/Seven-Up* (Fort Lauderdale, FL: Write Stuff Syndicate, 1995), 65.

"All of us badly . . ." John Sculley with John A. Byrne, *Odyssey: Pepsi to Apple* (Glasgow: Fontana Paperbacks, 1989), 50.

"Well, I'll be darned" . . . Quoted in Sculley, *Odyssey*, 73.

"The commercials on TV . . ." Pepsi-Cola, "The Pepsi Challenge at the C.N.E.," television advertisement, 1977, YouTube video posted by robatsea2009, September 13, 2011, www.youtube.com/watch?v=7Py_QMLFK0.

"I'm going to go with Pepsi for sure" . . . Pepsi-Cola, Pepsi Challenge television advertisement, 1983, YouTube video posted by GrubcoTV3, December 23, 2008, www.youtube.com /watch?v=v7lw_vhxtNc.

"pulling their wily tricks" . . . Quoted in Thomas Oliver, *The Real Coke, the Real Story* (London: Elm Tree Books, 1986), 47.

"Do you want to spend the rest of your life . . ." Quoted in Sculley, *Odyssey*, 135.

"We needed a campaign that would . . ." Sculley, *Odyssey*, 240.

"That was a John Sculley . . ." Andrea Cunningham, interview by Wendy Marinaccio, July 14, 2000, in Making the Macintosh (online collection), http://www-sul.stanford.edu/mac /primary/interviews/cunningham/trans.html.

"Look at orange juice advertising . . ." Quoted in J. C. Louis and Harvey Z. Yazijian, *Cola Wars* (New York: Everest House Publishers, 1980), 129.

"The fundamental change . . ." Quoted in Louis and Yazijian, *Cola Wars*, 130.

"The days are gone . . ." Quoted in Oliver, *The Real Coke*, 62–63.

"If you're number two . . ." Ibid., 51.

"This is Michael Jackson . . ." Quoted in Enrico and Kornbluth, *The Other Guy Blinked*, 92.

"What do you say . . ." Ibid., 102.

"I don't want you to show . . ." Ibid., 107.

"I was dancing down . . ." Michael Jackson, *Moonwalk* (London: William Heinemann, 1988), 236.

"That was where I learned . . ." Ray Kroc with Robert Anderson, *Grinding it Out: The Making of McDonald's* (London: St Martin's Paperbacks, 2011), 17.

"We will soon be unfolding . . ." Quoted in Pendergrast, *For God, Country & Coca-Cola*.

One reporter asked Goizueta . . . Quoted in Oliver, *The Real Coke*, 133.

"There are two things . . ." Quoted in Erik P. Smith, "Was the New Coke–Old Coke Skirmish Actually Planned?," *Spokesman-Review*, July 23, 1985.

"The sorrow is knowing . . ." Quoted in Hays, *Pop*.

"you boys made a BIG mistake" . . . Karen Raney, letter to Robert Woodruff, May 10, 1985, Robert Winship Woodruff Papers.

"You bastard! . . ." Quoted in Pendergrast, *For God, Country & Coca-Cola*.

"You have given us back our dream" . . . Quoted in Pendergrast, *For God, Country & Coca-Cola*.

"I feel like a lost friend . . ." Quoted in Pendergrast, *For God, Country & Coca-Cola*.

"phased out and totally eliminated" . . . Amanda Rosseter of the Coca-Cola Company, e-mail to the author, October 23, 2012.

"We are not that dumb . . ." "What the Coke Brass Had to Say," unattributed and undated news clipping, Coca-Cola Collection.

10. Beverage Backlash

Bon Jovi insisted . . . Associated Press, "Clients Make Peculiar Demands," *Beaver County Times*, May 25, 1988.

Stephen King turned the heroes . . . Stephen King, *Desperation* (London: Hodder & Stoughton, 1996).

"One glass and the jet lag . . ." "Selling Energy," *Economist*, May 9, 2002, www.economist.com /node/1120373?story_id=1120373.

"The only things we took back . . ." "Learning from the Super 7," *BevNET*, March 15, 2007, www.bevnet.com/magazine/issue/2007/2008-2-26-2008-super7.

Another part of its energy blend . . . Valeria Matinuzzi, Danielle Peterson, Sean Iacobone, and Salah Badjou. "Effects and Effectiveness of Energy Drinks," paper for the 2012 American Society for Engineering Education Northeast Section Conference, University of Massachusetts Lowell, April 27–28, 2012, http://acamedics.com/proceedings /aseene/2012/PM_3135.pdf; M.A. Heckman, K. Sherry, and E. Gonzalez de Meija, "Energy Drinks: An Assessment of Their Market Size, Consumer Demographics, Ingredient Profile, Functionality, and Regulations in the United States," *Comprehensive Reviews in Food Science and Food Safety* 9, no. 3 (May 2010), 303–17.

"When we launched in Germany . . ." "Learning from the Super 7."

"greatest marketing stunt of all time" . . . Jenny Shaw, "Reading Room: Red Bull Stratos," WPP, accessed February 23, 2013, www.wpp.com/wpp/marketing/digital/red-bull-stratos.

"We realized that if we . . ." Heather Landi, "A Mighty Force," *Beverage World*, January 15, 2009.

"Monster is about action sports . . ." Landi, "A Mighty Force."

"We allowed the labels . . ." "Keep up with the Jones, Dude!," *Bloomberg Businessweek*, October 25, 2005, www.businessweek.com/stories/2005-10-25/keep-up-with-the-jones-dude.

In the early 1960s . . . "Overweight, Obesity, and Healthy Weight Among Persons 20 Years of Age and Over, by Selected Characteristics," in *Health, United States, 2010* (Hyattsville, MD: Centers for Disease Control and Prevention, 2011) www.cdc.gov/nchs/data/hus/hus10.pdf.

But America led the pack . . . Organisation for Economic Co-operation and Development, "Obesity Update 2012," policy brief, accessed February 21, 2013, www.oecd.org /health/49716427.pdf.

"counter-offensive against attacks . . ." "Summary Outline of a Program for an Immediate Counter-Offensive Against Attacks on Coca-Cola on the Dental and Nutrition Fronts," unattributed and undated report, Robert Winship Woodruff Papers.

"We want to dislodge the cocksure . . ." "Summary Outline."

As soda sales peaked . . . Michael F. Jacobson, *Liquid Candy: How Soft Drinks Are Harming Americans' Health*, 2nd ed. (Washington, DC: Center for Science in the Public Interest, 2005).

"Orange Crush is served . . ." "Orange Crush and Kids—a 'Natural Promotion," *O-C News*, May–June 1951, Dr Pepper Museum Collection.

"Sorry, selling this juice . . ." Jacqueline Domac, "Sodas Out, Healthier Students In," *United Teacher Magazine*, August 2002, www.nojunkfood.org/media/goodbye_cocacola.html.

"It's unfair because . . ." Cara Mia DiMassa and Erika Hayasaki, "LA Schools Set to Can Soda Sales," *Los Angeles Times*, August 25, 2002, www.organicconsumers.org/school/0901 _schools_soda.cfm.

By the fall of 2009 . . . "Alliance School Beverage Guidelines Final Progress Report," American Beverage Association, March 8, 2010.

In 1986 Americans bought . . . Heather Landi, "State of the Industry Report '07: Bottled Water," *Beverage World*, April 15, 2007.

"We, Pepsi, would push . . ." Valerie Bauerlein, "PepsiCo Chief Defends her Strategy to Promote 'Good for You' Foods," *Wall Street Journal*, June 28, 2011, http://online.wsj.com/article/SB1 0001424052702303627104576412232408827462.html.

An examination of the obesity studies . . . Gail Woodward-Lopez, Janice Kao, and Lorrene Ritchie, "To What Extent Have Sweetened Beverages Contributed to the Obesity Epidemic?," *Public Health Nutrition* 14, no. 3 (March 2011).

Another review of the studies . . . Lenny R. Vartanian et al., "Effects of Soft Drink Consumption on Nutrition and Health: A Systematic Review and Meta-Analysis," *American Journal of Public Health* 97, no. 4 (April 2007).

"Is soda the new tobacco?" . . . Mark Bittman, "Soda: A Sin We Sip Instead of Smoke?," *New York Times*, February 13, 2010, www.nytimes.com/2010/02/14/weekinreview/14bittman.html.

"All over the United States . . ." Michael M. Grynbaum, "Bloomberg Plans a Ban on Large Sugared Drinks," *New York Times*, May 31, 2012, www.nytimes.com/2012/05/31/nyregion /bloomberg-plans-a-ban-on-large-sugared-drinks.html.

"This is the biggest step . . ." New York City Board of Health, "Mayor Bloomberg, Deputy Mayor Gibbs, Health Commissioner Farley and Bruce Ratner Announce Barclays Center Will Voluntarily Adopt Regulations to Limit Size of Sugary Beverages," news release, September 13, 2012.

"I can't say when it will be here . . ." Candice Choi, "Coke, Pepsi Racing for a Better No-Calorie Soda," *Huffington Post*, July 26, 2012, www.huffingtonpost.com/2012/07/26/coke-pepsi-no -calories-soda_n_1705083.html.

Bibliography

Books

Abbott, Elizabeth. *Sugar: A Bittersweet History*. London: Duckworth Overlook, 2008. Kindle ed.

Afri-Cola. *80 Jahre Anders Afri-Cola*. Stuttgart: Mineralbrunnen Überkingen-Teinach AG, 2011.

Allen, Frederick. *Secret Formula: How Brilliant Marketing and Relentless Salesmanship Made Coca-Cola the Best-Known Product in the World*. New York: HarperCollins, 1994.

Allen, Gary J., and Ken Albala. *The Business of Food: Encyclopedia of the Food and Drink Industries*. Santa Barbara, CA: ABC-CLIO, 2007.

Allen, Ida Bailey. *When You Entertain: What to Do, and How*. Atlanta: Coca-Cola Company, 1932.

Appleton, Nancy, and G. N. Jacobs. *Killer Colas: The Hard Truth About Soft Drinks*. Garden City Park, NY: Square One Publishers, 2011.

Barr, Robin, and Mark Jephcott. *Robert Barr, 1875–2001*. Glasgow: A. G. Barr plc, 2001.

Baumer, Jim. *Moxie: Maine in a Bottle*. Rockport, ME: Down East, 2011. Kindle ed.

Best, Gary Dean. *The Dollar Decade: Mammon and the Machine in 1920s America*. Westport, CT: Greenwood Publishing Group, 2003.

Blair, Pat, Dana Prater, and the Sheridan County Museum. *Sheridan*. San Francisco: Arcadia Publishing, 2008.

Blanding, Michael. *The Coke Machine: The Dirty Truth Behind the World's Favorite Soft Drink*. New York: Avery, 2011.

Bordowitz, Hank. *Bad Moon Rising: The Unauthorized History of Creedence Clearwater Revival*. Chicago: Chicago Review Press, 2007.

Bowers, Q. David. *The Moxie Encyclopedia*. Vol. 1, *The History*. Vestal, NY: Vestal Press, 1986.

Bridgforth, Dick. *Mountain Dew: The History*. North Charleston, SC: BookSurge, 2007.

Brogan, Hugh. *The Penguin History of the USA*. 2nd ed. London: Penguin Books, 1999.

Brown, John Hull. *Early American Beverages*. Rutland, VT: Charles E. Tuttle Company, 1966.

Cadbury, Deborah. *Chocolate Wars: From Cadbury to Kraft: 200 Years of Sweet Success and Bitter Rivalry*. London: HarperPress, 2010.

Capparell, Stephanie. *The Real Pepsi Challenge: How One Pioneering Company Broke Color Barriers in 1940s American Business*. New York: Wall Street Journal Books, 2007.

Cardello, Hank, with Doug Garr. *Stuffed: An Insider's Look at Who's Really Making America Fat.* New York: HarperCollins, 2009. Kindle ed.

Carpenter, Donna Sammons, and Maurice Coyle. *What You Can Learn from Pepsi.* Boston: New Word City, 2010. iBooks ed.

Coppin, Clayton A., and Jack C. High. *The Politics of Purity: Harvey Washington Wiley and the Origins of Federal Food Policy.* Ann Arbor: University of Michigan Press, 1999.

Debus, Allen G. *The Chemical Philosophy: Paracelsian Science and Medicine in the Sixteenth and Seventeenth Centuries.* Mineola, NY: Dover Publications, 2002.

Dick, Malcolm, ed. *Joseph Priestley and Birmingham.* Studley, UK: Brewin Books, 2005.

Dietz, Lawrence. *Soda Pop: The History, Advertising, Art and Memorabilia of Soft Drinks in America.* New York: Simon and Schuster, 1973.

Doyle, Arthur Conan. *The Adventures of Sherlock Holmes.* Lewes, UK: Vigo Essential Classics, 2011. iBooks ed.

Drowne, Kathleen Morgan. *Spirits of Defiance: National Prohibition and Jazz Age Literature.* Columbus: Ohio State University, 2005.

Drowne, Kathleen Morgan, and Patrick Huber. *The 1920s.* Westport, CT: Greenwood Publishing Group, 2004.

Eddy, Walter H. *The "Liquid Bite."* Dallas: Dr Pepper Company, 1944.

Ellis, Harry E. *Dr Pepper: King of Beverages.* Dallas: Dr Pepper Company, 1979.

———. *Dr Pepper: King of Beverages Centennial Edition 1885–1985.* Dallas: Dr Pepper Company, 1986.

Emmins, Colin. *Soft Drinks: Their Origins and History.* Princes Risborough, UK: Shire Publications, 1991.

Enrico, Roger, and Jesse Kornbluth. *The Other Guy Blinked: How Pepsi Won the Cola Wars.* London: Bantam, 1986.

Fisher, George P. *Life of Benjamin Silliman, M.D., LL.D.* New York: Charles Scribner and Company, 1866.

Foxcroft, Louise. *Calories and Corsets: A History of Dieting Over 2,000 Years.* London: Profile Books, 2011.

Fulton, John F., and Elizabeth H. Thomson. *Benjamin Silliman 1779–1864: Pathfinder in American Science.* New York: Henry Schuman, 1947.

Funderburg, Anne Cooper. *Chocolate, Strawberry and Vanilla: A History of American Ice Cream.* Bowling Green, OH: Bowling Green State University Popular Press, 1995.

———. *Sundae Best: A History of Soda Fountains.* Bowling Green, OH: Bowling Green State University Popular Press, 2002.

Gibbs, F. W. *Joseph Priestley: Adventurer in Science and Champion of Truth.* London: Thomas Nelson and Sons, 1965.

Greising, David. *I'd Like the World to Buy a Coke: The Life and Leadership of Roberto Goizueta.* New York: John Wiley & Sons, 1998.

Hardaway, Robert M. *No Price Too High: Victimless Crimes and the Ninth Amendment.* Westport, CT: Greenwood Publishing Group, 2003.

Hau, Michael. *The Cult of Health and Beauty in Germany: A Social History, 1890–1930.* Chicago: University of Chicago Press, 2003.

Hays, Constance L. *Pop: Truth and Power at the Coca-Cola Company.* London: Hutchinson, 2004. Kindle ed.

Hine, Thomas. *The Total Package: The Evolution and Secret Meanings of Boxes, Bottles, Cans, and Tubes*. New York: Little Brown and Company, 1995.

Hoffmann, Dr. Friedrich. *New Experiments and Observations upon Mineral Waters*. London: J. Osborn & T. Longman, 1731.

Holl, John, and Nate Schweber. *Indiana Breweries*. Mechanicsburg, PA: Stackpole Books, 2011.

Hollingworth, J. *The Modern Extractor: A Complete Treatise for Making of Extracts, Flavors, Syrups and Sundries*. Pittsburgh: The Extractor Co., 1923.

Isdell, Neville, with David Beasley. *Inside Coca-Cola*. New York: St. Martin's Press, 2011.

Ishizu, Dr. R. *The Mineral Springs of Japan*. Tokyo: Tokyo Imperial Hygienic Laboratory, 1915. http://archive.org/details/mineralspringsof00toky.

Issacson, Walter. *Steve Jobs*. London: Little Brown, 2011.

Jackson, Michael. *Moonwalk*. London: William Heinemann, 1988.

Jacobson, Michael F. *Liquid Candy: How Soft Drinks Are Harming Americans' Health*. 2nd ed. Washington, D.C.: Center for Science in the Public Interest, 2005.

Kahn, E. J., Jr. *The Big Drink: An Unofficial History of Coca-Cola*. London: Max Reinhardt, 1960.

Keegan, John. *The American Civil War*. London: Vintage Books, 2009.

King, Stephen. *Desperation*. London: Hodder & Stoughton, 1996.

Knowlton, Calvin H., and Richard P. Penna. *Pharmaceutical Care*. 2nd ed. Bethesda, MD: American Society of Health-System Pharmacists, 2003.

Kroc, Ray, with Robert Anderson. *Grinding It Out: The Making of McDonald's*. London: St. Martin's Paperbacks, 2011.

Kuisel, Richard F. *Seducing the French: The Dilemma of Americanization*. Berkeley: University of California Press, 1993. http://publishing.cdlib.org/ucpressebooks/view?docId=ft4w10060w.

Lamb, Robert. *Promising the Earth*. Abingdon, UK: Routledge, 1996.

Lears, Jackson. *Fables of Abundance: A Cultural History of Advertising in America*. New York: Basic Books, 1994.

Lender, Mark Edward, and James Kirby Martin. *Drinking in America: A History*. New York: The Free Press, 1987.

Lerner, Michael A. *Dry Manhattan: Prohibition in New York City*. Cambridge, MA: Harvard University Press, 2008.

Lloyd, John Uri. *Life and Medical Discoveries of Samuel Thomson and a History of the Thomsonian Materia Medica*. Cincinnati: The Lloyd Library of Botany, Pharmacy and Materia Medica, 1909.

Louis, J. C., and Harvey Z. Yazijian. *Cola Wars*. New York: Everest House Publishers, 1980.

Mack, Walter, with Peter Buckley. *No Time Lost: The Autobiography of Walter Mack*. New York: Atheneum, 1982.

Mariani, Angelo. *Coca and its Therapeutic Application*. 3rd ed. New York: J. N. Jaros, 1896.

Martin, Milward M. *Twelve Full Ounces*. New York: Holt, Rinehart and Winston, 1962.

Mason, Mark. *The Political Economy of Japanese Capital Controls, 1899–1980*. Cambridge, MA: Harvard University Press, 1992.

Mayhew, Henry. *Mayhew's London: Being Selections from "London Labour and the London Poor."* London: Spring Books, 1851.

McNeil, Legs. *Pop Culture: Stories from Pepsi-Cola's First 100 Years*. Singapore: Byron Preiss Multimedia Company, 1998.

McQueen, Humphrey. *The Essence of Capitalism*. London: Profile Books, 2001.

M'Elory, A. *A. M'Elory's Philadelphia Directory*. Philadelphia: A. M'Elroy, 1839. http://books .google.co.uk/books?id=4sklAAAAMAAJ.

Mieszkowski, Sylvia, Joy Smith, and Marijke de Valck, eds. *Sonic Interventions*. Amsterdam: Rodopi, 2007.

Mills, Robert Lockwood, with Harry Maurer. *Thomas Elmezzi: The Man Who Kept the Secret*. Great Neck, NY: JET Foundation Press, 2004.

Mishima, Yukio. *The Decay of the Angel*. London: Vintage Books, 2001. Originally published 1971.

Moore, Lucy. *Anything Goes: A Biography of the Roaring Twenties*. London: Atlantic Books, 2008.

Moritz, Charles P. *Travels, Chiefly on Foot, Through Several Parts of England in 1782*. London: G.G. and J. Robinson, 1797.

Morrison, Tom. *Root Beer: Advertising and Collectibles*. West Chester, PA: Schiffer, 1992.

Moskos, Peter. *Cop in the Hood: My Year Policing Baltimore's Eastern District*. Princeton, NJ: Princeton University Press, 2009.

Musto, David F. *The American Disease: Origins of Narcotic Control*. 3rd ed. New York: Oxford University Press, 1999.

Nishizawa, Iwata. *Japan in the Taisho Era: In Commemoration of the Enthronement*. Tokyo, 1917. http://archive.org/details/japanintaishoera00nishrich.

Offitzer, Karen. *Diners*. New York: Metro Books, 1997.

Oliver, Thomas. *The Real Coke, the Real Story*. London: Elm Tree Books, 1986.

Olsen, Kirstin. *Daily Life in 18th-Century England*. Westport, CT: Greenwood Press, 1999.

O'Neil, Darcy. *Fix the Pumps: The History and Recipes of the Soda Fountain*. London, Ontario: Art of Drink, 2009.

Ozersky, Josh. *The Hamburger: A History*. New Haven, CT: Yale University Press, 2008.

Peeters, Evert, Leen Van Molle, and Kaat Wils, eds. *Beyond Pleasure: Cultures of Modern Asceticism*. New York: Berghahn Books, 2011.

Pendergrast, Mark. *For God, Country & Coca-Cola: The Definitive History of the Great American Soft Drink and the Company That Makes It*. 3rd ed. New York: Basic Books, 2013. Kindle ed.

Platt, Jerome J. *Cocaine Addiction: Theory, Research and Treatment*. Cambridge, MA: Harvard University Press, 2000.

Potter, Frank N. *The Moxie Mystique*. Virginia Beach: Donning Company/Publishers, 1981.

Priestley, Joseph. *An Appeal to the Public on the Subject of the Riots in Birmingham*. London: J. Thompson, 1791.

———. *Directions for Impregnating Water with Fixed Air*. London: J. Johnson, 1772.

———. *Experiments and Observations on Different Kinds of Air*. 2nd ed. London: J. Johnson, 1775.

———. *The Importance and Extent of Free Inquiry in Matters of Religion*. London: J. Johnson, 1785.

Reichardt, Eike. *Health, "Race" and Empire: Popular-Scientific Spectacles and National Identity in Imperial Germany, 1871–1914*. Raleigh, NC: Lulu, 2008

Richmond, Lesley, Julie Stevenson, and Alison Turton, eds. *The Pharmaceutical Industry: A Guide to Historical Records*. Aldershot, UK: Ashgate Publishing, 2003.

Riley, John J. *A History of the American Soft Drink Industry: Bottled Carbonated Beverages 1807–1957*. New York: Arno Press, 1958.

Rodengen, Jeffrey L. *The Legend of Dr Pepper/Seven-Up*. Fort Lauderdale, FL: Write Stuff Syndicate, 1995.

Rouch, Lawrence L. *The Vernor's Story: From Gnomes to Now*. Ann Arbor: University of Michigan Press, 2003.

Rowland, Sanders, with Bob Terrell. *Papa Coke: Sixty-Five Years Selling Coca-Cola*. Asheville, NC: Bright Mountain Books, 1986.

Rush, Benjamin. *Experiments and Observations on the Mineral Waters of Philadelphia, Abington, and Bristol, in the Province of Pennsylvania*. Philadelphia: James Humphreys Jr., 1773.

Schutts, Jeff. "'Die Erfrischende Pause': Marketing Coca-Cola in Hitler's Germany." In *Selling Modernity: Advertising in Twentieth-Century Germany*, edited by Pamela E. Swett, S. Jonathan Wiesen, and Jonathan R. Zatlin. Durham, NC: Duke University Press, 2007. Kindle ed.

Scott, Robert L. *God Is My Co-Pilot*. Broomfield, CO: Summa Iru Speciality Publishing, 2011. Kindle ed.

Sculley, John, with John A. Byrne. *Odyssey: Pepsi to Apple*. Glasgow: Fontana Paperbacks, 1989.

Shavin, Norman, and Bruce Galphin. *Atlanta: Triumph of a People*. Atlanta: Capricorn Corporation, 1982.

Sherman, William Tecumseh. *Memoirs of General W. T. Sherman*. New York: Library of America, 1990. Originally published 1886.

Simmons, Douglas A. *Schweppes: The First 200 Years*. London: Springwood Books, 1983.

Sinclair, Charles. *Dictionary of Food: International Food and Cooking Terms from A to Z*. London: A & C Black, 2005.

Slavicek, Louise Chipley. *The Prohibition Era: Temperance in the United States*. New York: InfoBase Publishing, 2008.

Smith, Andrew F. *Encyclopedia of Junk Food and Fast Food*. Westport, CT: Greenwood Press, 2006.

Smith, Andrew F., ed. *The Oxford Companion to American Food and Drink*. Oxford: Oxford University Press, 2007.

Smith, Edgar Fahs. *Priestley in America, 1794–1804*. Philadelphia: P. Blakiston's & Co., 1920.

Steel, John H. *An Analysis of the Mineral Waters of Saratoga and Ballston*. Saratoga Springs, NY: G.M. Davison, 1831.

Steen, David P., and Philip R. Ashurst, eds. *Carbonated Soft Drinks: Formulation and Manufacture*. Oxford: Blackwell Publishing, 2006.

Stoddard, Bob. *Pepsi-Cola: 100 Years*. Los Angeles: General Publishing Group, 1997.

Stokes, Henry Scott. *The Life and Death of Yukio Mishima*. New York: Cooper Square Press, 2000.

Swiderski, Richard. *Poison Eaters: Snakes, Opium, Arsenic, and the Lethal Show*. Boca Raton, FL: Universal-Publishers, 2010.

Takabuki, Matsuo. *An Unlikely Revolutionary: Matsuo Takabuki and the Making of Modern Hawai'i: A Memoir*. Honolulu: University of Hawaii Press, 1998.

Teed, Peter. *Dictionary of Twentieth-Century History, 1914–1990*. Oxford: Oxford University Press, 1992.

Thomas, Mark. *Belching Out the Devil: Global Adventures with Coca-Cola*. London: Ebury Press, 2008.

Thomson, Samuel. *New Guide to Health, or Botanic Family Physician*. London: Simpkin, Marshall & Co., 1849.

Thorpe, Thomas Edward. *Joseph Priestley*. London: J.M. Dent & Co, 1906.

Wang, Jing. *Brand New China: Advertising, Media, and Commercial Culture*. Cambridge, MA: Harvard University Press, 2008.

Weinstein, Jay. "Bottling." In *The Oxford Companion to American Food and Drink*, edited by Andrew F. Smith. Oxford: Oxford University Press, 2007.

Welby, Adlard. *A Visit to North America and the English Settlements in Illinois, with a Winter Residence at Philadelphia.* London: J. Drury, 1821.

Wiley, Harvey. *The History of a Crime Against the Food Law.* New York: Arno Press, 1976. Originally published 1929.

Wilson, Bee. *Swindled: The Dark History of Food Fraud, from Poisoned Candy to Counterfeit Coffee.* Princeton, NJ: Princeton University Press, 2008.

Wingbermühle, Annika. "A Wee Bit Different: Socio-cultural Influences on Scottish Marketing." In *Cultural Industries: The British Experience in International Perspective*, edited by Christiane Eisenberg, Rita Gerlach and Christian Handke. Berlin: Humboldt University, 2006. http://edoc.hu-berlin.de/conferences/culturalindustries/wingbermuehle-annika/PDF/wingbermuehle.pdf.

Wright, Karen. *The Road to Dr Pepper, Texas: The Story of Dublin Dr Pepper.* Abilene, TX: State House Press, 2006.

Young, James Harvey. *The Toadstool Millionaires: A Social History of Patent Medicines in America before Federal Regulation.* Princeton: Princeton University Press, 1961.

Young, William H., and Nancy K. Young. *The Great Depression in America: A Cultural Encyclopedia.* Vol. 2. Westport, CT: Greenwood Publishing Group, 2007.

Memos and Letters

Acklin, A. A. Letter to Robert Woodruff, February 6, 1940. Robert Winship Woodruff Papers.

Adams, Charles W. "PepsiCo Activity in the Soviet Union." Letter, May 22, 1974. Robert Winship Woodruff Papers.

Austin, J. Paul. Letter to the directors of the Coca-Cola Company, October 20, 1969. Robert Winship Woodruff Papers.

———. Letter to Robert H. Finch, April 14, 1970. Robert Winship Woodruff Papers.

———. Letter to Robert Woodruff, September 27, 1971. Robert Winship Woodruff Papers.

———. Letter to Robert Woodruff, May 4, 1973. Robert Winship Woodruff Papers.

———. Letter to Robert Woodruff, February 15, 1977. Robert Winship Woodruff Papers.

———. Letter to Robert Woodruff and Lee Talley, June 17, 1965. Robert Winship Woodruff Papers.

———. Letter to Robert Woodruff and Lee Talley, July 1, 1968. Robert Winship Woodruff Papers.

———. Letter to Robert Woodruff and Lee Talley, November 28, 1969. Robert Winship Woodruff Papers.

———. Letter to Samuel N. Gardner, October 25, 1967. Robert Winship Woodruff Papers.

———. Report for Robert Woodruff, taken by phone by J. W. Jones, April 22, 1970. Telephone conversation transcript. Robert Winship Woodruff Papers.

———. Telegram to the directors of the Coca-Cola Company, July 16, 1979. Robert Winship Woodruff Papers.

Barber, E. R. Letter to W. H. Warwick, August 26, 1954. Robert Winship Woodruff Papers.

Bielski, Walt, et al. Letter to Robert Woodruff, September 8, 1943. Coca-Cola Company Archives.

Biedenharn, J. A. Letter to Harrison Jones, September 11, 1939. Robert Winship Woodruff Papers.

Bledge, E. D. Letter to John L. Tewksbury, October 8, 1963. Robert Winship Woodruff Papers.

Brock, Pope F. Letter to W. J. Hobbs et al, October 3, 1950. Robert Winship Woodruff Papers.

Callahan, Robert L., Jr. Letter to J. Paul Austin, February 2, 1972. Robert Winship Woodruff Papers.

Candler, Asa Griggs. Letter to Warren Candler, April 10, 1888. Asa Griggs Candler Papers.

Chason, A. L. "Check of Calories in Pepsi-Cola." Letter to Dr. O. E. May, August 6, 1953. Robert Winship Woodruff Papers.

Ching, Joan C. Letter to W. T. Jarrett, July 29, 1944. National Archives of the United Kingdom.

Clifford, Martha L. "To Those Concerned with the Health and Welfare of School Children," Letter, December 6, 1950. Robert Winship Woodruff Papers.

Coca-Cola Company, New York. Letter to John L. Harvey, January 14, 1965. Robert Winship Woodruff Papers.

Coca-Cola Export Corporation. Letter to Robert Woodruff, January 26, 1940. Robert Winship Woodruff Papers.

Corbyn, F. J. H. Letter to D. R. Lamb, May 8, 1944. National Archives of the United Kingdom.

———. Letter to E. M. Hugh-Jones, May 9, 1944. National Archives of the United Kingdom.

Coste, Felix W. Letter to H. B. Nicholson, May 28, 1954. Robert Winship Woodruff Papers.

Dorsey, William T. Letter to Bernard M. Culver, September 23, 1938. Robert Winship Woodruff Papers.

Fleck, H. J. Letter to Duke Ludwig, August 17, 1953. Robert Winship Woodruff Papers.

———. Letter to Duke Ludwig, August 24, 1953. Robert Winship Woodruff Papers.

Forbes, Lt. W. J. Letter to Mrs. Williams, August 15, 1949. Coca-Cola Company Archives.

Forio, E. J. Letter to Lee Talley, March 27, 1964. Robert Winship Woodruff Papers.

———. Letter to Robert Woodruff, April 15, 1952. Robert Winship Woodruff Papers.

———. Letter to Robert Woodruff, January 23, 1953. Robert Winship Woodruff Papers.

———. Letter to Robert Woodruff, April 1, 1957. Robert Winship Woodruff Papers.

———. Letter to Robert Woodruff, November 26, 1965. Robert Winship Woodruff Papers.

Foster, G. N. "Concentration of the Soft Drink Industry." Letter to G. E. Todd, July 31, 1942. National Archives of the United Kingdom.

Frazer, Gordon. Letter to the Coca-Cola Company, March 3, 1944. Coca-Cola Company Archives.

Gaddis, Lt. W. P., Jr. Letter to his mother in Berkeley, California, undated. Coca-Cola Company Archives.

Goizueta, Roberto. Letter to members of the board of directors of the Coca-Cola Company. March 11, 1981. Robert Winship Woodruff Papers.

Goodloe, John D. Letter to Thomas J. Deegan, April 9, 1966. Robert Winship Woodruff Papers.

Haldi, John. Letter to Lucien Harris Jr., September 3, 1963. Robert Winship Woodruff Papers.

Harris, Lucien, Jr. Letter to John Haldi, February 7, 1964. Robert Winship Woodruff Papers.

Hayes, Ralph. Letter, September 8, 1938. Robert Winship Woodruff Papers.

———. Letter to A. A. Acklin, October 4, 1940. Robert Winship Woodruff Papers.

———. Letter to Lee Talley, December 18, 1961. Robert Winship Woodruff Papers.

Hirsch, Harold. "Trade Mark Coca-Cola." Letter to Robert Woodruff, July 7, 1931. Robert Winship Woodruff Papers.

Hogan, Daniel E. Letter to J. Paul Austin, June 3, 1968. Robert Winship Woodruff Papers.

Hoppers, V. G. "A Proposal to Establish a Plant in the Free Zone of Port Said for the Production of Coca-Cola Concentrate and Other Beverage Bases." Letter to A. T. El Bakry, October 4, 1966. Robert Winship Woodruff Papers.

———. Letter to John R. Talley, June 28, 1966. Robert Winship Woodruff Papers.

———. Letter to John R. Talley, June 30, 1966. Robert Winship Woodruff Papers.

———. Letter to John R. Talley, July 20, 1966. Robert Winship Woodruff Papers.

———. Letter to John R. Talley, July 27, 1966. Robert Winship Woodruff Papers.

———. Letter to John R. Talley, October 18, 1966. Robert Winship Woodruff Papers.

Hugh-Jones, E. M. Letter to F. J. H. Corbyn, May 6, 1944. National Archives of the United Kingdom.

Johnson, W. T. Memo to Hunter Bell, March 3, 1953. Robert Winship Woodruff Papers.

Jones, Harrison. Letter to Robert Woodruff, July 5, 1932. Robert Winship Woodruff Papers.

———. Memo to Robert Woodruff, August 22, 1932. Robert Winship Woodruff Papers.

———. Letter to Robert Woodruff, February 18, 1933. Robert Winship Woodruff Papers.

———. Letter to Robert Woodruff, December 30, 1942. Robert Winship Woodruff Papers.

———. Memo to Robert Woodruff, undated. Robert Winship Woodruff Papers.

Jones, J. W. Letter to Robert Woodruff, September 11, 1973. Robert Winship Woodruff Papers.

Lamb, D. R. Letter to F. J. H. Corbyn, May 8, 1944. National Archives of the United Kingdom.

Law, Thomas C., Jr. "Status of TAB." Letter to J. Lucien Smith, September 22, 1965. Robert Winship Woodruff Papers.

Lee, Archie. letter to Robert Woodruff, November 21, 1945. Robert Winship Woodruff Papers.

Leonard, Earl T., Jr. "Saccharin Strategy." Letter to Roberto Goizueta, March 9, 1981. Robert Winship Woodruff Papers.

Ludwig, I. C. Letter to J. F. Curtis, July 24, 1953. Robert Winship Woodruff Papers.

Mack, Walter S. "Re: End of Sugar Rationing." Letter to all members of the Pepsi-Cola family, September 17, 1947. Robert Winship Woodruff Papers.

Makinsky, Alexander. Letter to John Talley, July 9, 1966. Robert Winship Woodruff Papers.

———. Letter to John R. Talley, July 11, 1966. Robert Winship Woodruff Papers.

———. Letter to Robert Woodruff, July 30, 1931. Robert Winship Woodruff Papers.

———. Letter to Steve Ladas, June 11, 1949. Robert Winship Woodruff Papers.

Marshall, G. C. "Supply of Equipment and Supplies for Preparation and Bottling of Soft Drinks in Oversea Commands." War Department circular no. 51, February 4, 1944. Robert Winship Woodruff Papers.

Nicholson, H. B. Letter to Robert Woodruff, February 8, 1940. Robert Winship Woodruff Papers.

Nixon, Richard. Letter to Robert Woodruff, December 15, 1959. Robert Winship Woodruff Papers.

Oehlert, B. H., Jr. Letter to Dr. Harold Rowe, April 7, 1942. Robert Winship Woodruff Papers.

———. Letter to J. A. Sibley, October 6, 1941. Robert Winship Woodruff Papers.

———. Letter to J. Paul Austin, April 22, 1966. Robert Winship Woodruff Papers.

———. Letter to J. Paul Austin, April 28, 1966. Robert Winship Woodruff Papers.

———. Letter to J. Paul Austin, November 22, 1966. Robert Winship Woodruff Papers.

———. Letter to James H. Bahti, August 11, 1966. Robert Winship Woodruff Papers.

———. Letter to John R. Talley, April 25, 1966. Robert Winship Woodruff Papers.

———. Letter to Ralph Hayes, April 7, 1942. Robert Winship Woodruff Papers.

———. Letter to Robert Woodruff, December 12, 1941. Robert Winship Woodruff Papers.

———. Letter to Robert Woodruff, June 1, 1942. Robert Winship Woodruff Papers.

———. Letter to Robert Woodruff, November 20, 1942. Robert Winship Woodruff Papers.

———. Letter to Robert Woodruff, January 20, 1954. Robert Winship Woodruff Papers.

———. Letter to Robert Woodruff, January 26, 1954. Robert Winship Woodruff Papers.

Powers, Ray. Letter to Robert Woodruff, October 7, 1930. Robert Winship Woodruff Papers.

———. Letter to Robert Woodruff, February 24, 1931. Robert Winship Woodruff Papers.

———. Letter to Robert Woodruff, May 14, 1937. Robert Winship Woodruff Papers.

———. Letter to Robert Woodruff, April 23, 1938. Robert Winship Woodruff Papers.

———. Telegram to Robert Woodruff, November 12, 1936. Robert Winship Woodruff Papers.

Pinkerton's National Detective Agency. Letter to A. A. Acklin, June 27, 1933. Robert Winship Woodruff Papers.

Randolph, W. H. Letter to Robert Woodruff, October 24, 1967. Robert Winship Woodruff Papers.

Raney, Karen. Letter to Robert Woodruff, May 10, 1985. Robert Winship Woodruff Papers.

Schumacher, J. A. Letter, May 1955. Robert Winship Woodruff Papers.

Smith, Eugene C. Memo, June 30, 1967. Robert Winship Woodruff Papers.

Smith, J. Lucien. Letter to members of the Coca-Cola Family, undated. Robert Winship Woodruff Papers.

Spears, Francis H. Letter to all bottlers of Coca-Cola, October 19, 1969. Robert Winship Woodruff Papers.

Stalnaker, John M. "Pepsi-Cola Scholarship Board Announcement." Letter, October 14, 1948. Robert Winship Woodruff Papers.

Stansfield, A. F. "Background About Sugar Rationing in the UK for Soft Drinks." Letter, November 1, 1944. National Archives of the United Kingdom.

Talley, John R. Letter to J. Paul Austin, June 19, 1968. Robert Winship Woodruff Papers.

Tewksbury, John L. Letter to the president of the Coca-Cola Company, October 4, 1963. Robert Winship Woodruff Papers.

US Office of the Military Attaché, Pretoria, Transvaal. Letter to R. Stuttaford, September 18, 1942. Coca-Cola Company Archives.

Wilson, J. A. Letter to Paul Austin, November 7, 1977. Robert Winship Woodruff Papers.

Woodruff, Robert. Letter to Richard Nixon, December 21, 1959. Robert Winship Woodruff Papers.

Newspapers, Magazines, and Other Periodicals

Advertising Age. "Ad Age Advertising Century: Top 10 Slogans." March 29, 1999. http://adage.com/article/special-report-the-advertising-century/ad-age-advertising-century-top-10-slogans/140156.

———. "Sales, Profits of 4 Major Bottlers." October 17, 1955. Coca-Cola Collection.

Albers, John R. "Concentration." *Clock Dial*, September–October 1978. Dr Pepper Museum Collection.

Albright, Joe. "Lawyers Study Question of Duncan's Coke Stock." *Atlanta Constitution*, undated news clipping. Robert Winship Woodruff Papers.

American Dental Association. "Diet and Tooth Decay," *Journal of the American Dental Association* 133 (April 2002).

Ammunition. "The Pause That Erodes." August 1951. Robert Winship Woodruff Papers.

Aris, Stephen. "How Pepsi Beat Coke to Moscow." *Sunday Times*, November 26, 1972.

———. "Things Went Better for Pepsi Than for Coke in Moscow." *Age*, December 5, 1972.

Asa G. Candler & Co. Print advertisement. *Atlanta Journal*, May 1, 1889. Robert Winship Woodruff Papers.

Associated Press. "Clients Make Peculiar Demands." *Beaver County Times*, May 25, 1988.

———. "Cola Wars." *Jacksonville Times-Union and Journal.* April 22, 1984.

———. "Designer Lacks Full Credit for Coke Bottle." *Atlanta Journal and Constitution*, undated. Coca-Cola Collection.

———. "NYC Ban on Big Sodas Could Face Legal Test." KOLOtv.com, June 14, 2012. www.kolotv.com/home/headlines/NYC_ban_on_big_sodas_could_face_legal_test _159073315.html.

Atlanta Constitution. "B'nai B'rith Raps Coke's Israel Franchise Denial." April 8, 1966.

———. "Bottled Water Booms." October 14, 1970. Robert Winship Woodruff Papers.

———. "Coca-Cola Ban in Arab World Goes in Effect." August 2, 1968.

———. "Ecologists Try to Halt Plastic Bottle Use." November 7, 1975.

———. "India's Cola Conflict." May 30, 1980.

———. "Ray R. Powers Dies in Berlin Hospital." December 14, 1938. Robert Winship Woodruff Papers.

———. "Tasty Happiness a Hit in Peking." July 10, 1981.

Atlanta Journal. "Austin to Give Up Coke Posts by February." July 15, 1980. Robert Winship Woodruff Papers.

Battista, O. A. "Why Sugar is Scarce!" *News & Views*, September 1946. Dr Pepper Museum Collection.

Bauerlein, Valerie. "PepsiCo Chief Defends Her Strategy to Promote 'Good for You' Foods." *Wall Street Journal*, June 28, 2011. http://online.wsj.com/article/SB100014240527023036271 04576412232408827462.html.

Becker, L.A. "The Soda Fountain Industry." *Pharmaceutical Era*, February 1913.

Bennett, Eileen. "Local Historians Argue Over the Root of the Story of How Hires First Brewed Beer that Made Millions." *Press of Atlantic City*, June 28, 1998. www.co.cumberland .nj.us/content/163/241/597.aspx.

Bennicoff, Jan. "The Secret Ingredient in Many a Tasty Batter." *(Nashua) Telegraph*, March 11, 1992.

BevNET. "Learning from the Super 7." March 15, 2007. www.bevnet.com/magazine /issue/2007/2008-2-26-2008-super7.

Bittman, Mark. "Soda: A Sin We Sip Instead of Smoke?" *New York Times*, February 13, 2010. www.nytimes.com/2010/02/14/weekinreview/14bittman.html.

Blackman, M. C. "Reverse in Coke War: Israel to Bottle Drink." *New York Herald Tribune*, April 16, 1966.

Bloomberg Businessweek. "Keep up with the Jones, Dude!" October 25, 2005. www.businessweek .com/stories/2005-10-25/keep-up-with-the-jones-dude.

Brady, Thomas F. "Arabs Vote to Bar Ford, Coca-Cola." *New York Times*, November 21, 1966.

Brooker, Katrina. "The Pepsi Machine." *Fortune Magazine*, January 30, 2006. http://money.cnn .com/magazines/fortune/fortune_archive/2006/02/06/8367964/index.htm.

Brooklyn Eagle. "Revolution in the Soft-Drink Industry." March 21, 1954.

Business Week. "Coke's Formula: Keep the Image Fresh." April 25, 1970. Robert Winship Woodruff Papers.

Cadbury. Print advertisement. *Illustrated London News*, October 22, 1898.

———. Print advertisement. *Illustrated London News*, November 23, 1901.

Canaseraga Times. "National Drinks: Queer Beverages Peculiar to Some Countries." November 11, 1887.

Cantrell & Cochrane. "Now! Your Favorite Soft Drinks in Cans!" Print advertisement for Super Beverages. *Daily Mirror*, June 10, 1953. Robert Winship Woodruff Papers.

Changing Times: The Kiplinger Magazine. "The Story Behind . . . Coca-Cola." November 1959.

Chapman, Fred'k L. Op-ed. *Ram's Horn.* August 31, 1897. Dr Pepper Museum Collection.

Choi, Candice. "Coke, Pepsi Racing for a Better No-Calorie Soda." *Huffington Post*, July 26, 2012. www.huffingtonpost.com/2012/07/26/coke-pepsi-no-calories-soda_n_1705083.html.

Chun, Janean. "Red Bull Stratos May Change Future of Marketing." *Huffington Post*, October 15, 2012. www.huffingtonpost.com/2012/10/15/red-bull-stratos-marketing_n_1966852 .html.

Cicero, Linda. "Coca-Cola's New Flavor: Sweeter, Less Fizzy." *Kingsport Times-News*, May 8, 1985. Coca-Cola Collection.

Cincinnati Press. "Jake and Coca Cola Caused Several Arrests." March 8, 1929.

Cleveland Press. "Quits as Chairman of Pepsi-Cola Co." September 18, 1950.

Clock Dial. "Cookin' with Dr Pepper." January–February 1976. Dr Pepper Museum Collection.

———. "Dr Pepper Responds to Guidelines." January–February 1978. Dr Pepper Museum Collection.

———. "Great Potential Seen in P.E.T." January–February 1978. Dr Pepper Museum Collection.

———. "Paragould Sales Are HOT During Winter Promotion." January–February 1976. Dr Pepper Museum Collection.

———. "Saccharin Controversy Stirs Widespread Protest." March–April 1977. Dr Pepper Museum Collection.

———. "Save Saccharin." May–June 1977. Dr Pepper Museum Collection.

———. "This Winter: You and HOT Dr Pepper." November–December 1976. Dr Pepper Museum Collection.

———. "Why the President of Wendy's Is a Pepper Too." May–June 1978. Dr Pepper Museum Collection.

Coca-Cola Bottler. "Another Good Sign." September 1909. Asa Griggs Candler Papers.

———. "Archie Lee, D'Arcy Chairman, Dies After a Brief Illness." January 1961. Coca-Cola Collection.

———. "A Big Drink." September 1909. Asa Griggs Candler Papers.

———. "The Bottle . . . The Carton . . . The Cooler . . . Merchandising Magic." April 1959. Coca-Cola Collection.

———. "What Georgia's Chemist Says of Coca-Cola." September 1909. Asa Griggs Candler Papers.

Collins, Glenn. "Ya-hooo! A Marketing Coup; at 50, Mountain Dew Manages to Tickle Innards of Young Men." *New York Times*, May 30, 1995. www.nytimes.com/1995/05/30/business /ya-hooo-marketing-coup-50-mountain-dew-manages-tickle-innards-young-men.html.

Cony, Ed, and Lee Geist. "Canned Soda Pop." Unattributed and undated news clipping. Robert Winship Woodruff Papers.

Cray, Douglas W. "Battle over Sweeteners Turns Bitter." *New York Times*, June 1, 1969.

Crushygram. "Period Highlights." September 1954. Dr Pepper Museum Collection.

Diehl, Bill. "Coca-Cola's Project Alpha." *Atlanta Magazine,* May 1963.

DiMassa, Cara Mia, and Erika Hayasaki. "LA Schools Set to Can Soda Sales." *Los Angeles Times,* August 25, 2002. www.organicconsumers.org/school/0901_schools_soda.cfm.

Domac, Jacqueline. "Sodas Out, Healthier Students In." *United Teacher Magazine,* August 2002. www.nojunkfood.org/media/goodbye_cocacola.html.

Dundee Evening Telegraph. "'Drink More Fruit' the New Recipe." May 31, 1928.

Economist. "Selling Energy." May 9, 2002. www.economist.com/node/1120373?story _id=1120373.

Ellwood, David. "The American Challenge in Uniform: The Arrival of America's Armies in World War II and European Women." *European Journal of American Studies,* special issue 2012, document 8 (March 29, 2012): http://ejas.revues.org/9577.

Emporia Gazette. "The Crusade." March 12, 1929. Robert Winship Woodruff Papers.

Florence Times–Tri-Cities Daily. "Spruce Beer Has Roots in American Tradition." May 1, 1976.

Florida Times-Union. "Coca-Cola's Claim Its Diet Beverage Is Now No. 3 Disputed by Seven-Up." March 8, 1984.

Forbes. "Pepsi's Double Trouble." June 15, 1951.

Gallagher Report. "Cyclamate Ban Leaves Bitter Aftertaste." Vol. 17, no. 46 (November 12, 1969). Robert Winship Woodruff Papers.

Garner, Phil. "Have a Coke and a Smile. Or Else!" *Atlanta Journal and Constitution,* October 28, 1979.

Garrett, Franklin M. "Benjamin Franklin Thomas." Unattributed and undated news clipping. Coca-Cola Collection.

George, Dan. "For Coca-Cola, Bottle Was Shape of Things to Come." *Atlanta Journal and Constitution,* August 20, 1989. Coca-Cola Collection.

Gertner, David, Rosane Gertner, and Dennis Guthery. "Coca-Cola's Marketing Challenges in Brazil: The *Tubaínas* War." *Thunderbird International Business Review* 47, no. 2 (March/April 2005): 231–254.

Gladwell, Malcolm. "U.S. Expected to Lift Ban on Cyclamate: Sweetener Harmless, Most Experts Say." *Washington Post,* May 16, 1989.

Graham, Jane. "Made in Scotland from Patriotism." *Guardian,* June 3, 2008. www.guardian .co.uk/culture/tvandradioblog/2008/jun/03/madeinscotlandfrompatrioti.

Great Speckled Bird. "Earth Week April 17–26: It's the Real Thing." Vol. 3, no. 16 (April 20, 1970).

Grey, John S. "The Advertising of Hires' Rootbeer." *Printers' Ink* 24, no. 12 (September 21, 1898). Dr Pepper Museum Collection.

Grynbaum, Michael M. "Bloomberg Plans a Ban on Large Sugared Drinks." *New York Times,* May 31, 2012. www.nytimes.com/2012/05/31/nyregion/bloomberg-plans-a-ban-on-large -sugared-drinks.html.

Haden-Guest, Anthony. "The Carbonated Conquest." *Miami Herald Tropic,* August 24, 1973. Coca-Cola Collection.

Handelsblatt. "Sinalco—die Limonade." December 18, 2012. www.handelsblatt.com/marken -des-jahrhunderts/unternehmensportraet-sinalco-die-limonade/7536862.html.

Harless, William. "Richmond Soda Tax: Beverage Lobbyist Funds 'Community' Campaign Against Measure." *Huffington Post,* June 14, 2012. www.huffingtonpost.com/2012/06/14 /richmond-soda-tax_n_1598508.html.

Heckman, M. A., K. Sherry, and E. Gonzalez De Mejia. "Energy Drinks: An Assessment of Their Market Size, Consumer Demographics, Ingredient Profile, Functionality, and Regulations in the United States." *Comprehensive Reviews in Food Science and Food Safety* 9, no. 3 (May 2010): 303–317.

Heitner, Darren. "Red Bull Stratos Worth Tens of Millions of Dollars in Global Exposure for the Red Bull Brand." *Forbes*, October 15, 2012, www.forbes.com/sites/darrenheitner /2012/10/15/red-bull-stratos-worth-tens-of-millions-of-dollars-in-global-exposure-for-the -red-bull-brand.

Herndon, Keith. "Coca-Cola Plans to Serve New Taste 'Out of This World.'" *Atlanta Constitution*, May 8, 1985.

Hesse, Stephen. "Pepsi Pushes Coke in Soft-Drink Fray." *Atlanta Constitution*, July 29, 1980. Coca-Cola Collection.

Hightower, James, and Paul Troop. "Coke, Russia Sign Pact to Swap Technical Data." *Atlanta Journal*, June 26, 1974. Robert Winship Woodruff Papers.

Hires. "Yassuh . . . It's Genu-wine Hires." Print advertisement. *Life*, September 6, 1937.

Hires, Charles E. "Seeing Opportunities: How Charles E. Hires Laid the Foundation for his Commercial Success." *American Druggist and Pharmaceutical Record*, 1913.

Horrock, Nicholas M. "Carter, as Governor, Got Free Rides on Planes of Lockheed and Coca-Cola." *New York Times*, April 1, 1976.

Huey, John. "New Top Executives Shake Up Old Order at Soft Drink Giant." *Wall Street Journal*, November 6, 1981.

Hughes, Edward. "U.S. Has a Big Stake in the Middle East's Newest, Hottest Row." *Wall Street Journal*, October 12, 1951.

Hull Daily Mail. "House and Home." June 2, 1927.

Iezzi, Teressa. "Red Bull Stratos Shatters Records—and Traditional Notions of Marketing." *Co.Create*, October 15, 2012, www.fastcocreate.com/1681748/red-bull-stratos-shatters -records-and-traditional-notions-of-marketing

Illustrated London News. "The Alkaloid Theine . . ." January 21, 1865.

Independent. "French Branding Story Orangina Marks 75 Years of Ad Fizz." July 16, 2011. www.independent.co.uk/life-style/food-and-drink/french-branding-story-orangina-marks -75-years-of-ad-fizz-2314796.html.

"Industrial Philadelphia: The Charles E. Hires Company." Unattributed and undated news clipping. Dr Pepper Museum Collection.

Jacarrino, Mike, Celeste Katz, and Tina Moore. "President Barack Obama, Michelle Obama Surprise Blue Hill Patrons." *New York Daily News*, May 31 2009. www.nydailynews.com /news/politics/president-barack-obama-michelle-obama-surprise-blue-hill-patrons -article-1.374974.

Jeffcoat, A. E. "American Pop Pours in a Swelling Flood Down Throats Abroad." *Wall Street Journal*, May 1950. Coca-Cola Collection.

"John Thomas Lupton." Unattributed and undated news clipping. Coca-Cola Collection.

Johnson, Roy W. "The Story of Charles E. Hires." *Printers' Ink Monthly*, 1921. Dr Pepper Museum Collection.

Jones, Harrison. "Blessed Beginnings." *Coca-Cola Bottler*, August 1944. Robert Winship Woodruff Papers.

"Joseph Brown Whitehead." Unattributed and undated news clipping. Coca-Cola Collection.

Kinsella, J. Hixon. "Highlights of Coca-Cola Advertising During the First Half Century of the Coca-Cola Bottler." *Coca-Cola Bottler*, April 1959. Coca-Cola Collection.

Kramer, Julia. "Bottled Sodas—Trending." *Time Out Chicago*, June 14, 2012.

Kurtz, Wilbur, Jr. "Joseph A. Biedenharn." *Coca-Cola Bottler*, August 1944. Coca-Cola Collection.

Landi, Heather. "A Mighty Force." *Beverage World*, January 15, 2009.

———. "State of the Industry Report '07: Bottled Water." *Beverage World*, April 15, 2007.

Lefebvre, Thierry. "Un pharmacien espagnol à l'origine d'Orangina." *Revue d'histoire de la pharmacie* 348 (2005): www.persee.fr/web/revues/home/prescript/article /pharm_0035-2349_2005_num_93_348_5906.

Lewis, Carol. "The 'Poison Squad' and the Advent of Food and Drug Regulation." *U.S. Food and Drug Administration Consumer Magazine*, November–December 2002.

L'Express. "Jean-Claude Beton, inventeur d'Orangina et génie de la communication." July 8, 2011. www.lexpress.fr/actualites/1/economie/jean-claude-beton-inventeur-d-orangina-et -genie-de-la-communication_1010541.html.

Lieberman, Paul. "The Spy Who Came in from the Cola." *Atlanta Journal*, November 7, 1982.

Los Angeles Times. "Believes Nixon Still Has Business Support PepsiCo Chief Raps Watergate Tape Actions." November 8, 1973.

Ludington Daily News. "It's Pop Politics: Pepsi, Coke Battle Spills Over into NASA." July 13, 1985.

Lund, Morten, and Mary Hayes. "Skiing Comes to Aspen: Visionaries and Teachers." *Skiing Heritage* 10, no. 2 (1997).

Lustig, Robert H., Laura A. Schmidt, and Claire D. Brindis. "The Toxic Truth About Sugar." *Nature* 482 (February 2, 2012): 27–29.

Madden, Caroline. "Judge Finds Message in a Bottle." *Irish Times*, June 18, 2012. www.irishtimes.com/newspaper/finance/2012/0618/1224318130082.html.

Massmann, W. F. 'Bill'. "Government Intervention." *Clock Dial*, July–August 1978. Dr Pepper Museum Collection.

McCollum, Justin. "A Brief Historiography of U.S. Hegemony in the Cuban Sugar Industry." *The Forum: Cal Poly's Journal of History* 3, no.1, art. 8 (2011): www.digitalcommons.calpoly .edu/forum/vol3/iss1/8.

McEwan, Andrew. "Nixon Makes Things Go Better with Pepski." *Daily Mail*, November 2, 1975.

McPherson, Lynn. "Irn-Bru TV Advert Provokes String of Complaints." *Daily Record*, June 17, 2012. www.dailyrecord.co.uk/news/business-news/2012/06/17/irn-bru-tv-advert -provokes-string-of-complaints-86908-23897155.

Miami News. "Death Notices: Kirsch." May 15, 1976.

Molseed, John. "New York–Type Soda Ban Plan Gets Cold Response Locally." *Cedar Valley Business Monthly Online*, June 17, 2012. http://wcfcourier.com/business/local/new -york-type-soda-ban-plan-gets-cold-response-locally/article_ee594acc-b648-11e1-b327 -0019bb2963f4.html.

Montreal Gazette. "Spruce Beer Dates from 17th Century." August 13, 1986.

Morgan, Philip. "Soda Pop." *Tampa Tribune*, August 5, 1983. Dr Pepper Museum Collection.

Morris, Joe Alex, Jr. "Ford, Coca-Cola Afoul of Arabs." *New York Herald Tribune*, June 16, 1966.

Morrison, Joseph L. "The Soda Fountain." *American Heritage*, August 1962.

Munsey, Cecil. "Matches, Match Safes and the History and Relics of Koca-Nola." *Federation Glass Works*, January 1992.

———. "Mrs. Diva Brown: 'Original Coca-Cola Woman.'" *Bottles and Extras*, summer 2004.

———. "The Six-Pack Cometh." *Soda Pop Dreams Magazine* 5, no. 5 (Christmas 2002).

———. "Soda Pop Santas (1915–1964)." *Soda Fizz*, November–December 2007.

Museum News. "The Classic Contour-Shaped Bottle for Coca-Cola: Attributes and Characteristics, 1916–1969." December 1968. Coca-Cola Collection.

Mussell, Betty. "The Bottle." *American Heritage*, June–July 1986.

Nature. "The Cyclamate Bandwagon." Vol. 224 (October 25, 1969).

Nees, P. O., and P. H. Derse. "Feeding and Reproduction of Rats Fed Calcium Cyclamate." *Nature* 208 (October 2, 1965).

Nelson, Steven. "New York Soda Ban Struck Down, Bloomberg Promises Appeal." *US News*, March 11, 2013. www.usnews.com/news/articles/2013/03/11/new-york-soda-ban-struck -down-bloomberg-promises-appeal

Network. "Aqua-Chem Sale Completed." Vol. 2, no. 17 (September 15, 1981). Robert Winship Woodruff Papers.

———. "Beijing Plant Opens." Vol. 2, no. 8 (April 30, 1981). Robert Winship Woodruff Papers.

New Idea Woman's Magazine. "Coca-Cola: The Shoppers Panacea." 1907. Coca-Cola Collection.

New-York Daily Tribune. "Cocaine Sniffers: Use of the Drug Increasing Among Negroes of the South." June 21, 1903.

New York Post. "Mount Sinai Ends Coca-Cola Boycott." April 12, 1966.

———. "No Coke for Israel—Arab Pressure Denied." April 9, 1966.

New York Times. "Coke Embargoed a Day at Hospital." April 12, 1966.

———. "Personality: From Salesman to the Top Post." April 11, 1965.

———. "Who Put the Fizz in Soda Water?" September 13, 1913.

New York World-Telegram. "Pepsi's Profit, Sales Climb to New Highs." March 10, 1965.

New York World-Telegram and Sun. "Nathan's May Hold the Coke to Draw Some in Israel." April 9, 1966.

News & Views. "All Star Per Capita League." February 1945. Dr Pepper Museum Collection.

———. "Sugar—Still Rationed!" June 1947. Dr Pepper Museum Collection.

Newsday. "Shuttle Set for Launch." July 12, 1985.

———. "Sweet Talk to FDA Stirs Tempest in a Soda Bottle." October 23, 1969.

Oatman, Maddie. "Soda: Ban It? Nah. Tax It? Yep." *Mother Jones*, June 18, 2012. www .motherjones.com/environment/2012/06/soda-sugar-tax-richmond.

———. "A Timeline of Sugar Spin." *Mother Jones*, October 31, 2012. www.motherjones.com /politics/2012/10/sugar-industry-marketing-timeline.

O'Brien, James. "How Red Bull Takes Content Marketing to the Extreme." *Mashable*, December 19, 2012. http://mashable.com/2012/12/19/red-bull-content-marketing.

O-C News. "Delivering the Goods: The Know-How of Successful Merchandising." September 1949. Dr Pepper Museum Collection.

———. "Orange Crush and Kids—a 'Natural Promotion.'" May–June 1951. Dr Pepper Museum Collection.

O'Leary, Noreen. "Soft-Drink Consumption Continues to Decline." *AdWeek*, March 30, 2010. www .adweek.com/news/advertising-branding/soft-drink-consumption-continues-decline-107218.

Oliver, Thomas. "Classic's Return Good News to 'Coke Heartland' Bottlers." *Atlanta Journal*, July 11, 1985.

———. "Coke Just Entertain No-Caffeine War, But Guns for Top." *Atlanta Journal and Constitution*, May 8, 1983.

Oney, Steve. "Mello Marketing." *Atlanta Weekly Magazine*, June 8, 1980.

O'Toole, Thomas. "Cola Clash Is Taking to Heavens." *Washington Post*, July 12, 1985.

Paris Match. "The Greatest Commercial Mystery of the Century." Undated translation. Robert Winship Woodruff Papers.

Park, Alice. "The New York City Soda Ban, and a Brief History of Bloomberg's Nudges." *Time*, May 31, 2012. http://healthland.time.com/2012/05/31/bloombergs-soda-ban-and-other -sweeping-health-measures-in-new-york-city.

Pawley, Emily. "Powerful Effervescence." *Chemical Heritage Magazine* 26, no. 2 (summer 2008): www.chemheritage.org/discover/media/magazine/articles/26-2-powerful-effervescence.aspx.

Pepsi-Cola. "Pepsi One Way." Print advertisement. *Victoria Advocate*, June 3, 1966.

———. "Pepsi, the Light Refreshment." Print advertisement. *American Weekly*, January 25, 1953. Robert Winship Woodruff Papers.

———. "The Time Will Come . . ." Print advertisement. *Bath Chronicle and Weekly Gazette*, July 15, 1944.

Printers' Ink Monthly. "The Story of My First Job: Charles E. Hires' Experience." Undated news clipping. Dr Pepper Museum Collection.

Pure Water Co. Ltd. Print advertisement. *Illustrated London News*, April 14, 1894.

Refresher. "Bob Woodruff." April 1960. Coca-Cola Collection.

———. "Fanta & Sprite." January–February 1962. Coca-Cola Collection.

———. "Ike Herbert Finds New Products Exciting." July–August 1966. Coca-Cola Collection.

———. "Minute Maid Company: A Look at the Leader." March–April 1965. Coca-Cola Collection.

Refresher USA. "Fifty Fabulous Years of Overseas Growth for Coca-Cola, 1926–1976." Vol. 8, no. 3 (1976). Coca-Cola Collection.

Reynolds, Barbara. "Soda, Food, Movies—It's All Refreshment." *USA Today*, August 7, 1984.

Richmond Times. "Greenway Found a Deranged Man." July 25, 1902.

Rolett, Burl. "Hoping for a Humdinger." *Richmond BizSense*, June 21, 2012. www.richmondbizsense.com/2012/06/18/hoping-for-a-humdinger.

Rudin, Max. "Beer and America." *American Heritage*, June–July 2002.

San Francisco Chronicle. "Ban on Carbonated Drinks Is Urged in S. F. Schools." March 9, 1949.

Scotland on Sunday. "Scotland's Other National Drink Gets a Carpeting." June 10, 2012. www.scotsman.com/scotland-on-sunday/scotland/scotland-s-other-national-drink-gets-a -carpeting-1-2347451.

Siegel, Benjamin. "Sweet Nothing—the Triumph of Diet Soda." *American Heritage*. June–July 2006. www.americanheritage.com/content/sweet-nothing—-triumph-diet-soda-0.

Sims, Calvin. "Lima Journal; Peru's Pride That Refreshes." *New York Times*, December 26, 1995. www.nytimes.com/1995/12/26/world/lima-journal-peru-s-pride-that-refreshes-kola-of-a -local-color.html.

Smith, Erik P. "Was the New Coke–Old Coke Skirmish Actually Planned?" *Spokesman-Review*, July 23, 1985.

Soft Drink Industry. "Root Beer in Big Sales Leap as Drive to Build Image Wins New Customers." January 2, 1968. Dr Pepper Museum Collection.

Subramanian, Samanth. "The Real Thing." *PORT Magazine*, winter 2011.

Sutcliffe & Co. "Aerated Lemonade." Print advertisement. *York Herald and County Advertiser*, March 14, 1807.

Tappy, Luc. "Q&A: 'Toxic' Effects of Sugar: Should We Be Afraid of Fructose." *BMC Biology* 10, no. 42 (May 2012): www.biomedcentral.com/1741-7007/10/42.

Taubman, Philip. "The Great Soft-Drink Shoot-Out." *Esquire*, March 27, 1979.

Tecumseh News. "Where Spruce Beer Is Made." November 29, 1912.

Thos. Christy & Co. Print advertisement. *Illustrated London News*, December 6, 1890.

Time. "The Sun Never Sets on Coca-Cola." May 15, 1950.

Today's Advertising. "Pepsi-Cola Hits the Spot Again! This Time It's with 12-oz. Cans." Vol. 1, no. 72 (February 27, 1950).

Trimingham, Adam. "Awash with History." *Argus*. June 27, 2011. www.theargus.co.uk /magazine/nostalgia/9107878.print.

Vartanian, Lenny R., Marlene B. Schwartz, and Kelly D. Brownell. "Effects of Soft Drink Consumption on Nutrition and Health: A Systematic Review and Meta-Analysis." *American Journal of Public Health* 97, no. 4 (April 2007).

Victoria Advocate. "Novel System of Internship of Youths to Start." July 2, 1940.

Wall Street Journal. "Pepsi-Cola Co." December 11, 1952.

———. "Pepsi-Cola Test-Markets New Dietetic Soft Drink." March 9, 1964.

Watchman. "Do You Advocate Temperance?" June 29, 1899.

Watin-Augouard, Jean. "Orangina, la petite boisson secouée." *Histoire d'entreprises* 7 (July 2009).

Welsh, Jean A., Andrea J Sharma, Lisa Grellinger, and Miriam B Vos. "Consumption of Added Sugars Is Decreasing in the United States." *American Journal of Clinical Nutrition* 94, no. 3 (September 2011): 726–734.

Western Morning News and Mercury. "Britain Adopts the Soda-Fountain." June 30, 1931.

"What the Coke Brass Had to Say." Unattributed and undated news clipping. Coca-Cola Collection.

Willard, J. J. "Some Early History of Coca-Cola Bottling." *Coca-Cola Bottler*, August 1944. Coca-Cola Collection.

Wilson, Dr. Andrew. "Science Jottings." *Illustrated London News*, June 25, 1898.

Wolverine Citizen. "Pleasant Drinks." July 30, 1859.

Woodward-Lopez, Gail, Janice Kao, and Lorrene Ritchie. "To What Extent Have Sweetened Beverages Contributed to the Obesity Epidemic?" *Public Health Nutrition* 14, no. 3 (March 2011).

Yates, Don. "Charles E. Hires Company 1870–Present Philadelphia, Pennsylvania." *Bottles and Extras*, summer 2005. www.fohbc.org/PDF_Files/HiresRootBeer_DonYates.pdf.

Zeldes, Leah A. "Two Rivers: Drinking Green in Chicago This St. Patrick's Day." *Dining Chicago*, March 9, 2010. www.diningchicago.com/blog/2010/03/09/two-rivers-drinking -green-in-chicago-this-st-patricks-day.

Online Resources

Ben Shaws. "Refresh Your Memories." Accessed February 23, 2013. www.benshawsdrinks .co.uk/ben-shaws-history.

Bottlebooks.com. "Big Bottles Big History: Demijohns and Carboys." 2008. www.bottlebooks .com/demijohn/big_bottles_big_history_demijohn.htm.

Bottles & Bygones. "The Story of Schweppes." Accessed February 25, 2013. http://mikesheridan.tripod.com/schweppes1.htm.

Cambridge World History of Food. S.v. "The Coming of the Colas." 2000. www.credoreference
.com/entry/cupfood/the_coming_of_the_colas.
———. S.v. "Fruit-Flavored Drinks." 2000. www.credoreference.com/entry/cupfood/fruit
_flavored_drinks.
———. S.v. "Kola Nut." 2000. www.credoreference.com/entry/cupfood/kola_nut.
———. S.v. "Kola Production." 2000. www.credoreference.com/entry/cupfood/kola
_production.
———. S.v. "The Kola Trade." 2000. www.credoreference.com/entry/cupfood/the_kola
_trade.
———. S.v. "Lemons and Scurvy." 2000. www.credoreference.com/entry/cupfood/lemons
_and_scurvy.
———. S.v. "Soft Drink Packaging." 2000. www.credoreference.com/entry/cupfood/soft
_drink_packaging.
———. S.v. "Temperance Drinks." 2000. www.credoreference.com/entry/cupfood
/temperance_drinks.
———. S.v. "Uses of Kola." 2000. www.credoreference.com/entry/cupfood/uses_of_kola.
Cawthon, Bill. "A Century of Flavor." Promotex Online. April 1, 2005. www.promotex.ca
/articles/cawthon/2005/2005-04-01_article.html.
City of Kawanishi. "Around Hirano and Shinden—Series 3 Around Hirano and Shinden."
Accessed February 20, 2013. www.city.kawanishi.hyogo.jp/pre/english/tales3.htm.
———. "Hirano Mineral Spring." Accessed February 20, 2013. www.city.kawanishi.hyogo.jp
/english/7515/guidance/sightseeing/hirano_m.html.
———. "Vol.1 'Kuzuryu' a Dragon with Nine Heads." Accessed February 20, 2013. www.city
.kawanishi.hyogo.jp/english/7515/legends/doragon.html.
CliffNotes.com. "Postwar America." Accessed May 2, 2013. http://www.cliffsnotes.com/more
-subjects/history/us-history-ii/the-rise-of-the-cold-war-19451953/postwar-america.
Complete Dictionary of Scientific Biography. S.v. "Hoffmann, Friedrich." 2008. www.encyclopedia
.com/topic/Friedrich_Hoffmann.aspx.
Davemanuel.com. "Inflation Calculator." Accessed February 26, 2013. www.davemanuel.com
/inflation-calculator.php.
Davies, Graham. "The Week the Wall Came Down." December 1, 1989. www.camsoftpartners
.co.uk/berlin.htm.
Despain, David. "Fate of Fructose: Interview with Dr. John Sievenpiper." *Evolving Health* (blog),
May 26, 2012. http://evolvinghealthscience.blogspot.co.uk/2012/05/fate-of-fructose
-interview-with-dr-john.html.
Ellen MacArthur Foundation. "Recycling and the Circular Economy." Accessed February 20,
2013. www.ellenmacarthurfoundation.org/explore-more/think-differently/recycling-and
-the-circular-economy.pdf.
Energy Fiend. "Caffeine Content of Drinks." Accessed February 20, 2013. www.energyfiend
.com/the-caffeine-database.
Gilder Lehrman Institute of American History. "Guided Readings: American Foreign Policy in
the 1970s." Accessed February 25, 2013. www.gilderlehrman.org/history-by-era/seventies
/resources/guided-readings-american-foreign-policy-1970s.
Hartings, Matthew. "I Love Gin and Tonics." *Science Geist* (blog), January 28, 2011.
http://sciencegeist.net/i-love-gin-and-tonics.

International Directory of Company Histories. "Asahi Breweries, Ltd." Vol. 52 (2003). www.company-histories.com/Asahi-Breweries-Ltd-Company-History.html.

———. "Sapporo Breweries Limited." Vol. 36 (2001). www.company-histories.com/Sapporo -Breweries-Limited-Company-History.html.

Kloeris, Vickie. "Eating on the ISS." NASA Quest, May 1, 2001. http://quest.arc.nasa.gov /people/journals/space/kloeris/05-01-01.html.

Kresser, Chris. "Ask Chris: Is Fructose Really That Bad?" Chris Kresser, June 15, 2012. http://chriskresser.com/ask-chris-is-fructose-really-that-bad.

McConchie, Alan. "Generic Names for Soft Drinks by County." Department of Cartography and Geography, East Central University, Oklahoma. Accessed February 22, 2013. http://popvssoda.com.

McKellar, Allen, Jr. "Pepsi's Real Challenge: Integrating Corporate America." Walker Speaker Series, Webster University. Accessed February 23, 2013. http://blogs.webster.edu /webstertoday/2012/02/17/walker-speaker-series-integrating-corporate-america-at-pepsi.

Munsey, Cecil. "Cocaine, Coca-Cola, Recipe, Colicky Infants & Contraceptive." CecilMunsey. com, October 2011. www.cecilmunsey.com.

———. "Nehi 'n High Heels." CecilMunsey.com, April 2011. www.cecilmunsey.com.

———. "A Short Family History of Chero-Cola, Nehi & Royal Crown Cola (RC)." CecilMunsey.com, June 2011. www.cecilmunsey.com.

———. "A Short History of Canada Dry Ginger Ale." CecilMunsey.com, November 2011. www.cecilmunsey.com.

My Brighton and Hove. Bradstreet, Andrew. "History of the Spa." June 26, 2006. www.mybrightonandhove.org.uk/page_id__7459_path__0p115p203p818p.aspx.

National Cancer Institute. "Artificial Sweeteners and Cancer." August 5, 2009. www.cancer.gov/cancertopics/factsheet/Risk/artificial-sweeteners.

Nierhoff, Maximilian H.. "Red Bull Stratos and Felix Baumgartner Breaking Real Life and Social Media Records." Quintly blog, October 2012. www.quintly.com/blog/2012/10/red -bull-stratos-and-felix-baumgartner-breaking-real-life-and-social-media-records.

Orangina. "The History of Orangina." Accessed February 20, 2013. www.orangina.eu/en /our-history.

Pesticide Safety Education Program. "The Delaney Paradox and Negligible Risk." Accessed January 7, 2013. http://psep.cce.cornell.edu/issues/delaney-negrisk.aspx.

Prodimarques. "Saga Orangina." October 1996. www.prodimarques.com/sagas_marques /orangina/orangina.php.

RandomHistory.com. "Clean Water for All: A History of Drinking Water Treatment." April 30, 2007. www.randomhistory.com/1-50/001water.html.

Raturi, Prerna. "And This Is How Parle Bisleri Began." Rediff.com. June 10, 2005. www.rediff .com/money/2005/jun/10spec.htm.

Red Bull Stratos. "Mission History." Accessed February 23, 2013. www.redbullstratos.com/the -mission/mission-history.

Rockstar Energy Drink. "Original Rockstar Product Ingredients." Accessed February 19, 2013. http://rockstarenergy.com/productIngredients.php?pdt=1. Page discontinued; archive copy available at http://web.archive.org/web/20120616112037/http://rockstar69.com /productIngredients.php?pdt=1.

Schwarcz, Dr. Joe, ed. "Dr. Nooth's Apparatus." *Chemically Speaking* (blog), May 13, 2010. www.chemicallyspeaking.com/archive/2010/05/13/dr.-nooths-apparatus.aspx.

Science Museum (London). "Nooth's Apparatus, Europe, 1774–1831." Accessed February 23, 2013. www.sciencemuseum.org.uk/broughttolife/objects/display.aspx?id=6698.

Shaw, Jenny. "Reading Room: Red Bull Stratos." WPP. Accessed February 23, 2013. www.wpp.com/wpp/marketing/digital/red-bull-stratos.

Sinalco International Brands. "History." Accessed February 20, 2013. http://sinalco.in/web /cms_de/front_content.php?idcat=7.

Soda Depot. "Green River Soda." Accessed January 27, 2013. www.dggpro.com /TheSodaDepot/browse.asp?page=415.

White Rock Products Corporation. "About Us." Accessed February 19, 2013. www.whiterockbeverages.com/AboutUs.cfm.

White Rocking. "Does Santa Claus Still Drink White Rock?" Accessed February 19, 2013. www.whiterocking.org/santa.html.

———. "History of Psyche." Accessed February 19, 2013. www.whiterocking.org/pwc.html.

TV, Film, and Video

Advertising Educational Foundation. "Giants of Advertising: Alan Pottasch." Accessed February 26, 2013. www.aef.com/industry/industry_leaders/giants_of_advertising.

Backer, Bill. "Bill Backer Interviewed About 'I'd Like to Buy the World a Coke.'" Interview by the Coca-Cola Archives, 2007. YouTube video posted by CokeConversations, October 7, 2011. www.youtube.com/watch?v=tSNU1TvF4pc.

BBC HD. *The Men Who Made Us Fat*. London, June 14, 2012.

CNBC. *Pepsi's Challenge*. Englewood Cliffs, New Jersey. November 10, 2011.

Griffith, D. W., dir. *For His Son*. Originally released 1912. YouTube video posted by GriffithMovies, November 3, 2007. www.youtube.com/watch?v=TJaToCF0tIU.

Horne, James W., dir. *College*. Originally released 1927. Tunbridge Wells, UK: Cornerstone Media, 2010. DVD.

ITV. *Burp! Pepsi vs Coke in the Ice Cold War*. Birmingham, UK, May 22, 1984.

Pepsi-Cola. "The Pepsi Challenge at the C.N.E." Television advertisement. 1977. YouTube video posted by robatsea2009, September 13, 2011. www.youtube.com/watch?v=7Py _QMLFK04.

———. Pepsi Challenge television advertisement. 1983. YouTube video posted by GrubcoTV3, December 23, 2008. www.youtube.com/watch?v=v7lw_vhxtNc.

Rogers, Heather, dir. *Gone Tomorrow: The Hidden Life of Garbage*. 2005.

Sheridan Channel. "BrewFest in Sheridan, Wyoming: Can-a-Pop." YouTube video, September 4, 2012. www.youtube.com/watch?v=1mSXUrAtbBU.

Wilder, Bill, dir. *One, Two, Three*. Originally released 1961. Beverly Hills: MGM Home Entertainment, 2004. DVD.

Other Sources

Abram, Morris B. Statement, April 15, 1966. Robert Winship Woodruff Papers.

Apple Computer Inc. "Macintosh Product Introduction Plan." October 7, 1983. In Making the Macintosh (online collection). http://www-sul.stanford.edu/mac/primary/docs/pip83 .html.

American Beverage Association. "Alliance School Beverage Guidelines Final Progress Report." March 8, 2010.

Anheuser-Busch InBev. "Paper Guaraná Antarctica." Undated product biography. Provided to author by company.

Atlanta Coca-Cola Bottling Company. *Preparedness*. Leaflet, 1942. Robert Winship Woodruff Papers.

Austin, J. Paul. "Advertising in the World Community." Speech to the Advertising Federation of America Convention, June 17, 1963. Robert Winship Woodruff Papers.

———. "Environmental Renewal or Oblivion . . .Quo Vadis?" Speech to the Georgia Bankers Association, April 16, 1970. Robert Winship Woodruff Papers.

———. "The International Company Looks at the Changing World Markets." Speech to the Association of National Advertisers International, April 18, 1963. Robert Winship Woodruff Papers.

———. Statement Before the Senate Select Committee on Nutrition and Human Needs, July 28, 1969. Robert Winship Woodruff Papers.

Bache & Co. "Pepsi-Cola." Report, June 12, 1947. Robert Winship Woodruff Papers.

Centers for Disease Control and Prevention. *Health, United States, 2010*. Hyattsville, MD: Centers for Disease Control and Prevention, 2011. www.cdc.gov/nchs/data/hus/hus10.pdf.

———. "Overweight and Obesity." Accessed February 19, 2013. www.cdc.gov/obesity.

Charles E. Hires Company. "Between You and Us." Pamphlet, 1910. Dr Pepper Museum Collection.

———. Fact sheet, 1962. Dr Pepper Museum Collection.

———. *Hires Advertising Campaign for 1920*. 1920. Dr Pepper Museum Collection.

———. *Hires Advertising Campaign for 1921*. 1921. Dr Pepper Museum Collection.

———. *Hires "How To."* Undated booklet. Dr Pepper Museum Collection.

Chero-Cola. Bottling franchise contract, 1919. Coca-Cola Collection.

"Chronological Highlights: Robert Winship Woodruff." Unattributed report, June 1, 1963. Robert Winship Woodruff Papers.

"Chronological Listing: Countries with Coca-Cola Bottling Operations and Year Introduced, 1906 Through April, 1969." Unattributed and undated report. Coca-Cola Collection.

"Coca-Cola Bottling Co. (Thomas) Inc.: A Salute to the World's Most Famous Bottle." Unattributed speech to Golden Anniversary Dinner, Waldorf-Astoria, New York, October 4, 1949. Coca-Cola Collection.

Coca-Cola Bottling Company of Minnesota v. The Coca-Cola Company. US District Court, District of Minnesota, 4th Division. Court transcript, February 12, 1957. Robert Winship Woodruff Papers.

Coca-Cola Company. *Annual Report 1985*. Coca-Cola Company, 1985

———. "The Coca-Cola Company and Corporation Inca Kola Announce Global Partnership for Inca Kola Brands." News release, February 23, 1999. Coca-Cola Company Archives.

———. "Coca-Cola, Minute Maid Boards Vote Merger Approval Benefits to Both Companies Cited." News release, September 22, 1960. Coca-Cola Collection.

———. "Coca-Cola Re-enters China." News release, December 19, 1978. Coca-Cola Collection.

———. "Foreign Comparative Operations in Per Cent of Sales Year 1939–1938." Undated report. Robert Winship Woodruff Papers.

———. "Haddon Sundblom." Undated biography. Coca-Cola Collection.

———. "Officially Approved Statement of Agreement Between the Coca-Cola Company and the China National Cereals, Oils and Food Stuffs Import-Export Corporation." News release, December 13, 1978. Coca-Cola Collection.

Coca-Cola Company, The, v. The Koke Company of America. Supreme Court of the United States. No. 101, October term 1920. Legal decision, December 6, 1920. Robert Winship Woodruff Papers.

Coca-Cola Company, The, et al. v. Harmar Bottling Company et al. Supreme Court of Texas. Legal decision, November 9, 2004. www.supreme.courts.state.tx.us/historical/2006/oct/030737.htm

Coca-Cola Company of Canada Ltd. v. Pepsi-Cola Company of Canada Ltd. Transcript of Privy Council hearing, December 19, 1940. Robert Winship Woodruff Papers.

———. Privy Council Appeal No. 14 of 1941. Legal decision. Robert Winship Woodruff Papers.

Coca-Cola Company Statistical Department. "Decline in Sales." Report, October 19, 1933. Robert Winship Woodruff Papers.

"Coca-Cola Is Unique." Unattributed and undated report. Robert Winship Woodruff Papers.

Coca-Cola USA. "History of Glass Package for Coca-Cola." Report, February 2, 1970. Coca-Cola Collection.

"Coca-Cola?—What Is It and Where Does It Come From?" German leaflet, trans. September 4, 1936. Robert Winship Woodruff Papers.

Coming Events. Strange Case of Loft vs. Guth, The. Coming Events Inc., 1939. Coca-Cola Collection.

Cook, George R. "Jolt: America's Original Energy Drink (Past & Future)." Case study, Simon Graduate School of Business, University of Rochester, July 2009.

Cook, Joe. "The Story of the Hires Company." Report, 1966. Dr Pepper Museum Collection.

Cunningham, Andrea. Interview by Wendy Marinaccio, July 14, 2000. In Making the Macintosh (online collection). http://www-sul.stanford.edu/mac/primary/interviews/cunningham/trans.html.

Donoghue v. Stevenson. House of Lords. Legal decision, May 26, 1932. British and Irish Legal Information Institute. www.bailii.org/uk/cases/UKHL/1932/100.html.

Dow-Jones Tape. Notice of Pepsi-Schweppes deal, December 10, 1952. Robert Winship Woodruff Papers.

E. F. Hutton & Company. "Pepsi-Cola Company: A Study Prepared for Institutional Investors." September 1964. Robert Winship Woodruff Papers.

Escola v. Coca Cola Bottling Co. Supreme Court of California. Legal decision, July 5, 1944. Stanford Law School. http://scocal.stanford.edu/opinion/escola-v-coca-cola-bottling-co-29248.

Farley, James A. Speech to the 23rd Annual Convention of American Bottlers of Carbonated Beverages, November 13, 1941. Robert Winship Woodruff Papers.

———. Statement, April 15, 1966. Robert Winship Woodruff Papers.

Forrestall, Daniel J. "The History of the Seven-Up Company." Unpublished manuscript, 1989. Dr Pepper Museum Collection.

Fuller & Smith & Ross Inc. Program presentation for Hires Root Beer, 1967. Dr Pepper Museum Collection.

Garrett, Franklin M. "Brief History of Advertising Media for Coca-Cola." Undated report. Coca-Cola Collection.

———. "The Development of the Soda Fountain in Drug Stores for the Past Fifty Years." Undated report. Coca-Cola Collection.

Goizueta, Roberto C. "The Emerging Post-Conglomerate Era: Changing the Shape of Corporate America, Insight to Roberto's Corporate Beliefs." Report, January 1988. Coca-Cola Collection.

———. Management stewardship report, 1981. Robert Winship Woodruff Papers.

History of spruce beer, root beer and birch beer. Unattributed and undated report. Dr Pepper Museum Collection.

"J. T. Lupton." Unattributed and undated biography. Coca-Cola Collection.

Keith, Max. Interview, June 29–30, 1966. Robert Winship Woodruff Papers.

Kofola. "Kofola Story." Company biography, 2010. Provided to author by company.

Kurtz, Wilbur G., Jr. "A Brief History of the Glass Package for Coca-Cola." Report, February 2, 1970. Coca-Cola Collection.

Kurtz, Wilbur G., Jr., and T. Clyde Edwards. "Interview with Mr. T. Clyde Edwards Relative to the Origin of the Patented-Design Coca-Cola Bottle." Undated. Coca-Cola Collection.

Ladas, Stephen P. "In Foreign Countries." Report, August 3, 1950. Robert Winship Woodruff Papers.

Law Courts Education Society of British Columbia. "'The Paisley Snail': Donoghue vs Stevenson; Teacher's Guide." Law Courts Education Society of British Columbia, 1996.

Lewis, Edwin N. "Biography of Walter Staunton Mack, Jr." Report, October 26, 1940. Robert Winship Woodruff Papers.

Mack, Walter S. Speech to the Pepsi-Cola Bottling Association Annual Meeting, November 21, 1975.

Mass Observation Ltd. "Carbonated Drinks: A Proposed Enquiry." Report, July 1950. Mass Observation Archives.

———. "Carbonated Drinks: Some Notes on a Pilot Enquiry." Report, August 1950. Mass Observation Archives.

Matinuzzi, Valeria, Danielle Peterson, Sean Iacobone, and Salah Badjou. "Effects and Effectiveness of Energy Drinks." Paper for the 2012 American Society for Engineering Education, Northeast Section Conference at the University of Massachusetts Lowell, April 27–28, 2012. http://acamedics.com/proceedings/aseene/2012/PM_3135.pdf.

Ministry of Food. "History of the Soft Drinks Industry (War-Time) Association Ltd." Report, 1946. National Archives of the United Kingdom.

New York City Board of Health. "Mayor Bloomberg, Deputy Mayor Gibbs, Health Commissioner Farley and Bruce Ratner Announce Barclays Center Will Voluntarily Adopt Regulations to Limit Size of Sugary Beverages." News release, September 13, 2012.

New York Obesity Task Force. "Reversing the Epidemic: The New York City Obesity Task Force Plan to Prevent and Control Obesity." Report, May 31, 2012.

New York Statewide Coalition v. New York City Department of Health. Supreme Court of the State of New York. Legal decision, March 11, 2013. *Wall Street Journal*. http://online.wsj.com/public/resources/documents/sodaruling.pdf.

Organisation for Economic Co-operation and Development. "Obesity Update 2012." Policy brief. Accessed February 21, 2013. www.oecd.org/health/49716427.pdf.

"Pepsi Net Profits, 1952–1958." Unattributed and undated graph. Robert Winship Woodruff Papers.

PepsiCo. *Annual Report 1998*. PepsiCo, 1998.

———. *Annual Report 1999*. PepsiCo, 1999.

———. *Annual Report 2000*. PepsiCo, 2000.

———. *Annual Report 2001*. PepsiCo, 2001.

———. *Annual Report 2002*. PepsiCo, 2002.

———. *Annual Report 2005*. PepsiCo, 2005.

Pepsi-Cola Company v. The Coca-Cola Company. Supreme Court of the State of New York, County of Queens. Motion for the defense, September 17, 1940. Robert Winship Woodruff Papers.

Pepsi-Cola USA. "Pepsi's 'Space Can' Brings American Lifestyle into the Outer Reaches." News release, July 25, 1985.

"Philosophy of Coca-Cola Advertising, The." Unattributed and undated report. Coca-Cola Collection.

Pruett, William. Coca-Cola USA news release, October 18, 1969. Robert Winship Woodruff Papers.

Richards, Evelyn. Interview by Wendy Marinaccio, July 10, 2000. In Making the Macintosh (online collection). http://www-sul.stanford.edu/mac/primary/interviews/richards/trans.html.

"Roberto C. Goizueta." Unattributed biography, June 1980. Robert Winship Woodruff Papers.

S. L. Stirling, Eastman, Dillon & Co. "Pepsi-Cola Company." Report, April 29, 1951. Robert Winship Woodruff Papers.

Seven-Up Company. "The Uncola: American Contemporary Graphics Exhibit." Undated booklet. Dr Pepper Museum Collection.

Smith, Henry, and Hiram F. Snow. Improved beverage. US Patent 56,458, filed May 31, 1866, and issued July 17, 1866.

Smith, Travis A., Biing-Hwan Lin, and Jong-Ying Lee. *Taxing Caloric Sweetened Beverages: Potential Effects on Beverage Consumption, Calorie Intake, and Obesity*. ERR-100. United States Department of Agriculture Economic Research Service, July 2010.

Soft Drinks Industry (War-Time) Association Ltd. "Range and Sizes of Beverages and Allotted Colours of Labels and Crown Corks." Report, December 31, 1942. National Archives of the United Kingdom.

Standard & Poor's. *Soft Drinks–Candy: Current Analysis*. Report, July 19, 1973. Robert Winship Woodruff Papers.

Steele, Alfred N. Speech to the New York Society of Security Analysts Inc., December 22, 1954. Robert Winship Woodruff Papers.

Stewart & Co. Menu, February 14, 1940. Mass Observation Archives.

"Story of Hires Root Beer, The." Unattributed report, 1972. Dr Pepper Museum Collection.

"Summary Outline of a Program for an Immediate Counter-Offensive Against Attacks on Coca-Cola on the Dental and Nutrition Fronts." Unattributed and undated report. Robert Winship Woodruff Papers.

"Switzerland: Campaign Against 'Coca-Cola.'" Unattributed report, February 23, 1949. Coca-Cola Collection.

"Through the Years in Cooperative Advertising." Unattributed and undated report. Coca-Cola Collection.

Trust Company of Georgia. "The Coca-Cola Company." Undated report. Robert Winship Woodruff Papers.

Unattributed and undated history of Hires Root Beer. Dr Pepper Museum Collection.

United States v. Forty Barrels and Twenty Kegs of Coca-Cola. US District Court, Eastern District of Tennessee, Southern Division, Chattanooga. Court transcripts, March 13, 1911. US National Archives Online Public Access. http://research.archives.gov/search?expression =parent-id-lnk:279312.

White Rock Beverages. "White Rock Beverages Celebrates 140th Birthday." News release, May 19, 2011. www.prnewswire.com/news-releases/white-rock-beverages-celebrates-140th -birthday-122232723.html.

Wilson, Ian. "Remarks for China Agreement News Conference." Undated. Coca-Cola Collection.

Woodruff, Robert. Speech to Coca-Cola marketing meeting, May 22, 1947. Robert Winship Woodruff Papers.

Special Collections

Candler, Asa Griggs, Papers. Manuscript, Archives, and Rare Book Library. Emory University, Atlanta, GA.

Coca-Cola Collection. Manuscript, Archives, and Rare Book Library. Emory University, Atlanta, GA.

Coca-Cola Company Archives. Coca-Cola Company, Atlanta, GA.

Dr Pepper Museum Collection. Dr Pepper Museum, Waco, TX.

Mass Observation Archives. University of Sussex, UK.

National Archives of the United Kingdom, London, UK.

Woodruff, Robert Winship, Papers. Manuscript, Archives, and Rare Book Library. Emory University, Atlanta, GA.

Index